Marx and Marxisms

ROYAL INSTITUTE OF PHILOSOPHY LECTURE SERIES: 14
SUPPLEMENT TO *PHILOSOPHY* 1982

EDITED BY:

G. H. R. Parkinson

CAMBRIDGE UNIVERSITY PRESS

CAMBRIDGE
LONDON   NEW YORK   NEW ROCHELLE
MELBOURNE   SYDNEY

Published by the Press Syndicate of the University of Cambridge
The Pitt Building, Trumpington Street, Cambridge CB2 IRP
32 East 57th Street, New York, NY 10022, USA
296 Beaconsfield Parade, Middle Park, Melbourne 3206, Australia

Library of Congress catalogue card number: 82–4424

British Library Cataloguing in Publication Data
Marx and Marxisms.—(Royal Institute of
Philosophy Lecture series)
1. Communism
I. Parkinson, G. H. R. II. Series
335.4′11   HX56
ISBN 0–521–28904–1

Printed in Great Britain by Adlard & Son Ltd, Bartholomew Press, Dorking

Contents

Notes on Contributors

Roy Edgley
  Professor of Philosophy, University of Sussex. Author of *Reason in Theory and Practice*.

D.-H. Ruben
  Lecturer in Philosophy, The City University, London. Author of *Marxism and Materialism: A Study in Marxist Theory of Knowledge*.

R. F. Atkinson
  Professor of Philosophy, University of Exeter. Author of *Knowledge and Explanation in History: An Introduction to the Philosophy of History*.

John N. Gray
  Fellow of Jesus College, Oxford.

Mary Warnock
  Fellow of St Hugh's College, Oxford. Author of *Ethics Since 1900*, *Existentialism*, *Imagination*, *The Philosophy of Sartre* and *Schools of Thought*.

W . J. Rees
  Formerly Senior Lecturer in Philosophy, University of Leeds.

Graeme Duncan
  Professor of Politics, University of East Anglia. Author of *Marx and Mill*.

Terry Eagleton
  Fellow of Wadham College, Oxford. His books include *Criticism and Ideology*, *Marxism and Literary Criticism* and *Walter Benjamin, or Towards a Revolutionary Criticism*.

Richard Kilminster
  Lecturer in Sociology, University of Leeds. Author of *Praxis and Method: A Sociological Dialogue with Lukács, Gramsci and the Early Frankfurt School*.

Steven Lukes
  Fellow of Balliol College, Oxford. Author of *Emile Durkheim: His Life and Work*, *Essays in Social Theory*, *Individualism* and *Power: A Radical View*.

Philip Pettit

Professor of Philosophy, University of Bradford. Author of *The Concept of Structuralism, Judging Justice: An Introduction to Contemporary Political Philosophy* and (with Graham Macdonald) *Semantics and Social Science.*

G.W. Smith

Lecturer in Politics, University of Lancaster. Contributor to *Philosophy, Philosophical Quarterly, Political Studies, Journal of the History of Ideas,* etc.

Timothy O'Hagan

Lecturer in Philosophy, University of East Anglia. Editor and translator of Nicos Poulantzas, *Political Power and Social Classes.*

Introduction

G. H. R. PARKINSON

In an essay first published in 1966, Charles Taylor remarked on the fact that Marxism has had very little impact on philosophy in Britain. It was true, he said, that a lively interest in Marxism was displayed in British universities, particularly by students of political thought. All this, however, represented 'a study of Marxism from the outside . . . Marxism may be of burning interest for all sorts of reasons, but never because it might be *true*'.[1] In the years since Professor Taylor wrote this, there has been a striking change. Numerous academic works have been published in Britain, often under the imprint of famous publishers, which argue for the truth of Marxist doctrines. Despite this, what Taylor wrote in 1966 remains substantially true as far as philosophy is concerned. Certainly, the last fifteen years have seen the publication of many works which defend Marxist philosophy; yet these works have had little impact on British philosophy in general, or on the philosophy of the English-speaking world as a whole. Marxists would have their own explanation of this. They would say that the majority of Western philosophers (whether they know it or not) work in the interests of the class that is dominant in their society, namely the bourgeoisie. It is understandable, then, that such philosophers should avert their eyes from a way of thinking that is fundamentally hostile to bourgeois interests; a way of thinking that (as Marx put it) is 'a scandal and an abomination to the bourgeoisie and its doctrinaire spokesmen'.[2] Non-Marxist philosophers, for their part, would probably reply that Marxist philosophy is scanty, stale and uninteresting. The aim of the Royal Institute of Philosophy lectures for 1979–80, which form the basis of this volume, was to bring the two sides together by asking both defenders and critics of Marxism to discuss Marxist philosophy.

The title of the book, *Marx and Marxisms*, draws attention to two main features of Marxist views. First, all who call themselves Marxists by that very fact acknowledge a debt to the ideas of Karl Marx. Probably no Marxist will claim that everything that Marx said is true; but every Marxist will claim that there is a core to Marx's thought that is both true

---

[1] Charles Taylor, 'Marxism and Empiricism', *British Analytical Philosophy*, B. Williams and A. Montefiore (eds) (London, 1966), 229.
[2] *Capital*, Afterword to 2nd edn, trans. E. and C. Paul (London, 1930), 874; Marx/Engels, *Werke*, XXIII (Berlin: Dietz Verlag, 1956–68) (abbreviated MEW), 27–28.

and important. So the question, 'What did Marx really mean?' is one that the Marxist constantly asks; and not out of a merely academic interest, but because he sees the correct answer to it as having an important bearing on the issues of the present day. Second, by speaking of 'Marxisms' the title draws attention to the fact that the question, 'What did Marx really mean?' has not received an agreed answer; Marxists have been, and still are, divided into a number of opposing groups, each of which claims to propound the real doctrines of Marx. Professor Edgley, in the first paper in this collection, remarks that 'Marxism is a historical movement', as indeed it is. But it is a movement in the sense in which Christianity is a movement; one in which there are important disagreements as to what the message of the founder really was.

The disagreement between Marxists about the true nature of Marxism has a history that is almost as long as that of Marxism itself; Marx himself is reported as having said, of some French Marxists of the 1870s, 'All I know is that I am not a Marxist'.[3] But during the years in which Stalin was dominant in the USSR, and the USSR was dominant in world communism, there was one generally accepted view about the nature of genuine Marxism, and this was Stalin's view. Dissentient opinions there were, but they were few and relatively ineffective. Since Stalin's death, and more especially since Khrushchev's denunciation of Stalin at the 20th Congress of the Communist Party of the USSR in 1956, the situation has changed radically. In a way, the new situation parallels the position in the Christian world in the period during which the Reformation was challenging the claim of the Roman Catholic Church to be the sole authentic interpreter of Christian doctrine. Just as numerous Protestant sects emerged, so the last twenty-five years have seen the emergence of many new versions (and sometimes the re-emergence of some older versions) of Marxism. These versions of Marxism are lumped together under the title of 'Western Marxism', as opposed to Russian or Soviet Marxism. It is, in the main, Western Marxism that is the subject of the papers in this volume. But it is important to realize that not all Western Marxists think that the views of Russian Marxists are completely wrong. This fact is illustrated by Professor Edgley's paper 'Revolution, Reform and Dialectic'.

Edgley considers some philosophical aspects of the movement known as 'Eurocommunism', a movement which has recently won some following among the communist parties of Western Europe. The movement is distinguished by the view that communism can and should be brought about peacefully, by parliamentary means—a view that it holds in conscious opposition to the Communist Party of the Soviet Union. Edgley writes as a Marxist, and as one who is by no means an out-and-out supporter of the USSR; at the same time, he argues that the views of the

[3] Quoted by Engels in a letter to C. Schmidt, 5 August 1890.

Eurocommunists are incompatible with genuine Marxism. Eurocommunism may only be a passing phase,[4] but whether this is so or not
does not affect the abiding relevance of Edgley's arguments. In essence, his
thesis is that Eurocommunism either fails to grasp, or actually rejects, the
true nature of Marx's philosophy, his 'dialectic'. Edgley argues that the
Eurocommunists, in rejecting violence as a means of social change, are at
one with the ethical socialists; and what is philosophically wrong with
ethical socialism is that it posits an absolute distinction between fact and
value. This leads Eurocommunists and ethical socialists alike to a kind of
moral scepticism, and to the view that all ideas should be tolerated and that
any social changes that are introduced should not be introduced forcibly.
The ethical socialists can take up this position consistently, in that they
reject Marxism; but the Eurocommunists claim to be Marxists. Now
Marxism, Edgley argues, is a science, the science of society, and this science
is not value-free. There is, then, no room for Marxist scepticism about
values, and no room for a rejection of violence that is based on such scepticism.

This gives rise to several questions. It will be asked why a denial of
moral scepticism should lead to a defence of violent revolution; it will
be asked, too, what are the grounds for the assertion that Marxism is a
science, and that this science is not value-free. Edgley does not discuss the
view that Marxism is a science; he doubtless assumes that Eurocommunists
will agree with him that it is. He answers the other questions by pointing
to the specific nature of Marxist dialectic. Hegel called his logic a 'dialectical' logic, or simply 'dialectic', and since for Hegel thought is reality, the
laws of logic are the laws of the world. Marxists reject Hegel's idealism,
but retain the view that reality can be called dialectical; the connection with
Hegel's dialectic is preserved through the idea that change proceeds by
way of internal contradiction. At this point, it is necessary to refer to a
problem which first became prominent in Marxist circles in the 1920s: the
problem of the *range* of dialectic. Engels followed Hegel in thinking that the
dialectic applies, not only to society, but also to the subject-matter of the
natural sciences. Later Marxists—notably Lukács, in his *History and
Class Consciousness* (1923)—argued that Engels had misrepresented Marx's
dialectic, which was intended to apply to society alone. Soviet philosophers
still follow Engels in this, but for Edgley, as for most Western Marxists,
there is a fundamental difference between the natural sciences and the
science of society, such that only the latter can properly be called 'dialectical'. To grasp this difference, it is necessary to consider further the
Marxist account of social change. When Marxists say that social change
proceeds by way of internal contradictions, they mean that such change

4 Since Professor Edgley read his paper in October 1979, the French Communist Party has given its support to the Russian invasion of Afghanistan, and it
has been argued that Eurocommunism has little political significance without
French support (*The Times*, 10 and 16 January 1980).

has to be explained in terms of conflict, conflict that occurs at various levels. There is a conflict within a society's class-structure, i.e. a conflict between classes; this in turn has to be explained in terms of a deeper conflict within the economic basis of society. These conflicts issue in revolutionary change; that is, in Edgley's words, in 'a sudden explosive change that is a change of structure, the destruction of the existing order'. But why should one not say, as Engels would have said, that such explosive changes, the result of internal contradictions, also occur in the subject-matter of the natural sciences? And if they do, why should not the natural sciences, too, be called dialectical? Some Western Marxists would reply that talk about internal contradictions has not proved fruitful in the field of the natural sciences; Edgley makes a different point. He argues that the *relation between* the science of society and the modern social revolution is different from that between (say) a revolution in climatic conditions and the science of geography. The modern social revolution, he says, *involves* the science that is Marxist dialectics. This science, unlike the natural sciences, does not merely reflect its subject matter, as in a mirror. Rather, it *expresses*, it *speaks for*, a social movement, and this is what Marxists mean when they speak of 'the unity of theory and practice'. It is now possible to see how Edgley can speak of a link between fact and value. The social movement for which dialectics speaks has as its aim the revolutionary transformation of society; dialectics, then, is critical, and not merely descriptive. This, says Edgley, is the point of Marx's famous eleventh thesis on Feuerbach (1845): 'The philosophers have only *interpreted* the world in various ways; the point is to *change* it'. This criticism, this call for society to be changed, is not based on *a priori* moral commands, as Eurocommunists suppose; it is bound up with the science of society.

Edgley's paper raises many questions. When he speaks of Marxism as the science of society, he outlines the theory commonly known as 'historical materialism'. One may ask: precisely what is historical materialism? Is it a science? Again, what Edgley says about fact and value is highly controversial. Many philosophers have denied any link between the two; is there really such a link in the case of Marxist dialectics and its subject matter? All these are important questions, which are taken up later in this volume. The next four papers—those of Dr Ruben, Professor Atkinson, Dr Gray and Mrs Warnock—are, in various ways, concerned with general aspects of historical materialism. Dr Ruben writes as a Marxist and, like Edgley, is concerned with inter-Marxist disputes. His paper 'Marx, Necessity and Science' discusses questions of ontology, in that it asks: given that Marxism is a science, what is there in reality that corresponds to the true propositions of this science? In particular, when a Marxist speaks of 'modes of production' and of 'tendencies', what is there in reality that corresponds to what he says? Dr Ruben argues, against the Marxist philosopher Roy Bhaskar, that tendencies are not ontologically basic; talk of tendencies merely indicates one's current inability to state sufficient conditions. Ruben also argues against a Marxist school of thought when he discusses 'modes of production', and here his arguments require more extensive comment. His criticisms are aimed at some of the views of Maurice Godelier, which show the influence of Althusser's ideas. The philosophy of Louis Althusser is one of the most important developments in recent Marxism, and it is fitting that three of the papers in this volume are concerned with various aspects of it.

Althusser writes in conscious opposition to what he calls the 'humanism' of some Marxists and interpreters of Marx. This view of Marx was particularly influential in the fifties; it laid great stress on some of Marx's early work, and especially the Paris Manuscripts of 1844, with their doctrine of human alienation. This was taken to be an *ethical* doctrine; Marxism, it was argued, is not a science, but is a moral point of view. Althusser replies that Marxism is a science. It is significant that one of his most important books (written in conjunction with Etienne Balibar, and published in 1965) was entitled *Lire le Capital*—the point being that Marxists should study the scientific doctrines of *Capital* and should not lay almost exclusive stress on Marx's earlier, and immature, work. Such a view is not peculiar to Althusser; it is shared, for example, by Soviet Marxists. What is distinctive about Althusser is the view that he takes of Marxist science, and it is this that is relevant to Ruben's paper. Marx's science, Althusser argues, is a study of *structures*, and such structures are not to be reduced to relations between men[5]. This view is reflected in what Godelier writes about 'modes of production'. This is one of the technical terms of historical materialism, and its meaning is not uncontroversial. However, there will be no harm (as far as the paper under discussion is concerned) in accepting Ruben's view that a mode of production is a type of economic structure, involving both producers and means of production. Now, it is Godelier's view that, within a mode of production, there is an internal relationship between structures, and also (and this is the important point) that these structures may be regarded as moving. Ruben replies that to say this is to ontologize structures. A structure is a universal, and as such it cannot change in time. Nor, he adds, did Marx ever suppose that it could; to suppose the existence and movement of such structures is to side with Hegel against Marx. In sum, it is societies, not structures, that change, and it is societies and their changes of structure that are the real subject matter of Marxist science.

Ruben's paper is not critical of historical materialism as such; his criticisms are directed against a mistaken view of its nature. The next two papers provide a critical examination of some of the basic doctrines of the theory. In a way, historical materialism has two faces, one looking

[5] Cf. *Lire le Capital* (*Reading Capital*), English translation (London, 1970), 180.

to the past and one to the future. On the one hand, it claims to explain the past, and it can therefore be considered as a theory of historical explanation. On the other hand, it claims (or is often thought to claim) to provide accurate predictions of the future, and one can consider the soundness of this claim. In his paper 'Historical Materialism', Professor Atkinson considers the theory as a thesis in the philosophy of history. He first tries to determine just what the thesis is, taking as his starting point Marx's famous summary of the theory in the Preface to the *Critique of Political Economy* (1859). Marx's observations are brief, and their correct interpretation is a matter of controversy. Stated in the very broadest way, the theory asserts that 'the mode of production of material life conditions the social, political and intellectual life process in general'. Filling in the detail, Marx draws a famous distinction between a 'basis' and 'superstructure', and this gives rise to serious problems of interpretation. (a) Precisely what is the basis? Does it consist simply of what Marx calls the relations of production—i.e. the relations into which people enter when they produce things? This, indeed, is what the passage appears to state; but did Marx perhaps mean that the basis also includes what he calls material productive forces—which seem to include, not just tools and machines, but the skills of those who make and use them? (b) How much is contained in the superstructure? Does it consist of legal and political institutions only, or does it also include what Marx calls 'definite forms of social consciousness'? And how are these related to the 'intellectual life process'? (c) What are the relations between basis and superstructure? It seems clear enough that the basis 'conditions' or 'determines' the superstructure; but is this a one-way affair? Can the superstructure affect the basis?

In response to question (a), Atkinson argues that material productive forces and relations of production together constitute the 'basis'. 'Economic factors generally, organizational as well as technical, are the fundamental causative factors in history'. With regard to (b), he remains agnostic; as to (c), he notes that Marxists themselves recognize that features of the superstructure not only escape economic determination, but even affect the development of the basis. Questions of interpretation answered, Atkinson goes on to ask how useful historical materialism is as a thesis in the philosophy of history. He agrees with Marxists that there are many historical questions the answers to which must be in economic terms; but, he says, these are not the *only* historical questions, nor are they always the most important ones. Intellectual history, for example, must appeal mainly to *internal* considerations, in the sense that the historian of (say) philosophy must explain philosophical change by reference to the arguments provided and not just, or even mainly, by reference to social forces. A historical materialist might concede this point, whilst claiming that the heart of the Marxist position is not touched. Historical materialism (he might say) is an account, not of the detail, but of the main lines of historical development—for example, the transition from feudalism to capitalism, which Marx explains in the first volume of *Capital*. Atkinson admits that nothing that he has said in his paper would refute such a a version of historical materialism. Philosophers influenced by Karl Popper might be inclined to say that the thesis, as so formulated, is so vague as to be unfalsifiable, and therefore meaningless or (as Popper himself would say) at best unscientific. Atkinson does not say that the thesis cannot be stated meaningfully, nor is he concerned with its scientific status; but he does say that its generality means that its truth is very hard to establish.

Dr Gray's discussion of historical materialism takes place in the context of an inquiry into Marx's views about human nature, entitled 'Philosophy, Science and Myth in Marxism'. Marx, Gray argues, had three concepts of of human nature, each of which requires a different kind of backing. These concepts may be called metaphysical, scientific and mythical respectively, and Gray considers them as they have been developed by three Marxists— Herbert Marcuse, G. A. Cohen and Georges Sorel. I will comment only briefly on that part of Dr Gray's paper that concerns Marcuse and Sorel. Though Marcuse claimed that he was a Marxist, there has been considerable controversy about the extent to which that claim was justified; however, Gray argues that Marcuse had a concept of man which is certainly to be found in Marx. This is the concept of man as producer both of himself and of his world, a being who has a vital need for productive labour. Present in Marx, too, is Marcuse's view that human self-determination implies the subjection of economic processes to the human will. In Marcuse, these views co-exist with a rejection of historicism; the socialist future becomes, not something which is vouched for by the science of history, but what Gray calls a 'free-floating possibility'. In saying this, of course, Marcuse is in the tradition of that Marxist humanism which is rejected by Althusser and many others. Gray's point is that this 'metaphysical humanism' is present in Marx's thought, and that those who reject it are rejecting some of Marx's ideas. As to Sorel, there can be no reasonable doubt that his Marxism was highly unorthodox. For him, revolutionary socialism was a non-rational social force; the Marxist offers, not a science, but a myth. The vast majority of Marxists would reject this account of their doctrines, but Dr Gray, writing as a critic of Marxism, thinks that Sorel was right. Whatever Marxists may think about the status of Marxist doctrines, those doctrines contain an element of myth.

Between his discussion of Marcuse and Sorel, Gray gives a critical account of a recent defence of historical materialism, G. A. Cohen's *Karl Marx's Theory of History: A Defence* (1978). What brings Cohen's book within Gray's purview is its recognition of the part played in Marx's theory of history by a concept of human nature. This concept is different from, and also thinner than, Marcuse's. It enters into one of two theses about the forces of production, which Cohen calls respectively the 'primacy thesis' and the 'development thesis'. The primacy thesis is Cohen's version of Marx's view that productive forces are the fundamental factor in human history; the development thesis asserts (Cohen, op. cit., 134) that productive forces 'tend to develop through history'. The second thesis is the one that is relevant here; for it is in defence of the development thesis that Cohen appeals (and suggests that Marx tacitly appealed) to premises which state certain facts about human nature. These are: that men are 'somewhat rational', and that their intelligence is such that they are able to improve their situation (op. cit., 152). This view of human nature may seem to be true, indeed to be almost a truism. Gray, however, argues that if the view is not to be almost entirely vacuous, certain assumptions have to be made; and these assumptions are by no means universally true, but are bound to a specific culture—namely, that of capitalist Europe. Cohen, like Marx, is preoccupied with human mastery over the natural environment, and writes this into his concept of rationality. But we are not entitled to say that rational conduct has only one ultimate goal; and unless there is agreement on goals, to talk of the more or less efficient use of productive forces, or of men 'improving their situation', makes no sense. Faced with such a criticism, a defender of historical materialism might answer by reducing the scope of the theory. Instead of saying that the theory is true of all human history, he could argue that it is true of the capitalist epoch alone; there could then be no objection to using a concept of rational behaviour that is peculiar to this period. But it is doubtful, to say the least, whether a Marxist would take this escape route. It is true that Lukács said (*History and Class Consciousness*, English trans. (London, 1971), 238) that historical materialism must be applied with great caution to pre-capitalist societies; but he did not deny that it could be applied to them.

Cohen's defence of Marxism takes the form of a careful exposition of Marx's writings; Sartre's *Critique of Dialectical Reason*, which is the subject of Mary Warnock's paper, is a work of a very different kind. In this book, Sartre proclaimed himself a Marxist, but he was ready to go far beyond Marx's text. Mrs Warnock concentrates on the task of clarifying the views on historical explanation presented in the *Critique*, and does not ask to what extent these views really belong within the Marxist tradition; consequently, a few remarks on this topic may be appropriate. Sartre criticizes Marx[6] for failing to give due weight to the element of negativity in history, an element which in turn has to be explained by *scarcity*. It is scarcity, Sarte says, that sets man against man; but it is important to

---

[6] The passage discussed by Sartre is Marx's account of the development of Roman society, contained in his letter to the editors of *Otechestvenniye Zapiski*, November 1877. Marx and Engels, *Selected Correspondence* (Moscow and London, n.d.), 379; MEW, XIX, 111.

realize that scarcity is a causal factor in history *only in so far as it is mediated through human grasp of it*. In other words, human actions have to be understood in the light of the human grasp of scarcity. But this grasp is not something timeless. In the *Critique of Dialectical Reason* Sartre insists, in opposition to the more static view of human nature taken in his earlier work, that human beings have to be seen in a socio-historical context. Mrs Warnock outlines the four types of social group recognized in the *Critique* and notes an important feature of Sartre's views about social change: namely, that he does not regard the progress from one type of group to another as inevitable. Each type emerges by reason of the actual projects pursued by the individuals who make up the group. Sartre concludes that biography, which presents the world through the eyes of the people who made history, is a major way of making history intelligible.

Much of this can be placed within some Marxist tradition or other. In stressing the element of negativity, Sartre is in the company of those Marxists (and they include the young Marx himself) who have developed Hegel's views about 'the labour of the negative'.[7] Again, what he says about scarcity can perhaps be fitted into a Marxist framework.[8] Even Sartre's view that progress from one type of group to another is not inevitable has some Marxist support; many Marxists (one may instance Lukács and Marcuse) have stressed the importance of the free decisions of oppressed groups. Again, in saying that historical change comes about by way of the actual projects pursued by individuals, Sartre is saying something that has been echoed recently by the Marxist historian E. P. Thompson.[9] But in saying that one of the chief ways of making history intelligible is by presenting the world through the eyes of the individual subjects of historical change, Sartre (as Mrs Warnock observes) is closer to Dilthey than to Marx. He seems to overlook the thesis, accepted by most Marxists, that a man's consciousness may be a *false* consciousness, and that it is the historian's business to replace this by a true presentation of the historical situation.

[7] Hegel, *Phänomenologie des Geistes*, 6th edn, Hoffmeister (ed.) (Hamburg, 1952), 20, 29. Cf. H. Marcuse, *Reason and Revolution*, 2nd edn (London, 1955), 282: 'For Marx, as for Hegel, the dialectic takes note of the fact that the negation inherent in reality is "the moving and creative principle". The dialectic is "the dialectic of negativity".' See also Marx, *Economic and Philosophical Manuscripts* (1844); Marx and Engels, *Collected Works*, III (Moscow and London, 1975–), 332.

[8] Cf. Cohen, op. cit., 152. In defending his 'development thesis' Cohen appeals, not just to the view about human nature discussed by Dr Gray, but to 'one fact about the situation human beings face in history'—namely, that the historical situation of man is one of scarcity.

[9] In his book *The Poverty of Theory* (London, 1978). This point is made by a Marxist critic of Thompson, Perry Anderson, in his *Arguments within English Marxism* (London, 1980), 49ff.

The four papers just discussed have considered historical materialism in its general aspects; the next three consider particular aspects or applications of the doctrine. W. J. Rees discusses a problem about the pattern of social development outlined in Marx's *Capital*, whilst Professor Duncan and Dr Eagleton consider two problems about the 'superstructure', in the shape of Marxist views about the state and literature respectively. Discussing the specific nature of Russian Marxism, Mr Rees points out that the Russian Marxists of the late nineteenth and early twentieth centuries found themselves faced with the problem of 'exceptionalism'. The problem was, whether the path of development traced in Marx's *Capital*—from feudalism to socialism, by way of capitalism—was applicable to all countries, or whether some countries, and in particular Russia, could avoid the capitalist phase. The problem was put to Marx and Engels, who did not provide a clear answer; however, the influential Russian Marxist Plekhanov argued against the 'exceptionalist' thesis. Capitalism could not be bypassed; there would have to be two revolutions in Russia, the first bourgeois and the second proletarian. Lenin's attitude to exceptionalism was complex, in that he rejected it as an economic doctrine but preserved many of its political consequences. Like Plekhanov, he conceived of a revolution in two stages, but these stages were different from those of Plekhanov. Lenin saw no need for a capitalist era, which would be rendered superfluous by an alliance between the urban proletariat and the poor peasantry. Rees argues that in saying that a socialist revolution could be carried through with the help of the poorer peasants, Lenin was returning to views advanced by the Russian 'Populists'; at the same time Lenin asserted, against the Populists and in line with the doctrines of *Capital*, that the major revolutionary force would be the urban working class. Rees notes also that Lenin's views about the part to be played in the revolution by the peasants exercised an important influence on his ideas about the nature of the Russian Communist Party. If the party was to express the interests of the poorer peasants, who were largely illiterate and scattered over a wide area, it must be paternalistic; it must guide rather than follow.

From problems about the nature of Russian Marxism we turn to the Marxist theory of the state in general, which is the subject of a paper by Professor Graeme Duncan. Duncan argues that the classical Marxist theory of the state is neither consistent nor complete. The theory in question asserts that the state is initially the product of class conflict, coming into existence to resolve the conflict of classes, and that it later becomes an organ of class conflict, a 'machine for the oppression of one class by another'.[10] It is the latter part of the theory—the view of the state as a class instrument—on which Duncan concentrates. He argues that the

---

[10] Lenin, *Proletarian Revolution and the Renegade Kautsky*; Lenin, *Selected Works*, VII (London, 1937), 149.

theory is acceptable only in a modified form. It is true, he says, that the state has a class bias, but this does not mean that the state is nothing but a class instrument. For example, the politico-legal regulation of capitalism in Britain shows that the state is capable of at least some manipulation by subjected groups. Moreover (and it is here that the inconsistency in Marxist theory becomes manifest), Marx himself, in *The Eighteenth Brumaire of Louis Bonaparte*, gave an example of a state which did not express an exclusive class domination, but which asserted its own independence. This was the Bonapartist state which emerged in France after the collapse of the Second Republic. Duncan adds that although this state was not the tool of a particular class, this is not to say that it did not serve class interests. In fact it served the interests of a class—the bourgeoisie—better than the bourgeoisie could have done if it had taken power in its own name. The point is, however, that it was not a tool of the bourgeoisie.

It will be worth while to compare Duncan's criticism of the Marxist theory of the state with Atkinson's criticism of the Marxist theory of history in general. In effect, both critics argue that Marxists inflate what is true in some cases, or to some extent, into a truth that is universal or unqualified. Atkinson agrees that many historical questions have to be answered in economic terms, but says that these are not the only historical questions. Duncan is prepared to say that the state always has a class bias, i.e. is always in the interest of a particular social class, but he adds that this is not to say that it is always a class instrument (cf. the Bonapartist state) or that it acts exclusively in the interests of the dominant class (cf. the regulation of British capitalism).

I said that according to Duncan, the classical Marxist theory of the state is not only inconsistent; it is also incomplete. In saying that it is incomplete, Duncan has in mind that part of the theory that sees the state as belonging to the superstructure, conditioned in the last analysis by productive forces. His point is that the correspondence between state forms and the economic basis can only be very general. As Marx himself noted, there are many variations in the economic and class configurations on which the state depends, nor is there a single state form appropriate to capitalism in all its phases of development. The view that the dominant mode of production conditions the form of the state is, Duncan says, the starting point of analysis and not its end result.

The next paper is in the field of Marxist aesthetics. Dr Eagleton, himself a Marxist, discusses the literary theory of Pierre Macherey, whose ideas owe much to Althusser. This brings us to another aspect of Althusser's views: namely, his objection to what he regards as the undue reverence for Hegel displayed by many Marxists. For Althusser, the most important philosophical ancestor of Marx is not Hegel, but Spinoza. Macherey has written on Spinoza (*Hegel ou Spinoza* (Paris, 1979)), and although one cannot say that the influence of Spinoza is obvious in his literary theory, his opposition to what Eagleton calls 'neo-Hegelian' Marxist criticism is clear. The neo-Hegelianism that Macherey opposes is perhaps best illustrated by the views of one of its leading exponents, the Hungarian critic and philosopher Georg Lukács. Like Hegel, Lukács sees art as a kind of knowledge of reality, or at least as involving such knowledge. Like Hegel, again, Lukács stresses the importance of the whole; a work of art is a totality which represents a totality. But whereas for Hegel the totality of which art gives knowledge is *Geist* ('spirit' or 'mind'), for Lukács the totality is a developing social whole. Sketchy as it is, this account is sufficient for a useful contrast with Macherey to be made. For Macherey, a literary work is *not* a unity, is *not* a complete and harmonious totality; rather, there is within it a conflict of meanings. Macherey means that the author, in trying to say one thing, is constrained by the ideology of his epoch to say another. This ideology has internal contradictions; these are not *stated* by the literary work—such a statement would presumably be the concern of historical materialism—but they are *shown*, shown by the work's own internal stresses. The task of the literary critic, Macherey argues, is not to complete what the work leaves unsaid, but is to explain why the work has to be incomplete; why it can only show, and cannot state, the contradictions that it displays.

Implicit in the account just given, and emphasised by Macherey, is the thesis that the critic is not concerned to establish norms. The attempt to set up standards of what a work should be, Macherey argues, would be a denial of the 'determinateness' of the work. The normative critic assumes, wrongly, that the work could have been different from what it is. Two comments may be made on this—one philosophical, one historical. The philosophical comment is that Macherey's reason for rejecting normative criticism seems a poor one. It is not clear why normative criticism should be incompatible with determinism. Even a rigid determinist like Spinoza uses terms such as 'good' and 'bad' in his philosophy, and there seems to be no reason why a determinist should not have a use for such terms in his aesthetics. The historical comment is that many Marxists have viewed art in normative terms. Following Engels, they have said that the mark of a good work of art is its realism, and they praise or blame works of art for their realism or lack of it.

Though Dr Eagleton finds Macherey's literary theory stimulating, he thinks that a weakness in the theory is its neglect of the concrete historical situation of the literary work. Macherey assumes that a literary work will automatically be subversive, in that it displays the contradictions of the ideology of its epoch, but Eagleton points out that it is possible for a work to underwrite an ideology. I take this to mean that it is possible for an author not to be constrained by the ideology of his epoch and for his work to have no internal tensions. The upshot of the argument is that Macherey's theory is not true of all literary works. We seem, in fact, to have another example of the tendency among Marxists, noted by Atkinson and Duncan, to inflate into a universal truth something which is true only in some cases.

After these discussions of various aspects of historical materialism we come to a topic which links historical materialism with the Marxist philosophy of action, and ultimately with Marxist views about ethics. Professor Edgley's paper drew attention to the Marxist thesis that theory (historical materialism) and practice (Marxist political activity) form a unity. When Marxists speak of that 'practice' which is united with theory, they commonly refer to it by the word 'praxis'; Dr Kilminster's paper 'Theory and Practice in Marx and Marxism' is concerned with some philosophical aspects of this concept. In Marx's early theory of knowledge, as stated in the rough notes that are known as the 'Theses on Feuerbach' (1845), 'praxis' means ordinary human social activity. Marx uses this concept in his argument that the idealism and the materialism defended by previous philosophers have elements of the truth, but that neither by itself gives the whole truth. Conscious man moulds nature by his labour, and to that extent idealists are justified in saying that the mind is not in a passive relation to the world; but conscious man is also a part of nature, and to that extent materialists are justified. But, as Kilminster notes, Marx is not interested in epistemology for its own sake. Since mankind makes its own world, it can also change that world, and this is where the political aspect of praxis enters. This aspect can be introduced by way of an answer to the question: 'Marx has insisted that people can, and do, change their world. But how *ought* they to change it?' Marx's answer, Kilminster argues, involves a view about the nature of human social activity, and more specifically about the way in which this activity develops in the course of history. It is a teleological view; history is a process which has a *telos*—an end or goal—and this telos is socialism, the rational social order. This means that human beings have a potentiality for rational social organization; but this potentiality is fettered by archaic class relations, in the way that historical materialism describes and explains. These archaic class relations not only ought to be, but will be, destroyed by 'revolutionary praxis'— political activity which is not purely spontaneous, but is impregnated by, 'informed by', theory. So, in Kilminster's words, 'the theory articulating the process' on the one hand, and 'a moral indictment of society' on the other, are necessarily the same thing.

If one views human history in this teleological (and, one might add, Hegelian) way, then one can bridge the gap between fact and value. But some Marxists would deny that Marx argued in this way; or they might say that, if Marx did argue like this, then Marx was wrong. It is not clear to me from Professor Edgley's paper how he views the matter, but it is clear that Dr Kilminster thinks that those Marxists who abandoned the teleological view of social reality were right.[11] But this left them with a problem:

how is the gap between fact and value to be bridged if teleology is set aside? Kilminster concludes his paper by considering some answers given by two members of the 'Frankfurt school' of Marxism, Adorno and Habermas. These attempts at bridging the gap are, he thinks, failures, in that they lead respectively to nihilism and to the postulation of an ideal state of affairs which is unrealizable in practice. Kilminster's paper does not raise the question whether Marxist attempts to bridge the gap between fact and value are fundamentally mistaken, or whether the gap can be bridged, but by equipment which is different from that which Marxists use. In fact, he appears to hold the second view;[12] but this is a subject outside the scope of this book.

In his paper on Marxist dialectic, Professor Edgley stressed the difference between Marxism and ethical socialism; yet he would hardly deny that Marxists themselves often use ethical terms. What makes this interesting is the fact that, in using these terms, they may seem to contradict their own theories. On the one hand, Marxists say that concepts such as 'duty', 'right' and 'justice' have no independent validity, but are relative to economic and social conditions; on the other hand, they proclaim the coming of a new form of society which is not merely different from, but is also higher than, the old, and they are loud in their condemnation of the evils of capitalism.[13] In his paper 'Marxism, Morality and Justice', Dr Steven Lukes asks whether this is only an apparent contradiction, or whether a consistent Marxist approach to morality is impossible. He concentrates on Marxist accounts of the nature of justice. He points out that Marx and Engels regarded concepts of justice as relative to class interests and to the mode of production; that being so, they had to say that there need be nothing unjust about the way in which the capitalist exploits labour. The same can be said of the principles of *Recht* (roughly speaking, legal or moral rules) in general. They do not provide an independent set of norms by means of which one can evaluate social relations; rather, they arise from these relations. Now, as long as these principles are regarded merely in this relativistic fashion, there seems to be no way of reconciling the Marxist theory of moral concepts with Marxists' use of moral terms. But, Dr Lukes argues, there is in Marxism another approach to moral

[11] He calls this teleological view a 'mythological strand' in Marx's thought.

[12] In his book *Praxis and Method* (London, 1979), 259, he says that sociologists are mistaken in affirming that the analysis of society is one thing and that the making of value-judgments is another. But Marxists have been prevented, by the conceptual baggage that they have taken over from Marx, from developing a new theory that is appropriate to the present day.

[13] A recent and eloquent example of this is Dr G. A. Cohen's 1980 Isaac Deutscher Memorial Lecture, 'Freedom, Justice and Capitalism' (*New Left Review*, No. 126 (March/April 1981), 3–16).

concepts. Marxists often criticize systems of *Recht* on the ground that they are abstract and one-sided, in that they apply the same standard to different cases. But human beings are not condemned to be treated in this way for ever. In a communist society, there will be no more *Recht*—which is not to say that such a society will be without a morality of any kind. A communist society will recognize a fundamental human good, but this will not be abstract; it will be the concrete human good that is proclaimed by what Dr Gray calls 'Marxist metaphysical humanism'—'self-realization in community, freedom as the overcoming of alienation, mastery over nature and the maximization of welfare' (Lukes). Dr Lukes concludes that the Marxist is able to present a self-consistent view of morality.

Lukes does not, however, find the view a plausible one; in fact, he raises no fewer than five objections to it. To these five I should like to add another, which is related to the problem of fact and value in Marxism. The Marxist theory of morality sketched by Dr Lukes owes much to Hegel. For Hegel, the advance of thought (which is also the self-development of reality) is a movement both from the fragmentary to the whole and from the abstract to the concrete. Similarly, the Marxist would (according to Lukes) claim superiority for his moral concepts because they are more concrete than those of *Recht*. Faced with these assertions, one might ask why one *ought* to prefer the concrete to the abstract. Hegel has an answer, which involves his metaphysics. There is, he would say, no gap between fact and value; the concrete is superior because reality is moving in the direction of greater concreteness, and this movement is a movement towards greater rationality. But can a Marxist argue along these lines? To do so would be to accept a teleological view of reality, and we have seen from Dr Kilminster's paper that, although there may be elements of such a view in Marx, it is rejected by several modern Marxists.

One of these Marxists is Jürgen Habermas, who was discussed in Kilminster's paper. Habermas has paid attention to the problem that justice poses for the Marxist, and his answer is the subject of a paper by Professor Philip Pettit. As we saw, the problem for the Marxist is that on the one hand he wants his own criteria to be objective, but on the other hand he wants all concepts of justice to be relative to socio-economic conditions. Habermas' solution takes the form of a consensus theory of justice. A just social scheme, he argues, is one that would attract rational consensus. Now, there is nothing subjective about such a scheme; it is not one on which people of any sort happen to agree, but is one on which *rational* people *would* agree. This preserves the objectivity of justice; at the same time, however, we do not know *what* scheme would attract rational consensus, so such schemes as are offered can consistently be regarded as economically or socially determined.

Habermas' consensus theory of justice is paralleled by a consensus theory of truth, and this theory of truth provides Professor Pettit with his starting point. Habermas does not say that to call a proposition true *means that* it has secured agreement, or even that it has secured rational agreement. Rather, truth is a property of propositions, their 'warranted assertibility', which Habermas connects with the concept of an 'ideal speech situation'. He means that if a proposition is to warrant assertion, it must be able to stand up to criticism of the most radical kind. That is, the proposition must be discussed within the context of an ideal speech situation, in which questioning is permitted at every level. Pettit finds some obscurities in Habermas' formulation of his consensus theory of truth, but he concludes that the theory enables Habermas to preserve an agnosticism as to *what* is true; for if one is to establish that a theory would command rational assent one must have all the relevant evidence, and this is never available. But, Pettit argues, there is no good reason to suppose that a similar agnosticism can be retained in the case of a consensus theory of justice, where we are concerned, not with theoretical, but with practical discourse. There is a vital difference between the two sorts of discourse—in short, between talk about truth and talk about justice—in that what makes us agnostic about truth is the fact that we do not have all the relevant evidence. But in the case of practical discourse, our arguments are not vulnerable in the same way to novel empirical discoveries. Pettit concludes that this attempt to go between the horns of the Marxist's dilemma—moral objectivity on the one hand, socio-economic determinism on the other—is a failure.

Professor Pettit's criticisms of Habermas' argument—and his criticisms, in the concluding pages of his paper, of some supplementary arguments for agnosticism about justice—seem to me to be very powerful. One might also raise a further criticism: namely, that it is hard to see how Habermas' views about justice can be reconciled with what Professor Edgley has said about the revolutionary character of Marxism. Habermas leaves one in the position of being unable to say, in concrete terms, what the just course of action in a given situation really is. There is, he says, a just course of action; i.e. there is a course of action on which rational people would agree. But we cannot know of any course of action which is actually recommended as being just, that it really is just. In short, Habermas defends a kind of moral scepticism; but it will be remembered that, for Edgley, moral scepticism is an integral part of Eurocommunism (which claims falsely to be Marxist) and of ethical socialism (which does not even claim to be Marxist). It is because the Eurocommunists and the ethical socialists believe that the right course of action is not known that they argue that all points of view must be tolerated, and that no social changes should be brought about by violent means. It may well seem to Marxists such as Edgley that Habermas, in trying to reconcile moral objectivity with historical materialism, has abandoned Marxism.

Dr Lukes mentioned, as one of the components of the Marxist concept of the fundamental human good, the idea of freedom. Marx's views about

freedom are discussed by Dr G. W. Smith in his paper 'Marxian Metaphysics and Individual Freedom'. Dr Smith points out that Marx made two
important claims about freedom: first, that the revolutionary proletariat is
more free than the bourgeoisie, and second, that the members of a future
classless society will enjoy complete and absolute freedom. The revolutionary proletariat is more free than the bourgeoisie in that the proletariat
alone can change the conditions that determine it, and so can change itself.
But the proletariat is only relatively, and not absolutely, free; for although
it can change circumstances, its actions are determined by its position in
society as a whole. Only in the classless society, i.e. only under communism,
will there be complete freedom, for only there will social circumstances be
brought wholly under control, and human beings will live and work
within conditions that they alone have set. There will then be no opposition between man and society; society will be the medium through which
men express themselves rather than an external obstacle to their activity.

Superficially, the freedom enjoyed in the classless society might not
seem to differ in kind from that of the revolutionary proletariat; the difference might appear to be only one of degree, in that human beings in a
classless society have *more* power than the revolutionary proletariat.
However, Dr Smith argues persuasively that different concepts of freedom
are involved. Freedom under communism is not a matter of the ability to
change circumstances; it is a matter of self-determination, as opposed to
determination by external factors. Smith places this concept within the
idealist tradition of Kant and Hegel, but in fact it goes further back than
this; we are dealing with what Isaiah Berlin, in his essay 'Two Concepts
of Liberty',[14] calls the concept of positive freedom, which includes
Spinoza among its adherents. To be free, in this sense, is to be one's own
master. I am free if I am 'a doer—deciding, not being decided for, self-
directed and not acted upon by external nature or by other men as if I were
a thing, or an animal, or a slave incapable of playing a human role' (Berlin,
op. cit., 131). Berlin objects that this concept has been used to justify
totalitarian regimes (some of them claiming to be Marxist); Smith approaches the concept from another angle and asks whether, in a free
society of this kind, there can be any place for the concept of an individual
person. The problem arises in this way. Marx sees the common-sense concept of the individual person as an abstraction. It assumes that social
relations are external to the individual; but this, says Marx, is not so.
Rather, the individual is constituted by them, in the sense that he would not
be *what* he is if he were isolated from his social relationships. A problem
arises when we ask: how can an individual be said to remain the same
through the series of changing relationships that constitute him as an
individual? Dr Smith argues that Marx, with his theory of freedom under

[14] Reprinted in Isaiah Berlin, *Four Essays on Liberty* (Oxford, 1969).

communism, does what Spinoza and Hegel have been accused of doing—that is, he dissolves the individual in the whole.

The final paper in the volume—Dr O'Hagan's 'Althusser: How to be a Marxist in Philosophy'—brings us back to some important issues discussed earlier: that is, historical materialism and the revolutionary character of Marxist philosophy. O'Hagan is concerned with Althusser's views about the nature of philosophy, or at any rate with his most recent views. These are closely related to classical Marxist sources, and it will be helpful to approach Althusser by way of Engels. Engels argued that philosophy, in the sense of a speculative account of the nature of things, came to an end in the nineteenth century—to be exact, it ended with the philosophy of Hegel; its place had been taken by science, 'real positive knowledge of the world'.[15] However, there was still a place for philosophy in one sense of the term, namely as a kind of logic, the theory of thought and its laws.[16] Althusser agrees with Engels that a sharp distinction must be drawn between science and philosophy, and also that there is still a place for philosophy. But he disagrees with Engels' view that this philosophy is really logic. Logic, he says, is itself a science,[17] so the nature of Marxist philosophy still has to be clarified. His answer to the problem is that philosophical 'propositions' are not propositions in the strict sense of the term, in that they cannot be called true or false. Rather, they are disguised injunctions and as such should be called, not 'true' or 'false', but 'correct' or 'incorrect'. They are correct in so far as they further the development of science, and incorrect in so far as they hinder it. This may seem to be a form of pragmatism; Althusser may seem to be denying the possibility of any rational argument in philosophy, and to be saying that a philosophical utterance is to be judged solely by reference to its utility. It would be suprising if this were what Althusser did mean; Marxists usually oppose pragmatism, and in fact O'Hagan argues that Althusser really means something else. In saying that philosophical assertions are not true or false, Althusser really means that they are not *demonstrable*; philosophical argument is not deductive argument, but resembles legal reasoning, where the lawyer is trying to influence action (i.e. secure a favourable verdict), but is doing so by means of rational argument. This is a much more plausible (though less dramatic) thesis than that with which we seemed to begin. The philosopher, it now appears, *does* state propositions; Althusser is saying that the arguments by which he supports these are of a special kind. What is lacking in Althusser is any detailed account of the nature of these arguments.

[15] Engels, *Ludwig Feuerbach and the End of Classical German Philosophy*, MEW, XXI, 270; Marx and Engels, *Selected Works*, II (Moscow and London, 1950), 331.

[16] Engels, Anti-Dühring, MEW, XX, 24; English trans. (London, 1934), 31.

[17] Althusser, *Lenin and Philosophy*, English trans. (London, 1971), 59.

So far, it has emerged that when Althusser says that a correct philosophical argument is one that furthers scientific progress, he does not imply that 'correct' *means* 'furthering scientific progress'. His view is that a philosophical argument is assessed by rational, though non-deductive criteria, and if it is a good argument it will also further scientific progress. There may seem to be nothing distinctively Marxist about such a view; long before Marx, Locke had argued that in giving an accurate account of the human understanding he was clearing away rubbish that stood in the way of scientific progress. What makes Althusser's view a Marxist view is the fact that it involves a reference to the influence of social class on ideas. Althusser's position is linked with another well-known thesis about the nature of philosophy stated by Engels. Philosophers, said Engels, fall into two classes: idealists and materialists.[18] When he, and other Marxists who defend this view, speak of 'materialism' they seem to mean what would generally be called 'realism'; for them, 'matter' is (in Lenin's phrase) 'objectively real being', which is 'independent of the consciousness of humanity'.[19] Engels adds that materialism is the world-view of science;[20] it follows that any philosophical argument in favour of materialism will help science, and any philosophical argument in favour of idealism will hinder science. Althusser, like other Marxists, adds the important proposition that idealism is the philosophy of the bourgeoisie, and materialism the philosophy of the proletariat. So, in Althusser's words, philosophy 'represents politics in the field of theory'; philosophy is 'basically a political struggle: a class struggle'.

This must not be misunderstood. Althusser is not saying that materialism is true because it is the philosophy of the proletariat; he says that he agrees with Spinoza that truth is its own standard, which means, in effect, that philosophical arguments are to be evaluated by philosophical, and not by political standards. His point seems to be that the truth of materialism is something that the bourgeoisie *cannot* recognize, and which it must therefore try to obfuscate by means of ideology. Conversely, the truth of materialism is something that the proletariat can recognize and must try to further. Althusser seems to have in mind here, not materialism as a general philosophical theory, but *historical* materialism, i.e. the Marxist theory of society. It is the existence of the class struggle, and the factors that determine it, that the bourgeoisie cannot recognize without abandoning its own position of domination within society as a whole.

Commenting on this view of philosophy, Dr O'Hagan notes that much work will have to be done if it is to be made acceptable. There is need of

[18] Ludwig Feuerbach, MEW, XXI, 275; Marx and Engels, *Selected Works*, II, 335. Compare Althusser, *Lenin and Philosophy*, 55.

[19] Lenin, *Materialism and Empirio-Criticism*; Lenin, *Collected Works*, XIV, English trans. (Moscow and London, 1962), 326.

[20] *Anti-Dühring*, MEW, XX, 129; English trans., 155.

(i) a general explanation, within the framework of historical materialism, of the roles of science and ideology; it has to be shown that the ruling bourgeoisie necessarily relies on mystificatory ideologies. There is also need of (ii) particular explanations of the role of philosophy in relation to politics and the sciences. Dr O'Hagan is, I believe, quite right in his statement of what Althusser's view needs if it is to be established; there is the further problem of whether what it needs can ever be provided. One may be reminded of Professor Atkinson's comments on historical materialism, viewed as an account of the main lines of historical development: namely, that the thesis is so very general that complete verification is extremely difficult.

University of Reading

Revolution, Reform and Dialectic

ROY EDGLEY

Marx and Marxism

Marxism is the tradition of thought and practice founded by Marx. To be identifiable as Marxism any phase of this tradition must have important resemblances to Marx's own work, and those resemblances must be conscious and acknowledged. Anti-Marxists tend to interpret this relation according to a derogatory religious model. Marxists, they suppose, treat Marx as an authority and follow their leader wherever he leads, instead of following the argument wherever it leads. On this view Marxism has an essentially scholarly relation to Marx and a polemical relation to everything else: it seeks to identify exactly what Marx said and thought, to preserve the master's teaching in all its original purity, and to appeal to it for correct answers to the substantive questions that we face. In other words, Marxism is that tradition which treats the works of Marx as a bible and imagines that it can clinch substantive arguments with the words 'Marx has said it'.

Of some Marxists and some phases of the Marxist tradition this view may be near the truth, though any such dogmatic fundamentalism would be contrary to Marx's own practice and would therefore cast doubt on the appropriateness of the 'Marxist' label. It is of course the case that Marxists regard Marx as a great and original thinker and spend time studying his work in the belief that he sheds more light than anybody else on the general nature and history of our society. But this is not a specifically religious attitude and is in any case not in the least irrational. All thinkers, in philosophy, science, or whatever, work within historically established intellectual and social traditions, as Marx and Marxists insist. They may acknowledge their debts by identifying some of their predecessors as superior to others, and they may identify themselves by reference to those predecessors, as Platonists, Aristotelians, Copernicans, Cartesians, Newtonians, Kantians, Hegelians, Freudians, or Wittgensteinians. They will certainly accept some theories from the past, such as empiricism, functionalism, behaviourism, quantum mechanics or psycho-analysis. Not acknowledging these matters or being ignorant of these predecessors may obscure the debts but is not, I take it, a condition of rationality. There is, in sum, nothing specially suspect about identifying one's intellectual position in terms of a past theory or theorist.

In particular, to do this is not to be uncritical. On the contrary, the work of Marx and of Marxism is essentially critical and oppositional, and if these things can be quantified it seems evident that in terms of the sheer range, historical tenacity, and common popularity of the items it objects to this work is far more critical than that of its opponents. From this judgment, of course, a thorough-going scepticism would have to be excepted. But such scepticism, especially of the philosophical sort, is more of a fantasy for the intellectual's study than a reality for the games of backgammon in the real life world outside, and tends to mask a real credulousness about that world that Marx and Marxism vigorously oppose. In any case, scepticism also is a position with a long history, and contemporary exponents, whether they know it or not, are most of them following lines of argument laid down long ago. Their position does not for that reason cease to be their own. It is not for that reason the property of somebody else, whom they follow with the irrationality of blind faith.

I am implying that originality is not a necessary condition of rationality or scientificity, not that it is impossible. Marx's work itself, of course, is highly original. Nevertheless, it draws on various traditions, such as Aristotelianism, Hegelianism, science, political economy, and socialism and the working-class movement, and Marx was generous in acknowledging his debts to predecessors, as the early parts of *Capital* prove. The point is that these traditions were not dead, not historical relics to be worshipped by the devout, but living elements of the present, and in working to absorb them he at the same time develops and transforms them. In a similar way Marx's work is a living presence in Marxism. Marxism develops and transforms Marx's work, and in doing so remains faithful to certain well-known ideas in Marx himself: the polemics against 'eternal truths', the changing nature of society, and the need for theory to be in close contact with that changing social reality.

Fifteen years ago, especially in England and most other parts of the English-speaking world, and in particular in intellectual and academic circles, there would have been some excuse for thinking that Marxism was moribund, a prostrate form before the ossified relic of Marx's remains. Today the revival of Marxism is everywhere evident, even in England, even among intellectuals, and even, it has to be said, in English philosophy. Part of the proof of that is the actuality of this present series of Royal Institute of Philosophy lectures. Their mere existence testifies to the emergence of Marxism as a subject for philosophical debate. More than that, I shall argue, Marxism is a philosophical issue, because it challenges the *status quo* not only at the most obvious level of political practice, not only at the level of political and economic theory, of social science, but also at the theoretically more fundamental level of philosophy itself. More specifically still, it is actually in the process of opposing the *status quo* at the levels of politics and economics that it also opposes it philosophically. I hope to exemplify this claim with respect to the relation between the aim of Marxist political practice, revolution, and the basic philosophy of Marxism, the materialist dialectic.

Dialectic and Revolutionary Change

Marx himself more than once asserts a connection between his dialectic and revolution. In the *Theses on Feuerbach* the word 'dialectic' does not occur, but this is precisely the text in which Marx contrasts his materialism with the undialectical materialism of Feuerbach; and in no less than three of the eleven theses Marx explicitly connects this contrast with the distinction between a revolutionary and a non-revolutionary approach. In the first thesis Marx identifies what he calls 'the chief defect of all hitherto existing materialisms (that of Feuerbach included)' and attributes to this Feuerbach's failure to 'grasp the significance of "revolutionary" . . . activity'. The third tells us that 'the materialist doctrine concerning the changing of circumstances and upbringing forgets that circumstances are changed by men and that it is essential to educate the educator himself', and that this 'coincidence of the changing of circumstances and of human activity or self-changing can be conceived and rationally understood only as *revolutionary practice*' (Marx's italics). Thesis IV comments on Feuerbach's work on religion, which 'consists in resolving the religious world into its secular basis. But', says Marx, 'that the secular basis detaches itself from itself and establishes itself as an independent realm in the clouds can only be explained by the cleavages and self-contradictions within the secular basis. The latter must, therefore, in itself be both understood in its contradiction and revolutionized in practice.' The crucial implication of this claim in the early Marx that traditional materialism is non-revolutionary is brought out in the mature Marx nearly three decades later when in a famous passage in a preface to *Capital* he makes explicit the basis of his revolutionary approach in his form of the dialectic. 'In its rational form', he declares, 'it is a scandal and abomination to bourgeoisdom and its doctrinaire professors, . . . because it lets nothing impose upon it, and is in its essence critical and revolutionary'.

We have here the most general and abstract formulation of Marxism's specificity, of those features, in other words, that distinguish Marxism from everything else. The concept of Marxism, and thus of Marxism's relation to Marx, is of course, by comparison with the concepts of pure mathematics, vague and fluid. Marxism is a historical movement, related by temporal continuities to Marx, but in a changing world changing and developing in its concrete content in such a way as to raise continually the question 'Is this really Marxism?' One thing that Marxism must be is socialism. It must, that is, be against capitalism and for the working-class in the effort to transform class society into a classless society. The identity of Marxism, and its relation to Marx, is chiefly a matter of its specificity within the socialist movement. Such concepts as deviationist and revisionist Marxism indicate the fluidity of the distinctions within socialism, that broad stream within which Marxism relates in various ways to Utopian socialism, ethical socialism, social democracy, communism, Eurocommunism and so on. One thing that helps to distinguish Marxism within this stream is its revolutionary character. Other versions of socialism tend to be reformist. But in the connection he sees between dialectic and revolution Marx is also signifying a further distinctive feature. For the concept of dialectic, as is made clear in the preface to *Capital* already quoted, is meant to characterize Marx's science, and in particular what he calls his 'method'; and the *Theses on Feuerbach* are clearly epistemological, or at any rate outline a view intended as an alternative to the epistemological materialism attributed to Feuerbach. Marxist socialism, then, is distinguished by being both revolutionary and scientific, but also by the fact that in Marxism the science and the revolution are unified by or in the dialectic. The kind of socialism most sharply distinguished from Marxism at this general and philosophical level is ethical socialism. Ethical socialism is reformist, not revolutionary; and if its political practice is in any way guided by science, its conception of science will be undialectical. Being undialectical it will be 'theoretical' in the pejorative sense used in the *Theses on Feuerbach*, and it will then need to be related to practice by some ideological mediation, such as morality, which carries within itself ideological residues from religion and law.

One of the things that the Marxist dialectic is doing, therefore, is shaping a conception of science, in particular social science, that relates science to political practice without the mediation of morality. In the process, the political practice required by such a dialectical science is determined as revolutionary. What is meant by 'revolutionary' here?

A connection between science and revolution has entered the philosophical arena in recent years through Kuhn's *Structure of Scientific Revolutions*, and indeed the idea of the Scientific Revolution has been for a long time a familar aspect of the history of sixteenth and seventeenth century thought. The generic notion of revolution involved here is relevant to our concerns. It means a historical change of a fundamental and pervasive kind, a change of structure, a change of elements due to an overall change in their systematic relations. But a scientific revolution in this history-of-science sense is a revolution within science, or at least within thought or theory; and thus, being fundamental, pervasive and structural, it is a specifically *conceptual* change, a change in the basic categorial framework in terms of which reality is characterized or understood. Marxism is a revolutionary science in this sense.

Is such a change dialectical? According to dialectic, things change because of their internal contradictions. Certainly it is contradictions within a body of theory, and what Kuhn calls 'anomalies' between theory and observation, that generate the pressure for change, and these pressures eventually produce a new theory that also in some sense contradicts the old.

But though the opposition between new and old theory is such that accepting one necessarily requires rejecting the other, they do not contradict each other in the standard formal logical sense. The concept of incommensurability marks this distinction. The new theory negates not simply the truth of the statements of the old theory but the very appropriateness and applicability of its concepts, and it is because of this fundamental character of this type of negation that the new theory negates the old not statement by statement, not piecemeal and bit by bit, but as a single totality. It does not follow that the change from the old to the new theory, either for the scientific community as a whole or for any individual within it, is sudden, accomplished with the speed of a Gestalt switch or in a blinding flash of revelation as in religious conversion.[1]

That idea of dialectical change is specially present in what might be regarded as the standard 'diamat' version of the materialist dialectic. According to most non-Marxist doctrine, contradictions can occur only in thought, as in the account of scientific thought above, not in the reality that thought is about, e.g. in the solar system or in atomic reactions. Kant, for instance, distinguishes real from logical opposition, that is, conflict from contradiction, and to non-Marxists since this distinction has seemed so obvious as to constitute a simple and decisive objection to dialectical materialism. From this objection Hegel escapes, given his idealism: for if reality is constituted by thought and ideas it follows that contradiction, as a relation between ideas, can occur in reality. But Marx accepts the Hegelian dialectic of contradictions in reality while rejecting Hegel's idealism, and thus commits himself to the outrageous claim that there can be contradictions not merely in thought but in the material reality that thought is about. As distinguished from conflict by being a specifically *logical* relation, contradiction, it is argued against Marx, must be a kind of opposition between words, thoughts, or ideas, and in particular between items that can be true or false, propositions, statements, or theories. Oppositions in material reality, e.g. between forces such as gravity and inertia, can only be conflicts. To imagine otherwise would be to commit oneself to the nonsensical claim that such conflicts, being contradictions, would be truly described by contradictory statements. What is nonsensical about this of course is that a contradictory statement must be false, that is, the contradictory state of affairs that such a statement apparently describes is logically impossible.

If anything survives this assult on the materialist dialectic it can only be the view that thought must depict real change as the product of conflict. The task of scientific theory must then be to identify large-scale change and its explanatory mechanism in the basic material conflicts within that

---

[1] See John Krige's 'Revolution and Discontinuity', *Radical Philosophy*, No. 22 (Summer 1979).

reality. For social science in particular this large-scale change will be change in the social structure that identifies a type of society throughout a lengthy historical period, and its explanatory mechanism will be conflict in the basic, most material, part of that society's structure, i.e. its economy and specifically its mode of production. The structure that identifies a historical type of society must be relatively inert, the aspect of that society most resistant to change. What explains a change of structure must thus have great explanatory power. Now it is natural to suppose that the explanatory power of conflict is a function both of the fundamentality of that conflict and of the degree of conflict involved. A change of anything so inert as structure must be explained by a conflict that is both basic and intense. But for all pre-socialist societies, conflict is not only what *explains* structural change; it is also definitive of the structure that changes. In respect of this aspect of conflict, it is natural to suppose that the lower the degree of conflict characterizing a social structure the more stable the structure. Both of these considerations suggest a picture of social change according to which social conflict gradually intensifies, strengthening the transformative power of the base while it weakens the resistance of the structure in general to the point at which that structure collapses. What changes gradually here is the intensification of the conflict; until it reaches the point at which a sudden explosive change occurs in the social structure itself. A period of gradual piecemeal change builds up to a moment of revolutionary change, a sudden explosive change that is a change of structure, the destruction of the existing order.

Dialectic, Social Science and Social Revolution

In this very general form there is nothing that distinguishes this 'dialectical' account of social revolution from revolutionary change in natural systems. In other words, the concept of revolution in its relation to dialectic here involves nothing more than the idea of change of definitive structure, i.e. fundamental and pervasive change, occurring with relative swiftness as a result of gradual intensification of structural conflict. Changes of climate could be revolutionary in this sense. Such changes are temporal and capable of being depicted by natural science. They are not historical in the sense in which it is essentially men (and women) who make history, and for which a specifically social science is necessary.

The change of perspective consequently required is complicated. On the one hand the revolution must be social and political, involving the will and consciousness of a revolutionary class. On the other hand the social science that dialectically represents the contemporary movement of socialist revolution cannot stand in the same general relationship to it as does natural science to its real object, the external, detached relationship of objectively and neutrally depicting that revolutionary movement, like a reflection in a mirror. Earlier social revolutions, such as the English bourgeois revolution, were made by men whose consciousness of what they were doing was defectively ideological, and this situation was connected with the historical fact that at that period no adequate social science had been developed. By contrast, the working class movement grows contemporaneously, though not by coincidence, with the growth of social science. What the materialist dialectic does is to bring into convergence this scientific form of consciousness and the consciousness of the revolutionary class. Marx does indeed speak of his science as reflecting, as in a mirror, the social movement of his time. But he also formulates the relationship in ways open to a different interpretation:

> Just as the economists are the scientific representatives of the bourgeois class, so the Socialists and Communists are the theoreticians of the proletarian class ... in the measure that history moves forward, and with it the struggle of the proletariat assumes clearer outline, they no longer need to seek science in their minds: they have only to take note of what is happening before their eyes and to become its mouthpiece (*Poverty of Philosophy* (New York: International Publishers, 1963), 125).

Also:

> The theoretical conclusions of the Communists ... merely express, in general terms, actual relations springing from an existing class struggle ... (*Communist Manifesto* in *The Revolutions of 1848*, D. Fernbach (ed.), (Harmondsworth: Penguin, 1973), 80).

This relationship, according to which social scientific theory may *express* or be the *mouthpiece* of a social movement, could be regarded as construing that science as representing the reality of that movement not simply in the way in which a reflection in a mirror represents an external object, but rather as a representative, on its behalf: not simply as speaking *of* it, but as speaking *for* it. That the 'theoretical conclusions' of the 'scientific representatives' of the working class express in general terms the fully developed and articulated consciousness of that class is evident from the fact that having referred to the Communists (capital 'C') as 'theoreticians', Marx identifies proletarian class-consciousness as 'communist consciousness'. It is this convergence that determines the sense in which Marx's science is revolutionary. Marx identifies 'a class which forms the majority of all members of society, and from which emanates the consciousness of the necessity of a fundamental revolution, the communist consciousness': and he goes on to say '... for the production on a mass scale of this communist consciousness ... the alteration of men on a mass scale is necessary, an alteration which can only take place in a practical movement, a revolution' (*German Ideology*, C. J. Arthur (ed). (London: Lawrence and Wishart, 1970), 94–95). In more explicit conjunction with

3

the word 'science' itself, Marx says, after referring to the science of communist theoreticians as the 'mouthpiece' of the working-class movement: 'From this moment, science, which is a product of the historical movement, has associated itself consciously with it, has ceased to be doctrinaire and has become revolutionary' (*Poverty of Philosophy*, 126).

This dialectical convergence between science and its real object is made possible, at the philosophical level, by a structure of relations peculiar to social science. The traditional materialism associated with natural science regards material reality as external to and independent of scientific theory and thought in general, while scientific theory is dependent on material reality for its truth, conceived as a relation of correspondence or reflection between theory and real object. More specifically, this relation is a relation of description, explanation, and prediction. However, even in natural science a theory is related not only to the material reality it is about but also to other theory: in contradicting another theory it logically opposes it and in effect criticizes it, evaluating it as wrong, mistaken, in error, and thus calling for its rejection and replacement. This logical relation of contradiction between theories is thus, explicitly or by implication, a social and historical relation of conflict between people, between those who accept the theories. In social science this structure is considerably complicated. It is complicated by the general fact that in this field theory and real object are so to speak closer together than in natural science. This relative closeness is a function of the fact that for social science each of the two terms of the thought–object relationship draws toward the other. On the one hand, thought or theory is included in that social object: the ideas that people have in society are, of course, part of the real social object that social science investigates and seeks to understand, and these ideas must, in any adequate account, include social scientific theories themselves, both those that such an account opposes and criticizes and even that account itself. On the other hand, that real social object includes, as the material base of such thought or theory, not the material objects and processes of the natural science paradigm but: practice. Practice and thought, as the two chief elements of the social object, are moreover not simply conjoined in that object. Thought itself is a kind of practice, mental or intellectual practice, and material practice, which transforms physical nature, as in the production of food and buildings, necessarily involves thought. Marx's materialism in this way replaces the traditional philosophical problematic of the relation between thought and matter with the problematic of the relation between theory and practice. His social science both *depicts* the various historical modes of the unity of theory and practice and *requires* a particular mode of such unity in the revolutionary movement.

How is this requirement possible? Given that human thought is part of the social reality that social science seeks to understand by grasping its structural relation to the material practice of the social base, Marxism stands exposed to the temptation of 'the sociology of knowledge': the temptation of a sceptical relativism about thought in general, and thus of a self-refuting conception of science that fails to distinguish science from ideology. Such a move would be completely contrary to Marx's conception of science and his own theoretical practice embodying that conception. He does not make the mistake of imagining that a materialist explanation of theory is incompatible with its cognitive evaluation. On the contrary, his theoretical work is a work of relentless criticism of other theories, a resolute effort to reveal their irrationalities. He gives full and sometimes passionate expression to the necessity of scientific theory to contradict other existing theories, to engage in real logical opposition to the muddle and mystification generated by unscientific modes of thought. Retaining this essential critical function for science, but in accordance with his materialist conception of social science refusing to leave the cognitive defects of opposing ideas simply exposed as illusions or mistakes, he traces these defects to their explanatory conditions in material practice. But he does not represent those conditions as otherwise neutral causes of such cognitive defects. Rather, he characterizes these conditions themselves as defective: irrationalities of theory are due to irrationalities of practice. It is this common irrationality shared by both thought and practice that is categorized by the single dialectical conception of contradiction. The illogicality of self-conflicting thought reflects the irrationality of self-conflicting practice.

The Ideology of Moral Opposition

The critical scope of Marx's science thus as materialist dialectic extends from other theories to the material practices that necessitate those theories, taking as its target the whole social structure that is its real object. But this criticism of its real object is consequently not specifically *moral* criticism, in that sense of the word 'moral' that has become dominant in the modern period. The conception of morality that has developed under capitalism has evolved partly in response to the Scientific Revolution, in which natural science was constituted as a specialism in a new division of cultural labour, leaving morality, like the religion with which it has close connections, to develop by contrast and distinction. These contrasts are well enough known in the arguments of the philosophers. One of them is the contrast between the determinism of science and the free will of morality. Connected with that, and more directly relevant to our concerns, is the contrast between science as theory and fact, morality as practice and value. The general split that threatens here, given a materialist account of science conceiving it as a paradigm of rationality in contact with the real material world, involves a view of morality recognizably present in some of Marx's polemics: as utopian, out of touch with reality, inventing fantastic ideals that bear no relation to the historical situation and its real forces, and which thus stand no chance of realization but serve rather to distract people from effective action, with conservative consequences. Science meanwhile, on this theoreticist view, bears on practice in the only way such a con-conception logically allows it to, in the form of technological imperatives prescribing means to whatever ends it can be employed to serve: it therefore yields efficiency as the only rational practical value and finds its natural social site in the egoistic materialism of economic practice, as both productive technology and practice 'in its dirty-judaical manifestation' (first of the *Theses on Feuerbach*).

But this is the merest hint. What I want to suggest is that in representing his science, in virtue of its dialectical character, as revolutionary, Marx is rejecting as non-revolutionary both the traditional materialist conception of science, and morality conceived and necessitated as that science's complementary opposite; and he is shaping his science as an essential component in the human agency by which the social revolution of socialism is effected. Ethical socialism is non-revolutionary, a socialism of reform, because its practice is governed by morality in this sense outlined. In being governed by morality it is under the sway of bourgeois ideology, a system of thought and practice that helps to protect the social *status quo* by resisting the change called for as necessary by Marxist science. I shall try to trace some of the conceptual affinities between morality and opposition to revolution that make this view plausible in our time and place. These affinities do not amount to entailments and 'logical necessities'.[2] As far as 'pure logic' is concerned, to say nothing of actual particular examples, the separation of science as theory from practice as morality, together with the paradigmatic rationality of science, leaves morality a completely free hand, so to speak, to recommend anything whatsoever, revolution included. But such indeterminacy is impossible to live with and social need develops a rationale for eliminating all but a narrow range of these 'logical possibilities'. My concern is with actual socio-historical forms of thought and practice, and their rational reconstruction must in any case allow for their pervasive ideological character.

I have argued that Marx's dialectical conception of social science is a conception of scientific theory that is critical of its real object, society itself, and thus opposes society and calls for it, in the words of the eleventh of the *Theses on Feuerbach*, to be not merely interpreted but changed. At this level Marx's target is that 'theoretical attitude' associated with traditional materialism which conceives of the relation of scientific theory to its object as a relation of contemplation or interpretation. Such theory is purely descriptive and value-neutral. It seeks only to correspond or conform to its object, not to criticize and oppose it. As is evident from the passage

[2] A point made forcefully by Russell Keat in his reply (*Radical Philosophy*, No. 23) to an early draft of some of these ideas in *Radical Philosophy*, No. 21.

I have already quoted about his 'rational form' of the dialectic (*Capital*, Preface), Marx associates the critical character of his science with its revolutionary nature. But in *The German Ideology* he identifies a form of criticism that he labels specifically 'mental criticism' and says that 'not criticism but revolution is the driving force of history' (ed. C. J. Arthur, 58–59). Political and social change has two general modes, revolutionary and non-revolutionary, and revolutionary activity Marx at the end of the first of the *Theses on Feuerbach* identifies with what he calls ' "practical-critical" activity'. Given this structure of concepts, morality, as the necessary opposite of a neutral and non-critical science, must involve a point of view from which criticism of its object is possible, but as a critical activity that is not specifically practical. The implication is that morality's characteristic or preferred mode of opposition, by contrast with the materialist nature of practice, is theoretical, or better, mentalistic: activity in the idealist sense. As such, morality fulfils the classic function of ideology, opposing the *status quo*, when it does so at all, more in appearance than in reality, and thus, like its parent, religion, giving real discontent a form of expression that is mystified and ineffectual. Such an account accepts what is acceptable in what might be regarded as the dominant 'sociological' view of morality, as a social device for promoting social solidarity and conformity,[3] while acknowledging what that sociological view sometimes forgets, the conceptual space for and actual existence of moral opposition to the *status quo*, e.g. in the form of ethical socialism.

The non-practical and idealist character of moral criticism is thus constituted by its being a mode of opposition that is criticism and nothing else, i.e. by its predominantly verbal form, its character as 'moralizing', 'preaching', and 'exhortation', and more generally as arguing and reasoning with people. As opposition to an action or practice it calls for that practice to be changed; but it calls for it to be changed through a change of heart, mind, or attitude on the part of its agents, and this call itself has the force, in Austin's sense of illocutionary or perlocutionary force, of an activity whose point is to help bring about that change of attitude and thus of behaviour. Moral criticism is itself, in this way, conceived as a mode of effecting change, an idealist means of changing material practice. This is presumably what people have in mind when they talk of 'moral means' of changing something.

The tendency of morality under this conception to favour this specific means of effecting changes in practice expresses the general condition that restricts moral criticism to free action, i.e. action under the control of the agent's mind, his ideas, will, judgment and attitude. More particularly,

[3] Its many and varied resources in this respect are described and analysed in papers by A. Collier, R. Norman and A. Skillen in *Radical Philosophy*, Nos. 5, 6, 8 and 9.

if somebody morally ought to behave differently the implication is that he should behave differently because *he thinks* he should behave differently; and thus that the moral way of changing his behaviour is to convince him by persuasion that he should change it, if necessary by blaming him and thus getting him to feel shame and guilt, appealing to his conscience.

This idealist tendency has been strongly reinforced by another current developing within the conception of morality since the Enlightenment and coming to dominance in the twentieth century. As the example of Kant shows, the separation of science, as theory, from practice, and thus the development of the modern conception of morality as the regulator of practice, is not obviously incompatible with the claim that morality and practice can be rational.[4] But this conception of morality as distinguished from science has developed under the shadow of the powerful doctrine that only science can yield knowledge, i.e. rationally justified truth, and the consequence has been a prolonged scepticism, first clearly formulated by Hume, about the possibility of knowledge, truth, and rationality in moral judgment and action. This scepticism makes it less easy to suppose that the right method of changing things is to change other people's practices by changing their moral judgments into conformity with one's own. Nevertheless this scepticism has a similar effect in favouring, if not logically necessitating, idealist methods of change. If each person's moral values and interests are ultimately a matter of arbitrary and subjective choice, the universality and neutrality of reason, or at least its closest analogue, will be available not at the level of any individual's own particular moral judgment and interest but only in an uncommitted point of view above such judgments, at a so-to-speak philosophical meta-level above the fray. Since nobody's particular judgment or interest is more objective or true than anybody else's, each should be as free as possible to do what he thinks right. Toleration, of other people's moral values, interests and conduct, is thus the central value issuing from this attempt to preserve a semblance of rationality from scepticism about values in general. In conditions of disagreement and conflict the aim must be to seek agreement by dialogue, possibly by negotiation, bargaining, arbitration, and compromise, and if those fail we can at least agree to accept a majority verdict. For this to be workable the essential attitudes are moderation and flexibility. Those who, in conflict with others, refuse to compromise reveal themselves as dogmatists and extremists. Under this conception, indeed, specifically moral values at the ground level may wither away, their place taken entirely by the prudential value of interests, with morality confined to the second level values of freedom, toleration, compromise, and moderation.

This group of concepts, familiar to us all from their ubiquitous presence

---

[4] Another matter also stressed by Russell Keat in his reply (*Radical Philosophy*, No. 23) to my remarks on this subject in *Radical Philosophy*, No. 21.

in contemporary life, is central to modern liberal morality, and to the moralized form of politics characteristic of liberal societies, the politics of parliamentary democracy. Though this is one form of politics in competition with others, liberalism tends to represent itself as having the virtue of being apolitical or non-political. It sees its institutional forms, e.g. in the liberal state itself, or in the liberal university, as occupying the neutral level above the contending particularities on the ground below, as comprehending within themselves this pluralism of differing views and styles of life, and where necessary as arbitrating between them. In such a position, it is supposed, the state must represent 'the national interest', and it does so partly by sublimating conflict, including class conflict, into its idealist parliamentary form of parley, of dialogue and debate, and in the process moderating that conflict by subjecting it to the pressure of compromise. The Parliamentary opposition is also Her Majesty's loyal opposition. Necessary social change is effected politically in this sense, by state action, through legislation, that is, by reform.

Dialectical Opposition and Political Revolution

If morality, as potentially critical of the *status quo*, in these ways can oppose conflict and seek to reduce it through the medium of argument and ideas, idealistically, how does it differ from a dialectical social science, whose dialectical character also puts it in opposition to real contradictions, i.e. social conflicts, and whose mode of opposition, as science, is theoretical, also at the level of ideas and argument? In what way is this science unlike morality in being revolutionary, a critical activity whose mode of opposition is specifically practical? The dialectic here is inseparable from Marx's materialism, and this in its turn from science as concerned with what is fundamental. So far as concerns its peculiarly dialectical content, what distinguishes the Marxist from this moral mode of opposition to social conflict is its character as opposing such conflict by *taking sides* and *intensifying* the conflict, not ameliorating it by compromise from a position between or above the contending sides. Intensification of the conflict, not merely predicted but called for, leads to its resolution through the victory of one of the sides, of that side, namely, which is needed by the other but which does not in its turn need that other opposing side. Amelioration cannot resolve this conflict because the conflict being referred to is the class conflict, which is both pervasive and necessitated by the most fundamental aspect of society, the capitalist mode of production, and is thus an essential structural character of this type of society. Such a conflict is an 'irreconcilable contradiction', and not eliminable under capitalism. The change from capitalism to socialism is a deep-rooted structural change, requiring therefore to be effected by a massive practical power, the power of the masses in action against the capitalist structure, and thus against the class interests of the bourgeoisie. Purely moral means must be ineffective against such an obstacle.

Indeed, non-revolutionary methods, doing what they can with the limited means at their disposal, characteristically avoid the target. This is evident in the real practice of modern social democracy. The historical development of this social formation, especially by contrast with such contemporaneous outcomes of revolutionary socialism as Stalinism, has been largely responsible, both in thought and fact, for the failure that has always haunted Marxism, the failure of the revolution to materialize in its classic Marxist form in the agency of the working class of the advanced capitalist societies of Western Europe. The general condition that has frustrated the revolution in Western Europe, where it was most expected, has been the development of capitalism into a phase in which the working class has apparently been integrated into society and the class antagonism between workers and bourgeoisie thus moderated instead of intensified. This general condition divides into two, one political and the other economic. Universal suffrage, the growth of parliamentary democracy, has brought the working class a share of constitutional political power; and the working-class movement, using this political power in conjunction with the economic struggle of its trade union wing, has been able, under the increasing productive capacity of capitalism, to raise the workers' standard of living and to lift them out of the grinding poverty of their Victorian ancestors. Our advanced capitalist society, in other words, is apparently no longer 'two nations' but one: the irreconcilable contradiction between working class and bourgeoisie has been reconciled in the form of a society that is a compromise between socialism and capitalism, the welfare state and its 'mixed economy', in which, partly in accordance with Keynesian theories of demand management and partly through socialist policies of public ownership of the 'commanding heights' of the economy, the democratic state intervenes in the economy and thus, as representative of all the people, ensures 'fair shares for all'. Contemporary social democracy, as in the prevailing consensus, especially at the level of the main political parties, of Western Europe, no longer has a socialist commitment. In this respect it differs from its classical ancestor, the social democracy of Bernstein and the German party, and from the revival of classical social democracy, now known as democratic socialism, among the communist parties of the West in the form of Eurocommunism. What all forms share is Fabianism: change, if at all, by legal and constitutional means, the 'parliamentary road'. Is it not possible, in a democracy, for the working class majority to elect a government that will legislate the replacement of capitalism by socialism?

The social democratic form of change has recognized, with Marxism, the fundamental importance of the economy. But it has missed the specific target of Marxist theory and practice, the material base of the economy itself in the mode of production. Its nationalization programme has been largely a salvage operation: it has left the old hierarchies intact, and like its anti-monopoly legislation, has aimed at the efficient running of the capitalist system. Its welfare policies, progressive taxation, and even its characteristic activity at the point of production, trade union activity, have been aimed not at production but at distribution, the redistribution of the social product. This distinction between production and distribution, and the modes of change appropriate to them, have often been understood, or misunderstood, in ways that bear their undialectical character on their face.[5] The production process, as a means of producing goods for distribution, is thought of as changing progressively in terms of its efficiency, i.e. 'productivity', represented by its scientific technology and measured by the relationship between production (especially labour) as a cost and the value of the goods, or wealth, produced as an end. The specifically moral rather than scientific dimension of the economy, on this view, enters with distribution of that wealth, as fair and just or otherwise, and it is this moral question of distribution that the moral methods of social democracy address themselves to. In other words, the distinction between production and distribution has been aligned with the distinction between science and morality. Notoriously, however, production and distribution cannot be separated in this way. As Marx pointed out, in production people produce not only goods, commodities, but also themselves, and their jobs, class position, and general life-chances are goods (or evils) allocated like any others by a system of distribution. In any case, the causal connection between a mode of production and a pattern of distribution of commodities imposes strict limits on the degree to which distribution can be changed without a change in production. The rising standard of living of the working class has had as its chief necessary condition the overall growth of the economy, and the continuing capitalist structure of the mode of production has ensured two things: first, the survival of the class system and a distribution of the economic product, however expanded, along familiar class lines; and second, a historical path of economic growth which, within its long-term rise, fluctuates wildly between boom and slump, periodically bringing the system, its class structure explosively preserved, into crisis.

I am not of course suggesting that in a parliamentary democracy the working class majority has the power to effect by reform the revolutionary transformation of capitalism into socialism, and that the only thing that prevents this is the ideology of morality. On the contrary, the relatively weak power of the social democratic state as an agent of change in the face of the capacity of the capitalist mode of production to reproduce itself, moral ideology and all, provides support for the Marxist view that the

[5] For a philosophical example of this, see J. Rawls' *Theory of Justice*, and the critique of this by G. Doppelt, so far unpublished.

moralized version of politics constituted by the parliamentary form of democracy is itself an ideological appearance that conceals the real essence of this state. There are two general ways in which this appearance belies the reality of its material base. First, its democratic character is compromised by the fact that the capitalist economy produces and reproduces, through class structuration, gross inequalities of power, economic, political, judicial and ideological, that make the formal democracy of universal suffrage and freedom of discussion compatible with bourgeois class rule, or at least domination. Second, its parliamentary character, i.e. its form as a mode of political activity in which conflict is resolved by parley, by dialogue, serves to camouflage its other method of settling issues, by its legitimate monopoly of violence (Weber) through its legal system and repressive apparatus, the army and police force. Together these constitute the element of bourgeois class dictatorship within liberal social democracy. They make the state in capitalist society, whether a fascist state or a social democratic state, an essential target of revolutionary action.

This is the final specification of the Marxist conception of revolution. As so far explicated, revolution is a fundamental and pervasive change in the social structure effected by human agency. But Marx frequently distinguished what he called social revolution, in this sense, from what he called political revolution. Using this distinction, the Austro-Marxist philosopher Max Adler pointed out that though a social revolution must be a long revolution a political revolution could be relatively swift. Prepared for by a lengthy process of social change, including legislative reform, and followed by a lengthy process of social change, including legislative reform, this political revolution would constitute the moment at which specifically state power is taken over from the bourgeoisie by the working class. Given the constraints already mentioned, the change from non-socialist to socialist government is probably impossible by electoral means: political revolution may be necessary in the sense of an illegal and unconstitutional seizure of state power, involving the use of insurrectionary force and violence. Moreover, after such a seizure of power, the socialist government's legislation must be uncompromising, its aim the destruction of capitalism and its replacement by socialism. Partly because of this a gap will be opened up between legislation and implementation, and legislation will need to be forcibly implemented against the will of the bourgeoisie. For this reason, the existing bourgeois state apparatus, the parliamentary and representative form of democracy, the Civil Service, the military and security forces, and the legal system, will need to be attacked and replaced. These are the requirements distinguished by Marx's concept of the revolutionary dictatorship of the proletariat. What marks them all is: the specifically dialectical condition of intransigent and uncompromising opposition to the contradictions of capitalism, and the specifically materialist and practical condition of using, when the economic and political situation makes success possible, whatever means are necessary, not excepting force and violence.

The Eurocommunist parties of Western Europe now reject this specific form of Marxist revolution. Their Marxism, if it can still be called Marxism, is the socialism of 'the historic compromise' and 'the parliamentary road'. The key concept in their revision of Marx is the concept of democracy: in rejecting social democracy they identify their position as democratic socialism. In this way they seek to distinguish themselves sharply from the Russian model, rejecting both Leninist political revolution and Stalinist tyranny. Appealing to Engels' 1895 introduction to Marx's *Class Struggles in France*, and Gramsci, they argue that whether or not the Russian revolution was socialist, the state in Western Europe differs crucially from the Tsarist state that faced Lenin, and as such makes insurrectionary revolution and the dictatorship of the proletariat both impossible and unnecessary. On this subject I will draw attention to one central philosophical and political problem: the question of democracy. Eurocommunism has a strong tendency to identify democracy with its existing parliamentary form, and thus with the moral or at least mental and idealist mode of historical change; and its socialism is centrally the struggle of a parliamentary political party acting as representative of its mass supporters, whose participation in the struggle is chiefly of a trade union and economic kind. But we must both distinguish democracy from parliament and remember that the parliamentary form of the state depends on its monopoly of legal violence: a parliament is specifically a talking shop, and historically it precedes democracy, as universal suffrage, by many centuries. What Engels rejected in his 1895 introduction was minority revolution, seizure of state power by a minority of revolutionary activists. For Marx the socialist revolution is a mass movement, the mass movement whose communist consciousness is expressed in general terms by Marx's science. Though not exclusively or even primarily parliamentary, it is nevertheless democratic in being: the will of the majority. It is this distinction, though not explicitly formulated in this way, that lies behind the arguments of one of the most acute and critical representatives of Eurocommunism, Fernando Claudin (see his *Eurocommunism and Socialism* (London: New Left Books, 1977)). It is a distinction that enables us to say that 'the dictatorship of the proletariat' is democratic, though not liberal democracy. It is democratic in the old sense, the sense in which democracy was long feared by a historic succession of anti-democratic political philosophers, from Plato to Mill.

The association of political revolution with violence, and the opposition to such revolution from the point of view of morality in the manner indicated, invites an understanding of revolution that brings it within the general antithesis between reason and violence, and so represents it as essentially non-rational, and possibly as romantic and spontaneous.

Roy Edgley

Plenty of evidence of this view can be found in Neil Harding's 'Socialism and Violence', in *The Concept of Socialism* (Bhikhu Parekh (ed.) (London: Croom Helm, 1975)). This arrangement of the relevant categories is of course entirely contrary to Marx's conceptual framework. In particular, it ignores the peculiarity of the connection in Marx between science and revolution. It is this connection between theory and 'practical–critical activity' that is mediated by the materialist dialectic: for Marx, socialist revolution is not romantic and spontaneous but rational and scientific, in his dialectical sense.

University of Sussex

Marx, Necessity and Science

D.-H. RUBEN

Among the very many questions we might wish to ask of any particular science, two of them concern the nature of the objects of the science and the character of the laws which describe the behaviour of those objects. What I wish to do is to raise those two questions about historical materialism. That is, I want to ask *what it is* that one studies in *Capital* for example, and *in what ways of behaving* does the nomic or lawlike behaviour of those objects consist. Both are ontological questions of a sort, and, in particular, questions about what I call social ontology, although it is usual to restrict the term 'ontological' to the former question alone. The first question asks about the objects to whose existence historical materialism is committed; the second asks about the characteristic ways of behaving of those objects.

First, let us ask about the nature of the objects of Marxist science. Most commentators claim that *Capital* is not about any particular capitalist society. References in *Capital* to Britain, for instance, are meant to be illustrative, but the book itself is about capitalism and its development. Marx sub-titled the book 'a critical analysis of capitalist production', and thereby indicated that his discussion was at a higher level of abstraction than, say, one about the economies of Britain or France or Germany.

The object of study of *Capital* is a type of economic structure, capitalism. In general, historical materialism studies *types* of economic structures, capitalism, feudalism, socialism. Marx often called these types 'modes of production', although his use of that expression is not entirely unambiguous. 'In broad outline, the Asiatic, ancient, feudal, and modern bourgeois modes of production may be designated as epochs marking progress in the economic development of society'.[1] In discussing the various ways Marx used the expression 'mode of production', G. A. Cohen correctly points out that Marx did not identify modes of production with economic structures, 'for a mode is a way or manner, not a set of relations'.[2] Since an economic structure is a set of relations, it must be logically possible for two societies to share precisely the same economic structure. But in fact, since a description of a society's economic structure includes every economic relation

---

[1] Karl Marx, *Preface to a Contribution to A Critique of Political Economy* (London: Lawrence and Wishart, 1971), 21.

[2] G. A. Cohen, *Karl Marx's Theory of History: A Defence* (Oxford: Clarendon Press, 1978), 79.

in the society, such a description is far too detailed for it to be plausible to believe that any two societies ever will share precisely the same economic structure. Yet many societies do share a mode of production, and so modes of production cannot be economic structures. But from this it does not follow that Marx did not identify a mode with a *type* of economic structure, and this seems to be what Marx was doing in the following remark, itself quoted by Cohen: 'Whatever the social form of production [=type of economic structure, according to Cohen's earlier identification], labourers and means of production always remain factors of it ... The specific *manner* [my emphasis—D.H.R.] in which this union is accomplished distinguishes the different economic epochs of the structure of society from one another.'[3] A manner of production or mode of production is a way in which the immediate producers and means of production become united, and this is Cohen's own method for individuating types of economic structures. Thus, we can safely assert that historical materialism has, as its object, types of economic structure, or modes of production, at least in one of Marx's central uses of that expression. Marx says, in the preface to the first German edition of *Capital*: 'In this work I have to examine the capitalist mode of production . . .'

That a science investigates a certain 'object' does not by itself commit us to the ontological irreducibility of that sort of thing. We can study and formulate laws about the behaviour of ideal gases, perfect vacuums, and frictionless surfaces without believing that there are such things. Indeed, we can even believe that it is a physical impossibility that there be such things. We can construe statements which make apparent reference to these things as statements which make real reference to something else— for example, statements seemingly about ideal gases can be construed as really about real gases, statements which say of those gases that the more nearly they have certain properties, the more nearly they behave in certain ways.[4] So we can ask, similarly, if we are obliged to construe talk about modes of production realistically, or if we have, on the contrary, alternative construals which show us that our apparent references to modes of production are real references to something else. I do not here want to raise the quite general question of methodological individualism.[5] Let us

[3] Karl Marx, *Capital*, II (Moscow: Progress Publishers, 1967), 36–37.
[4] See W. V. O. Quine, *Word and Object* (Cambridge, Mass.: MIT Press, 1960), 248–251, on limit myths.
[5] I take methodological individualism, in so far as it is an ontological doctrine, to be the thesis that statements which appear to refer to any social things can be translated without remainder into statements which actually refer to material individuals and ascribe to those individuals *social* properties. Methodological individualism in this sense seems to me to be a very plausible doctrine. I think that the poor repute into which it has fallen in Marxist circles can be explained by its conflation with a far less plausible thesis, that statements which appear to

suppose for the sake of argument that methodological individualism is false. Suppose there are irreducibly such things as wars (and not just warring individuals) and societies or economies (and not just individuals in social or economic relations). What I want to ask is whether, once we admit at least some social entities, there are any further reasons not to admit into our ontology modes of production. I think there are such reasons, and that it would be salutary for many of those who are influenced by the Althusserian tradition of Marx interpretation to consider those reasons.

Notice that wars and economies and states, if such things there be, are not like the abstract objects (again, if such there be), numbers, universals, or propositions, which are neither the proper subjects of change or locatable in space or time. Abstract objects do not have a spatio-temporal mode of existence and, connectedly, can play no part in causal interactions. It is true that we say such things as that the number of people in a certain country has changed, but in cases like this we take the proper subject of change to be the country and not the number. Consider now the mode of existence of World War II, the Fourth French Republic, or the Great Depression of 1929. If methodological individualism is false, these names name irreducibly social events or things. World War II had a temporal beginning and end, the Great Depression of 1929 occurred at certain places and not others, the Fourth French Republic has a history of change and development. These sorts of social entities or events, which I call 'first-order', are quite unlike the abstract objects by being (more or less) spatio-temporal and subjects of change, much like the material individuals which, as some say, bear them. These first-order social entities or events can initiate changes ('The causal consequences of World War II were . . .')

refer to social entities can be translated without remainder into statements which actually refer to material individuals and ascribe to those individuals non-social (physical or material) properties. Thus the interesting division between methodological individualists and holists, at least on ontological rather than explanatory questions, seems to me to be over the question of whether there are social entities or only social properties of material entities. Either we double the kinds of objects or the kinds of properties in the world. For my part, I prefer to keep my cosmic furniture simple and to complicate only the colours I can paint it, but this seems to be the sort of ontological question that can be decided only by tracing out all the metaphysical and epistemological consequences each of the two choices has in philosophy. There is a strange, unremarked tension within much of Marxist theory between materialism and a predilection for methodological holism. Whatever precisely materialism is, one would have assumed it to be anti-Platonic, sceptical of the possibility of non-material things. Yet, methodological holism appears to be a variety of Platonism in its ontological commitments. One would have supposed that materialism and methodological individualism went together.

and be the subjects of change ('The French Republic changed as a result of . . .').

What about modes of production, which stand rather as universals to first-order social entities, since many individual societies can share a mode of production, and more than one mode can be co-instantiated in a single society? Do the modes of production change and develop like first-order social entities, or are they outside of space, time, and change rather like abstract objects? Cohen argues that the economic structure of a society can change without there being any change in the type of economic structure itself.[6] Indeed, Cohen denies that the type can be the proper subject of change at all, for change at this level is merely the society's changing by replacing one mode of production by another: '. . . *Changes of social form.* This is the revolutionary case in which the type of economic structure does change, because one dominant production relation supplants another.' Cohen treats the modes of production as abstract objects, for just as we say that the number of people in a country changed without implying that the change befell a number, so too we now say that a type of economic structure changed without implying that the change befell the type itself. It is worth noting that if the reason for which modes of production cannot change is that they are abstract objects,then the same reason would lead us to conclude that economic structures, which are sets of relations, are also incapable of change. The economy of a society may change, and a society may change its economic structure or mode of production (type of economic structure) for another, but if a mode of production is unable to be a proper subject of change, so is an economic structure.

Marx repeatedly does link change and mode of production, and this linkage provides the essential importance for Marx of the concept of a mode of production. Sometimes change is linked to the mode of production itself;[7] sometimes to various of its parts of features.[8] Modes of production, for the Marxist tradition, grow, change, and develop—and whatever grows, changes, or develops does so in time. Modes of production have stages, are efficacious in bringing about changes, and are themselves the causal consequences of changes.[9] The laws Marx formulates are about the characteristic developments of a mode of production. Now, it is not my intention to argue that such talk is in any way suspect or illicit. What I do want to argue is that, in order to account for Marx's talk, we have to see that a

[6] Cohen, op. cit., 85–87.

[7] 'This system presents everywhere an obstacle to the real capitalist mode of production and goes under with its development' (*Capital*, III (Moscow: Progress Publishers, 1966), 334).

[8] 'Like all its predecessors, the capitalist process of production proceeds under definite material conditions . . .' (*Capital*, III, 818–819).

[9] 'The capitalist mode of production is, for this reason, a historical means of developing the material forces of production . . .' (*Capital*, III, 250).

reduction is at least in principle possible, just as it is in talk about the number of something changing. We have to understand talk about changes that befall modes of production as convenient shorthand for talk about the changes that befall the proper subjects of change, either about changes in the economy, or about societies changing one economic structure or type of economic structure (mode of production) for another. Neither types nor sets of relations can be the proper subjects of change.

It is in these last remarks that I find reason to refuse to recognize modes of production in their own, irreducible, ontological right. First, there is the difficulty in swallowing such an odd ontological category—a universal which can change in time. Swallowing it would give Hegel his revenge on Marx, since Marx produced a critique of Hegel on just this point in *A Critique of Hegel's Philosophy of Right* and *The Holy Family*.[10] But even if this wasn't sufficiently indigestible, there is the issue of the total superfluity of modes of production. If we were to deny methodological individualism in general, it would be because we believed that we had something to say about some social entity that could not be completely captured by our talk of material individuals. But how does the matter stand with regard to modes of production? We said above that the importance of modes of production for historical materialism concerned their changes and developments. As a matter of fact, everything we want to say in this connection can also be captured in terms of the changes and developments that befall societies. How do we date such changes and developments? If we ask about the beginning of capitalism, we shall answer by specifying the dates of the first capitalist society. If we ask about the death of capitalism, we shall answer with details of the last capitalist society. If we ask at what point in time capitalism will manifest its tendency to a falling rate of profit, we shall reply by dating the manifestations of those tendencies in actual capitalist societies. If we ask about the causal consequences of capitalism, or the consequences of something on capitalism, we answer by listing some of the relevant causal consequences of capitalist societies (racism, for example) or the consequences of something on capitalist societies (incomes policies, for instance). All the changes and developments of capitalism, if not in principle reducible in the way I have proposed, would unnecessarily parallel and repeat the temporal changes and developments of the societies which instance them, if not actually, then at least 'in the limit' towards which those actual temporal changes and developments tend.[11] In reifying modes of production, we would not be adding to our power of saying anything about the social world that we could not say before. Rather, our reification would seem like a simple echo

[10] See, for instance, Karl Marx and Frederick Engels, *The Holy Family* in *Collected Works*, IV (Moscow and London: Lawrence and Wishart, 1975), especially 57–61.

[11] See again Quine, op. cit.

of what we can already say when we talk about societies. Thus, even if methodological individualism is rejected and we admit irreducible social entities, I want to propose the following principle: statements apparently about modes of production and their developments can be construed, without remainder, as statements about actual societies and their characteristic developments. Modes of production are types, and accepting the reality of social entities in general need not commit us ontologically into accepting these types, but only social entities (societies, or, in Marxist parlance, social formations) of certain types. Actual societies may be capitalist, feudal, or socialist, but there is no ontologically irreducible capitalism, feudalism, or socialism as modes of production. I think it is fair to say that the typical response of Marxists to Weber's conception of ideal types is one of hostility. Clearly, if my argument is sound, that hostility needs re-examination.[12]

The first reason I mentioned for refusing to admit modes of production in their own right was the difficulty in swallowing Hegelianesque universals which change in time. To see just how unattractive this is, one needs only to look at various texts written under the influence of Althusserian Marxist philosophy. A case in point is Maurice Godelier's *Rationality and Irrationality in Economics*.[13] Godelier understands that modes of production are meant to change and develop. Presumably, being convinced of their irreducible reality for scientific purposes, Godelier does not want to trivialize them by reading off their changes directly from the temporal changes that occur in actual societies. So we are presented by Godelier with a theory to explain the strange sorts of independent changes that can befall modes of production.

The initial idea is that, in a mode of production, there is a kind of *de re* logical or internal relationship between one structure and another—'the logic of the relations between one structure and another'.[14] Our thought leads us from one structure to another in order to grasp this connection between the parts of the mode of production; in any event, if anything can be said to 'move', it is the thought of men. It is an easy slide from thinking of our thought as moving from one structure to another in order to discover the logical relations between them, to thinking of the structures themselves as moving: 'The theory causes the structures to emerge ideally, so to speak, from one another, and our thinking seems to be present at this birth'

---

[12] See, for example, Russell Keat and John Urry, *Social Theory as Science* (London: Routledge and Kegan Paul, 1975), 112–113, or Ted Benton, *Philosophical Foundations of the Three Sociologies* (London: Routledge and Kegan Paul, 1977), 136–137. Part of the problem here is, I think, the tendency on the part of some Marxist philosophical realists to apply that realism too widely.

[13] Maurice Godelier, *Rationality and Irrationality in Economics* (London: New Left Books, 1972).

[14] Ibid., 146. Subsequent page references are to this book.

(p. 145). So the structures of the mode of production now move, in apparent imitation of human thought, although 'this movement cannot . . . be confused with the historical origin of capitalism, with its real origins' (p. 144). We might be forgiven for wondering how anything can move, but not in historical time, and the attempt to reply to this sort of difficulty explains the strange theory of logical time that one finds not only in Godelier but also in Balibar and Althusser:

> While, however, the relations between the categories is a logical one, it is also chronological, but the time of this chronology is wholly determined by the logic of the relations between one structure and another . . .
>
> Chronological time is thus altogether structured by the logic of the functional relations between economic structures. This time is logicized —which means that this logicized chronology both is, and, at the same time, is not concrete historical time. In the latter, what is successive in logicized time, is also simultaneous, and this is fundamental to understanding the relationship between abstract economic theory and concrete history (p. 146).

If accepting the irreducible reality of developing modes of production were to further saddle us ontologically with another, 'logical' time dimension, this would be a further reason against such initial acceptance. It is far easier simply to cut the Gordian knot for such problems by maintaining that all we want ultimately to say about modes of production or productive structures is better said by speaking of societies—ones that exist in historical time—which the more nearly they possess certain structural features or properties, the more nearly they develop or change in certain ways. Any supposed movement within a mode of production is a hypostatization of movements occurring within societies, just as modes of production are hypostatizations of societies of the same type.

Whatever we want to say about modes of production—their changes, developments—can be said in terms of the changes and developments of societies. Modes of production are ontologically expendable. There are capitalist societies, but no ultimately irreducible capitalist mode of production. There is no objection to talking about the set or class of capitalist societies. But the laws of motion which describe the changes of capitalist societies cannot be construed as being about the set of capitalist societies, any more than the laws of anthropology are about the set of men. Anthropology is about men, not about the set of them, and historical materialism is about human societies, and not the set of them. Talk of modes of production is merely a convenient linguistic device for summing up this information, a device which has all too often led Marxists into an unnecessary reification.

The second question I said I wished to raise about historical materialism concerned the ways of behaving of its objects of study. There are two points I want to focus on in this connection: (1) laws are about necessary changes; (2) laws are about tendencies to change.

(1) Marx very often speaks of the 'necessary' or 'inevitable' changes of a mode of production, or the 'necessary' or 'inevitable' character of the laws which describe those motions. For example, he speaks of the development of capitalism as displaying 'the inexorability of a law of nature',[15] and necessitarian talk is something he uses repeatedly in his description of the path of capitalist development: 'that the class struggle necessarily leads to the dictatorship of the proletariat'.[16] In the preface to the first German edition of *Capital*: '. . . It is a question of these laws themselves, of these tendencies working with iron necessity towards inevitable results'.[17]

These necessities are physical or natural necessities, not logical ones, and I want briefly to defend that conception not against those theorists who attempt to reduce physical necessity to some syntactic or epistemological feature of extensionally true generalizations, or perhaps to their degree of entrenchment within science, but against those 'friends' of necessity who try to collapse it into something still stronger, a variety of logical necessity. I want to distinguish logical and natural necessity. I do not assert that the 'source' of necessity is different in the cases of logical and physical necessity, for example that one is *de dicto* or conventional, the other *de re* or real. All that I wish to argue is that we need some sort of distinction between logical and physical necessity, that there is a difference—however we are to characterize it—between the necessities of capitalist development on the one hand and the necessities of self-identity on the other.

A plausible way in which some philosophers think of natural necessity is that what is naturally necessary holds in less than all possible worlds, but in more possible worlds (and there are alternative accounts of what that means!) than the actual world. In this way, natural necessity, although a stronger notion than actuality, is weaker than logical necessity, since what is logically necessary holds in all possible worlds. That physical necessity is weaker than logical necessity has been denied by Milton Fisk, who argues that there is 'no reason to distinguish logical from physical necessity as regards necessity'.[18] His argument against Popper's distinction between the two runs as follows: Popper's belief 'that though logical necessities hold in all possible worlds, physical necessities fail in some possible worlds' is false, since Popper does not see that physical necessities always involve three things, *viz.* two properties and a kind. Let us suppose that, of things

---

[15] Karl Marx, *Capital*, I (Moscow: Progress Publishers, 1965), 763.

[16] From Karl Marx's letter of 1852 to J. Weydemeyer, in Karl Marx and Frederick Engels, *Selected Correspondence* (Moscow: Foreign Languages Publishing House, undated), 86.

[17] Karl Marx, *Capital* I, 8 (the preface to the first German edition).

[18] Milton Fisk, 'Are There Necessary Connections in Nature?', *Philosophy of Science* **37** (1970), 385–400. All quotes are from 388.

of natural kind N, necessarily if they have property F, then they have property G. Is this true in all possible worlds, or in less than all?

Fisk argues that it is true in all possible worlds. Fisk is certainly right when he reminds us that to argue that this is true in all possible worlds is not to deny that there is a possible world in which F and G fail to be connected, because there are many possible worlds in which natural kind N has been replaced by natural kind N', in which kind F and G are not connected. But what is true in all possible worlds, according to Fisk, is that, in things of natural kind N, F and G are connected, and imagining a world without N but with N' is not to imagine that there is a possible world in which, in things of kind N, F and G are not connected. Fisk diagnoses Popper's error as arising from forgetting that physical necessities involve reference to kinds as well as to two properties. It does not follow from there being a possible world in which F and G are not connected that there is a possible world in which, in things of kind N, F and G are not connected and hence so far we have described no possible world in which 'Of things of natural kind N, if they have F, then they have G' is false.

Has Popper made any sort of error? Even recalling that these claims involve reference to the connection between two properties and a natural kind does not itself justify us in inferring that the claims are true in all possible worlds. This result follows only if the property of being G if F is essential to things of that kind. If this conditional property of being G if F is inessential even though nomic to things of the kind, then there will be a possible world in which F and G are unconnected, even in things of the kind in question. I am assuming that there is some distinction to be drawn between properties which things of a kind have essentially, and properties which things have non-essentially. At any rate, Fisk does not argue for the Leibnizian position which would deny this assumption. Thus, if being G if F is a property which a thing of kind N has essentially, then if a thing is of that kind, then it is G if F in all possible worlds. But the same result certainly does not follow if these properties are had non-essentially but nomically by things of kind N. We have been given no reason to believe that all physical laws are about only the essential properties had by things of natural kinds, and one cannot merely assume that this is so. If there are laws about the non-essential properties of natural kinds, then such laws are not true in all possible worlds, even when restricted to things of that natural kind. In 'Of things of natural kind N, necessarily if they are F, they are G', if the property of being G if F is physically necessary but not essential for things of that kind, then there is a possible world in which things of natural kind N might fail to be G when F.

This vitiates Fisk's argument to what I regard in any case as a truth, namely, that being of a natural kind is not a contingent matter. Fisk's argument is a *reductio* which begins by supposing that 'there were a world in which this object that is in actuality a grain of salt were a diamond'. He then infers that if it is a grain of salt in this world, then necessarily (in all possible worlds) it dissolves in water, and hence dissolves in water in the world in which it is a diamond. But since diamonds necessarily do not dissolve in water, 'we reach a contradiction', and thus if a thing is of a natural kind, then it is of that kind in all possible worlds. Again, Fisk's argument founders on the supposition that a grain of salt which dissolves as a matter of physical necessity in this world dissolves in water in all possible worlds. This would be so, I submit, only if this physically necessary property of salt, solubility in water, were had by it essentially, and for this stronger requirement Fisk offers no argument whatever. That logical and physical necessities are different in the range of possible worlds in which they hold seems to fit whatever intuitions we have in the matter, for it seems wrong to say that none of the scientific laws we in fact have—about our natural kinds—could have been different than they are, as long as they remain about the same natural kinds.

There is another account I want to look at, because there is in it a similar tendency to conflate physical and logical necessity. Colin McGinn has argued that 'properties of a kind come in two grades, one more fundamental than the other. Let us call properties of the more fundamental grade *primary* nomic properties, and let us call properties of the less fundamental grade *secondary* nomic properties . . . We know what the nature of a substance is when we have identified its primary properties and seen how they account for the more readily discernible secondary properties.'[19] McGinn then argues that such 'accounting' proceeds by reductive identification of the secondary properties with the primary properties, and, since true identities are necessary and 'property identities, though discovered *a posteriori*, are necessary', these secondary properties are as much part of the essence of a natural kind as are the primary properties with which they are identified. Since the primary properties are true of a natural kind in all possible worlds, so are the secondary properties. 'Whence it follows that if gold could not have lacked its atomic properties, it could not have lacked its dispositional properties either. For to lack one would just *be* to lack the other.' That McGinn is at least tempted by the doctrine that all natural laws are logically necessary is evidenced by his remarks in another article, although it is not a doctrine on which his argument finally relies.[20]

What McGinn's argument in fact shows is that *if* a natural kind has a primary property in all possible worlds, and if that primary property is identical with some secondary property, then the natural kind has that secondary property in all possible worlds. What McGinn never establishes

[19] Colin McGinn, 'A Note on the Essence of Natural Kinds', *Analysis* **35** (June 1975), 177–183. All quotes are from 179–181.
[20] Colin McGinn, 'Mental States, Natural Kinds, and Psychophysical Laws', *Aristotelian Society Supplementary Volume* **LII** (1978), 195–220. See 204.

is that natural kinds do have their primary nomic properties in all possible worlds. McGinn begins by characterizing the primary properties of a thing as those which 'underlie' or 'are responsible for' the secondary properties, or are those from which the secondary properties are derived. He then moves on to say, without argument, that the internal nature of a thing 'is constituted by its primary properties'. McGinn evidently takes his remark that 'we know what the nature of a substance is when we have identified its primary properties . . .' as licensing the inference that *all* the primary properties of a thing, in the sense of 'primary' which makes the primary properties the smallest set of properties needed to account for the others, are had by it essentially, in all possible worlds. But there seems nothing at all objectionable about the idea that primary nomic properties themselves come in two grades, the essential and the non-essential. Whether a secondary nomic property is had by things of a kind essentially or non-essentially, in all possible worlds or in less than all, depends on with which sort of primary property it is identified. I can see no *a priori* reason for believing that the nomic properties of a kind which are 'primary' in the sense that they constitute the smallest set of properties which can be used to explain or account for all the remaining properties are, all of them, had by that kind in all possible worlds. I conclude then, that neither McGinn nor Fisk has offered any compelling reason for thinking that all nomic properties are had by a kind in all possible worlds, and that there is no reason to agree with Fisk's refusal to distinguish between logical and physical necessities.

(2) At the beginning of this paper I said that both questions in which I was interested were ontological in some sense, that what interested me about the second question was the sort of commitment as to the ways of behaving historical materialism presupposed in describing the nomic or lawlike behaviour of whatever objects it studied. Marx and Marxists have often spoken of tendencies in this connection—the laws of development of modes or production are about tendencies. Marx speaks about 'the law of the tendency of the rate of profit to fall' (*Capital* III, 213), and about 'the historical tendency of capitalist accumulation' (*Capital* I, 761), and then in *Capital* III (234–235), he explains: 'This factor does not abolish the general law. But it causes that law to act rather as a tendency, i.e. as a law whose absolute action is checked, retarded, and weakened by counteracting circumstances.' Finally, in *Capital* III, 175:

> Such a general rate of surplus-value—viewed as a tendency, like all other economic laws—has been assumed by us for the sake of theoretical simplification. But in reality it is an actual premise of the capitalist mode of production, although it is more or less obstructed by practical frictions causing more or less considerable local differences . . . But in theory it is assumed that the laws of capitalist production operate in their

pure form. In reality, there exists only approximation; but, this approximation is the greater, the more developed the capitalist mode of production and the less it is adulterated and amalgamated with survivals of former economic conditions.

Failure to understand the tendential nature of Marx's conception of necessary development has given rise to countless misunderstandings of Marx's work. Claims about tendencies at work in society are often misread as categorical claims about the actual course of events. For example, Marx calls the increasing misery of the proletariat 'the absolute general law of capitalist accumulation'. If we understand this law as describing a tendency, we can see why it is useless to try to immediately verify or falsify the law by comparing its claims with actual social facts as they present themselves. Marx adds, after the statement of the law: 'Like all other laws it is modified in its working by many circumstances, the analysis of which does not concern us here'.[21] In a similar spirit, Sweezy describes 'the tendencies in capitalism which lead away from free competition among producers and towards the formation of monopolies . . .'[22] and Mandel asserts that 'the tendency of the average rate of profit to fall is thus a law of development of the capitalist mode of production.'[23]

What is a tendency, and what significance does talk of tendencies have? Although the importance of tendencies has been stressed by many who write on Marxist methodology, little has been done by way of making clear how we are to understand such talk. In particular, I want to ask whether or not such talk is onotologically revealing, tells us anything about the structure of the social world itself.

'Tendency' is not meant in any statistical sense, for a mode of production might rarely or even perhaps never develop in the way in which it tends to develop. Such laws cannot be read as categorical claims about the occurrence of events; that much I have already said. But they cannot be read as claims about the probable occurrence of events either.

Clearly, tendency statements do not state sufficient conditions for the occurrence of the phenomena for which there exists a tendency. But are they in any way incompatible for Marx with there being a set of sufficient conditions? I want to ask if the use of tendency talk reveals some ontological feature about the reality we are studying, or something epistemological about the state of our knowledge about that reality. I think that there is no textual evidence whatever to suggest that Marx thought that tendency talk marked anything other than something about our current inability to

[21] Karl Marx, *Capital*, I, 644.
[22] Paul Sweezy, *The Theory of Capitalist Development* (New York: Monthly Review Press, 1968), 254.
[23] Ernest Mandel, *Marxist Economic Theory* (London: Merlin Press, 1968), 166.

state sufficient conditions, and no suggestion whatever that there is no set of conditions sufficient for the occurrence of the phenomenon under investigation. I quoted Marx earlier as saying: the law 'is modified in its working by many circumstances, the analysis of which does not concern us here', and he also says that this actual 'approximation' to the tendency is 'the greater, the more developed the capitalist mode of production' and that 'it is only under certain circumstances and only after long periods that its effects become strikingly pronounced' (*Capital* III, 239). This last remark seems to say that, under some set of conditions, however complex, the event in question, the fall in the rate of profit, actually occurs, and not merely tends to occur. In so far as one can base an interpretation on these remarks, they support an epistemological rather than ontological interpretation of Marx's remarks on the operation of tendencies. So I propose that we understand Marx's laws of tendency in the following way. To say that under conditions of type C, an event of type E tends to occur is to say: (1) There exists a set of conditions of type $A_i \ldots A_n$, whether known or unknown, such that whenever conditions of $A_i \ldots A_n$ and of type C obtain, an event of type E does occur; (2) conditions of type C are not just any from the set of sufficient conditions, but ones which relate to essential structural features of the mode of production under study. This I think gives the sense in which Marx uses tendency talk in his formulations of the laws of modes of production. There may be other, perhaps statistical senses of 'tendency', again perhaps in certain areas of physics, and without a concomitant commitment to there being a set of sufficient conditions. But these are not the senses in which Marx uses that concept, and I offer the above only as an explication of Marx's use of 'tendency' in his scientific study of society.

I think one can identify a certain reluctance among Marxist theorists to admit that tendency talk must ultimately have an epistemological rather than an ontological significance. Usually, tendency claims are made in circumstances in which at least some of the remaining conditions which belong to the set of sufficient conditions are unknown. If tendency talk is, at least for Marx, epistemologically motivated, then under ideal epistemic conditions—in a state of 'full' knowledge of all the relevant conditions— tendency claims are in principle replaceable by claims about the conditions sufficient for the occurrence of the kind of event in question. In principle, historical materialism must admit that the events or ways of behaving of the objects it studies are capable of being predicted (or, retrodicted), although its present (and perhaps for the indefinite future) inability to do so is a characteristic of all those bodies of doctrine which compete with it for the status of being the science of society, and thus is a characteristic which is *per se* no more a telling criticism of it than it is of them. Under such ideal epistemic conditions, laws entail categorical claims about what actually does occur, and not just what tends to occur, and the laws of historical

D.-H. Ruben

materialism are no exception to this requirement. Yes, Professor Popper, in principle historical materialism is falsifiable—but not in its current state.

Perhaps part of the reluctance of Marxist theoreticians that I mentioned stems from an overwhelming fear of a mélange of doctrines often—with varying degree of historical accuracy—called 'empiricism', a fear which as often as not has led to the throwing-out of the baby with the bathwater. In the Althusserian corpus, just about every sort of error is an example of empiricism: 'But this definition is unsatisfactory, because, in its empiricist and mechanistic character, it is a return precisely to what Marx criticized in the economists ... : the study of "factors" called "independent" because of an inability to find their common origin in the unity of a structure ...'[24] Within British Marxist theory, fear of abiding by 'facts' perhaps in part has arisen in reaction to the 'falsifiability' attacks on Marxism by Popper, Lakatos, and others of the Popperian school.[25] The consequent disregard for facts has become cavalier: 'This book is a work of Marxist scientific theory. It must be judged in terms of that theory ... Our constructions and our arguments are theoretical and they can only be evaluated in theoretical terms—in terms, that is to say, of their rigour and theoretical coherence. They cannot be refuted by any empiricist recourse to the supposed "facts" of history.'[26] Perhaps more explicitly than any other Marxist writer, Roy Rhaskar, in his *A Realist Theory of Science*, has subscribed to an ontological interpretation of scientific laws of tendency: 'The normic character of laws [laws as tendencies—D.H.R.] are irreducible ontological features of the world'[27] and as such are incapable in principle of yielding categorical claims at the level of what Bhaskar refers to as 'actuality'.

Although I cannot see that Bhaskar has produced any convincing arguments against thinking that under ideal epistemic conditions, laws of tendencies could be replaced by laws giving the sufficient conditions for actual occurrences (or, borrowing an idea from John Mackie, perhaps sufficient in a certain assumed causal field),[28] we might still wonder if there

[24] Louis Althusser and Etienne Balibar, *Reading Capital* (London: New Left Books, 1970). See Balibar's remarks on 283–293. The quote is from 286.

[25] Well-known examples include Karl Popper, *The Open Society and Its Enemies*, II, (London: Routledge and Kegan Paul, 1969), 183–189, and Imre Lakatos, 'Science and Pseudo-Science', BBC talk for the Open University, 1973.

[26] Barry Hindess and Paul Q. Hirst, *Pre-Capitalist Modes of Production* (London: Routledge and Kegan Paul, 1975), 3.

[27] Roy Bhaskar, *A Realist Theory of Science* (Sussex: Harvester Press, 1978), 116.

[28] J. L. Mackie, *The Cement of the Universe* (Oxford: Oxford University Press, 1974), 34–35 and 63. Since Mackie's description of the causal field includes such qualifications as 'this block of flats as normally used and lived in', I cannot see how interesting reference to a causal field improves upon the statement of the

52

are any arguments for understanding laws of tendencies in my preferred way rather than his. I think that there is at least this *ad hominem* argument against Bhaskar: at varous points Bhaskar himself seems to be presupposing just this. Consider the following passage:

> If a system is closed, then a tendency once set in motion must be fulfilled. If a system is open, this may not happen due to the presence of 'offsetting causes'. But there must be a reason why, once a tendency is set in motion, it is not fulfilled . . . Once a tendency is set in motion, it is fulfilled unless it is prevented (op. cit., 98).

The difficulty is to see how we are to understand this sort of remark unless there are sufficient conditions, known or unknown, for the occurrence of whatever it is that tends to occur. And if there are such conditions, then it remains mysterious what there can be which is ontological about tendencies. Bhaskar tells us that if a tendency is not fulfilled, then there must be a reason. But what could 'reason' mean here? Presumably, the reason for a tendency's non-fulfilment is that *a* occurred if and only if the joint occurrence of not-*a* and whatever conditions did obtain would have been sufficient for the tendency's fulfilment. Indeed, it is hard to see how any position could deny this without lapsing into some form of indeterminism, something which I think Bhaskar does not wish to espouse. Bhaskar's picture of scientific laws of tendencies as not even in principle always about actual events detaches science and empirical reality in a wholly unacceptable way.

I agree with Ernest Mandel's accurate observations in *Late Capital*,[29] in which he notes and rejects the attempt to separate scientific laws and actual events which one finds increasingly in expositions of Marx's method:

> The laws of motion, it is argued, are only 'tendencies' in the very broad historical sense. They are therefore supposed to exclude the possibility of any causal connections with any temporal events in the short or medium term, and even in the long term are deemed not to be demonstrable in a materially identifiable, empirical way . . . Marx's treatment of the tendency of the rate of profit to fall . . . has been endlessly cited as the classic example of a tendency and counter-tendency which allegedly enable nothing to be said of the final outcome.
>
> From this, the conclusion is then drawn that it is scarcely possible to find empirical 'confirmation' for Marx's laws of development. Indeed, it is maintained that attempts to track down such 'empirical confirmations'

---

regularity with no mention of causal field but with a good, old-fashioned *ceteris paribus* clause. 'As normally . . .' seems merely an alternative way of saying the same thing.

[29] Ernest Mandel, *Late Capitalism* (London: New Left Books, 1975), 19–20.

reveal a fundamental 'positivist' understanding of Marx's method and intentions, since the two different levels of abstraction, that of the 'pure' mode of production and that of the 'concrete' historical process are so far removed from one another that there is virtually nowhere that they could come into contact.

I think that Mandel's criticism of those expositions of Marx's method which drive a wedge between theory and empirical facts is entirely well-founded. Marx himself would have seen little difference between those expositions and the method he imputed to Hegelian philosophy in his various critiques of it.

It is well worth carefully distinguishing several claims that one might make about the sufficient conditions for something's occurring and the consequences of this for science. I wonder whether simple failure to distinguish these claims is not in part responsible for making these 'anti-empirical' tendencies within contemporary Marxism appear to be more attractive than they are. To begin with, one might simply claim:

(1) For whatever occurs, there is some set of conditions sufficient for its occurrence.

I have claimed something stronger than (1), because I have talked about ideal epistemic conditions under which claims about a tendency for something to occur are replaceable by claims that something will occur. That is, I have claimed:

(2) For whatever occurs, there is some set of conditions, in principle knowable, sufficient for its occurrence.

(2) should be distinguished from the still stronger claim (3):

(3) For whatever occurs, there is some set of conditions, which human beings are capable of coming to know, sufficient for its occurrence.

It could be that the set of conditions jointly sufficient for the occurrence of something was so complicated or lengthy or whatever that human beings, with their limited memories and restricted intellectual capabilities, were in fact incapable of coming to know the set of conditions. In this case, (3) would be false but (2) would be true. And perhaps some, awed by the incredible complexity and interconnectedness of the factors which make up man's social existence, have come to despair and think (3) to be false. For my part, I think that (3) as well as (2) is true, although I can think of no arguments for my belief, other than reminding someone who denies (3) but accepts (2) of the ways in which certain limitations in man's intellectual powers have been offset by devices such as computers. Nor, by the way, does (3) commit us to believing that the set is knowable at a time *before* the time of the occurrence for which the set is sufficient. Because of the so-called paradoxes of self-prediction which arise in cases of attempting to predict one's own behaviour, such knowledge may only be available in the form of a retrodiction, after the occurrence in question has already taken place.[30] So (3) does not commit us to any *particular* time at which this knowledge is available.

Both (2) and (3) should be sharply distinguished from (4):

(4) Nothing can be a law unless it states such a set of sufficient conditions.

Although (4) has often been argued, I cannot see much in its favour, and thus I do not want to be interpreted as arguing in its favour. At any given stage in our acquisition of knowledge, we may have to accept laws of tendencies as the best we can do for the present, and I have even considered the suggestion that this could be some ineradicable feature of the specifically human predicament. I can see no objection to calling these interim laws 'laws', rather than 'proto-laws' or 'law-sketches'. As long as we are clear that they offer less than sufficient conditions, and that sufficient conditions do exist, it seems to me to be a not particularly interesting question what we call them.

Finally, consider (5):

(5) It must be the goal of science to attempt to discover lists of sufficient conditions for the occurrence of the events or phenomena that it studies.

First, I think it is obvious that (5) does not follow from any of (1)–(4). Perhaps part of the reluctance on the part of many Marxists to accepting any version of the sufficiency thesis stems from the misapprehension that so doing carries implications about the actual practice of science. Being highly critical—in my view, rightly so—of the often trivial investigations undertaken by the more orthodox 'social scientists', they fear that the acceptance of the sufficiency thesis will somehow legitimate the practice of investigating any factor present, regardless of how inessential or superficial it may prove to be. But neither (5) nor any other methodological directive about the practice of science follows from the acceptance of the sufficiency thesis, and it is salutary to remind ourselves that this is so.

Is (5) true? In the passage I quoted, Mandel appeared to assert that it was the goal of the political economy of capitalism to discover those conditions sufficient for the rate of profit to fall. But perhaps this is too strong, and did not really capture what Mandel had in mind. We can imagine a slightly more modified and modest claim:

(6) It must be the goal of political economy to discover all the economic

[30] Andrew Oldenquist provides an excellent summary of these paradoxes in 'Self-Prediction' in *The Encyclopaedia of Philosophy*, VII, (New York and London: Macmillan, 1972), 345–348.

conditions which would appear on the list of the conditions sufficient for the occurrence of the phenomena it wishes to explain.

Certainly, the kinds of 'countervailing causes' to the tendency of the rate of profit to fall that interested Marx were all internal to the science of political economy. Marx does not mention, for example: adverse weather conditions, natural geographic factors, or physiological features of the people involved—and yet any of these might affect whether, or by how much, the rate of profit actually falls. It is this, I suppose, that in part makes the acceptance of (5) seem so unreasonable. The list of sufficient conditions might seem to us so incorrigibly disparate and heterogeneous that it strikes us as unilluminating or unrewarding to try to discover the list. So, although I think that (6) may be true, I suspect that (5) could well turn out to be false. But, I dare say, this must be true: in so far as we are not also committed to (5), we cannot be committed to understanding why what occurs does occur. If we accept (6), we can understand why, e.g. rates of profit behave as they do economically speaking, or to whatever extent political economy can explain these things. But we cannot understand why rates of profit do or do not fall *tout court*. Perhaps it is rational for us not to want to know why they behave as they do *sans* qualification. But rational or no, if we do not accept (5), then this is something we cannot know.[31]

The City University, London

[31] I wish to thank G. A. Cohen, G. H. R. Parkinson and R. M. Sainsbury, whose comments on earlier drafts of this paper have made it better than it would otherwise have been.

Historical Materialism

R. F. ATKINSON

I. Introduction

Historical materialism I take to be the view expressed in the well-known Preface to the *Critique of Political Economy* (1859) and exemplified in *Capital* and in many other writings by Marx and by Marxists. I shall begin with a few introductory remarks, next sketch in the theory, and finally contend that, despite real attractions, it too far limits the scope of legitimate historical enquiry to be ultimately acceptable.

My chosen point of view is perhaps an eccentric one. I consider historical materialism (as I have also elsewhere considered methodological individualism) as a view to the effect that certain sorts of cause, roughly speaking economic causes, are fundamental, dominant or primary in historical enquiry. This is, in effect, to consider historical materialism as a thesis in the critical or analytical philosophy of history, thus extracting it, at least up to a point, from its place in a generally materialistic, even dialectically materialistic metaphysic, and from its place in the revolutionary political project. How far it is feasible to do this must, of course, be open to discussion; but it is, I believe, at least worth a try. A good reason for looking at historical materialism in this way is that so considered it appears to have some appeal to the practising historian, which gives it a good deal of credit in my philosophical book. Part of the task of philosophy is to 'place' the various human activities and enquiries with respect to one another. To do this one has to 'characterize' them; and here there is not infrequently a degree of tension between what seems theoretically appropriate or illuminating and what is acceptable to practitioners of the activity or enquiry in question. I am not asserting that philosophy is no more than the natural history of ideas. In the last analysis theoretical perspicuity is all. But the last analysis is a long way off; and meantime, when I think about history, I tend to put the emphasis on conformability to the attitudes and procedures of practitioners.

Although, on such grounds, I see real merit in historical materialism, the outcome of my own recent consideration of it was on balance negative. I concluded that economic factors, though manifestly important in relation to many questions in history, were not so in regard to all. (Like some Marxists, e.g. Plekhanov, and Lukács if I understand him aright, I am most doubtful of their importance in regard to a certain sort of history of ideas.) History generally I see as a very open, theoretically unstructured study, which consequently leaves room for very different directions of interest among historians, all of them equally legitimate. Economic factors connect with some of these, but not with others; and the ones with which they do not connect are just as legitimate as those with which they do.

All this is an expression of personal opinion, not an argument; and it is based on a pretty summary characterization of historical materialism, as were the opinions expressed in my recent book. I said there that I did not think that my criticisms would lose force in the face of more elaborate statements of historical materialism. One of the things I want to do here is to put that claim to the test by exposing in more detail what I take historical materialism to be.

II. Outline and Interpretation of the Theory

(i) There seems to be no alternative to re-quoting some of the well-known sentences from the 1859 Preface: 'In the social production of their life, men enter into definite relations that are indispensable and independent of their will, relations of production which correspond to a definite stage of the development of their material productive forces. The sum total of these relations of production constitutes the economic structure of society, the real foundation, on which arises a legal and political superstructure and to which correspond definite forms of social consciousness. The mode of production of material life conditions the social, political and intellectual life process in general. It is not the consciousness of men that determines their being, but, on the contrary, their social being that determines their consciousness. At a certain stage of their development, the material productive forces of society come in conflict with the existing relations of production, or—what is but a legal expression for the same thing—with the property relations within which they have been at work hitherto. From forms of development of the productive forces these relations turn into their fetters. Then begins an epoch of social revolution. With the change of the economic foundation the entire immense superstructure is more or less rapidly transformed' (op. cit., 181–182. Unless otherwise stated all page and chapter references are to the editions listed at the end).

This is about the minimum possible statement of the theory. One should note the threefold distinction between the *forces or powers of production* (often the *material* forces or powers), the *relations of production*, and the *legal and political superstructure* with the associated forms of social consciousness. (Arguably a distinction is intended between the institutional superstructure and the forms of social consciousness, in which case we should have a fourfold distinction.) I have supposed that the two former, the forces and relations of production, taken together constitute the economic basis of society, and have read the theory as maintaining that economic factors generally, organizational as well as technical, are the fundamental causative factors in history. (I will discuss different interpretations below.)

There are a few other sentences from the 1859 Preface that perhaps should be mentioned at this stage:

(a) One is this: 'In considering such transformations a distinction should always be made between the material transformation of the economic conditions of production, which can be determined with the precision of natural science, and the legal, political, religious, aesthetic or philosophic— in short, ideological forms in which men become conscious of this conflict and fight it out'. It will be apparent from what I say later on that I would like to interpret this as allowing some scope for non-materialistic perspectives in history.

(b) Another is this: 'No social order ever perishes before all the productive forces for which there is room in it have developed; and new, higher relations of production never appear before the material conditions of their existence have matured in the womb of the old society itself'. I cannot make much sense of the former part of this, and can therefore only read the sentence as a variant expression of the general historical materialist claim.

(c) There is also, of course, the sentence: 'In broad outlines Asiatic, ancient, feudal, and modern bourgeois modes of production can be designated as progressive epochs in the economic formation of society'.

(ii) Before coming to matters of interpretation, I should like to limit my topic, possibly in a non-Marxist fashion, by trying to distinguish the theory from, on the one hand, the conclusions hitherto drawn from it, and from Marxist social and political attitudes on the other.

(a) The former distinction is perhaps the less controversial; and it, or something like it, is drawn by some Marxist writers, e.g. by Lukács, for whom Marx's *method* alone is *de fide*, whilst his results are wholly revisable (p. xxvi and p. 1). It would seem that at any rate the story of the four epochs is very schematic, not obviously superior to, nor less vulnerable to criticism than, the conventional period divisions of old-fashioned political history. Marx himself, indeed, uses the expression 'In broad outlines'. Further, at the more detailed level, it would be extremely surprising if Marx, or his collaborator and followers, had everything exactly right. In the end, if the theory is an empirical one—and what else could it be?—it will have to be judged on its applications or results. But it seems to me that it ought to be able to survive a fair amount of revision—in the light of new information or simple hindsight—of the conclusions originally drawn. Perhaps no Marxist would want to deny this.

(There is also, it must be said, the opposite possibility that the *theory* is false or merely speculative although some of the original conclusions are sound. Marx appears to be more interested in the transition to capitalism than in earlier transitions, and he is more impressive on it. Is his theory merely an over-generalization from this one case? There are sug-

5

gestions with this tendency in Plamenatz's *Man and Society*, II; and, more surprisingly, some defensiveness on the matter in Lukács' *History and Class Consciousness* (238–239). The end result of this approach would be to give more credence to Marx the historian of capitalism than Marx the social theorist.)

(b) The latter distinction, between the theory and Marxist social and political attitudes, which seems clear enough to me, would I think be resisted by many Marxists, perhaps especially those who put their emphasis on the dialectic (see the strong claim by Mészáros, p. 23). I can see no logical impossibility in accepting the theory and the predictions based upon it without espousing the cause of the proletariat. Nor can I see anything irrational about this. One would indeed be opposing, seeking to delay, developments one believed would ultimately come to pass—but why not? The thing is pretty long term, and (if only from a bourgeois individualistic standpoint) a lifetime or two is a very long time in politics.

I am not disputing, of course, that historical materialism and Marxist practical attitudes go very well together. I emphasize the possibility of distinguishing them only because it is the *theory* that I want, in the end, to reject as one-sided. I am not *here* attacking Marx-inspired policies, though I am not in fact convinced that they will deliver a balance of what we cannot but regard as good.

I do not at all doubt that my social position and practical commitments might render me blind to the merits of historical materialism, just as a different position and commitments might blind one to the theory's demerits. But, if such contentions are to be significant, it must be supposed that objective truth is—whatever the difficulties in fact—in principle attainable and recognizable when attained. My impression is that Marx himself did, in the main, have this conception of objective truth, though I am less sure about some of his twentieth-century followers.

(iii) As regards matters of interpretation I have, as I have said, tended to run together forces and and relations of production, thus perhaps facilitating the criticism that talk of a causal connection between them is insignificant (see Cohen, II, i). Again, I have tended not to distinguish sharply between the institutional superstructure and forms of consciousness. I have also virtually ignored the dialectic, which would lead some to consider that I interpret historical materialism as crude economic determinism. I am not at all sure that 'determinism' is the right word, but I am inclined to think that without a pretty heavy emphasis on the economic, the theory is insufficiently distinctive to be assessable for truth or falsity.

I meant, in what I have just said, to allude to at least four issues of interpretation:

(a) The relationship between forces and relations of production;

(b) The relationship between economic base and superstructure, and the dialectic;

(c) The relationship between institutions and forms of consciousness;

(d) The sense in which the theory is deterministic.

I mention these problems, not because I have a ready solution for them, but mainly in order to convey some notion of the understanding of historical materialism presupposed in the critical remarks to be made later on.

(a) *Forces and Relations of Production*

Here it is desirable to separate the question of what Marx and/or his followers thought from the question whether what they thought was right. On the former there are remarks—including the famous one about the hand mill and the steam mill from the *Poverty of Philosophy* (1847), and the allegedly analogous suggestion in *Wage Labour and Capital* (1849) that military organization is determined by military techniques—remarks which certainly give the impression that Marx would have liked to mean by forces of production productive techniques, which he would have liked to regard as the ultimate determinants of history. Whether his writings taken as a whole are adequately characterized in this way is much harder to assess. There is indubitably much in them which supports Bober's contention (Chap. 1; see also Rader, Chap. I, 5) that Marx's productive forces are wider than productive techniques. Acton tends to favour the technological interpretation because it makes the theory definite and discussable and, it must be said, as such implausible or false (p. 137). Cohen is equally keen on falsifiability, but thinks the theory plausible or true (op. cit.). I am inclined to agree with them both that the most fruitful line is to see what can be made of the technological interpretation. It seems generally recognized not to be the case that technological innovations have invariably *preceded* changes in economic organization. But it is at least more plausible to maintain that certain sorts of economic organization are more congenial to the exploitation of certain techniques than are others: and that such sorts of organization will accordingly tend to persist and to spread. I cannot, however, see any reason in principle why there should not be different schemes of organization equally congenial to a given constellation of productive forces. In which case, there would be features of economic systems—features in which historians might interest themselves—which would elude determination by productive forces.

(b) *Base, Superstructure and Dialectic*

I would expect the same to be true of the relationship between the economic base and the institutional superstructure. Even if certain sorts of legal and political institutions are more congenial to certain sorts of economic structures than are others, it would not follow that each economic structure determines a unique institutional superstructure. If this is right, there will be features of an institutional set up which are not to be explained in economic terms, but rather perhaps by the earlier history of the institutions themselves. It is to be expected that the legal system of a capitalist economy will facilitate private investors obtaining a return on their investments, the development of limited liability companies, the geographical mobility of labour, etc. Again, political institutions are likely to allow a great measure of influence to the owners of the means of production, distribution and exchange. But such uniformities as there pragmatically and definitionally *must* be in capitalist institutions surely leave room for very many differences. (My conventional illustrations probably understate the institutional variety possible in a capitalist economy.) So much would presumably not be denied by any Marxist. What might, however, be maintained is that the differences are less important than the economically determined uniformities. But this, it seems to me, is more a *conclusion* from historical materialism than an *independent* reason for accepting it. One cannot deny to historical materialists the right to view institutions and their development in a certain perspective; but this does not entail that anybody else should or must do so, or that this is the only perspective available.

There will, then, be features of the superstructure which escape economic determination and exert an independent influence of their own—even an influence on the development of the substructure itself. This is not only not denied, but actually emphasized by some Marxists: by Engels and Plekhanov, and by Lukács in those of his writings I know. The idea that determination might be one way only is dismissed as crude economic determinism, vulgar mechanism. If a breakthrough can be made to dialectical thinking, it will be seen that determination can run both ways and that everything influences everything else. (I realize that I am using 'determination' quite uncritically, but it may serve well enough for the time being.)

I am not disputing that a dialectical way of looking at society (here taking together what Rader distinguishes as simply and organically dialectical views) may be an improvement on a mechanistic one. In any case my present concern is with matters of interpretation, about which I can only say that it seems very hard to do equal justice to both dialectics and economic materialism. Engels, for instance, tends to go so far down the dialectical road that he approaches self-contradiction when he reverts to emphasizing the dominant influence of economic factors. Much the same applies to Plekhanov, though the flavour of contradiction is perhaps less marked, and he seems readier to allow the possibility of genuinely independent developments in the realm of ideas. In Lukács—in the bits I know and maybe do not understand very well—the emphasis on the dialectic seems extreme. We are told, for instance (p. 27), that the important thing in Marx is not the primacy of economic factors but the point of view of totality; and yet, later on (p. 58), we find him asserting that the 'motor of history' is economic class interest. As regards Marx himself, what always impresses me is his splendid concreteness when considering actual situations, his willingness to give weight to any factor whatever which seems to be influential in the particular case. But in his more theoretical pronouncements I am inclined to think that the materialism, the economic emphasis, is more prominent than the dialectics. In *The Eighteenth Brumaire*, for example, political conflicts are detailed, whilst explanations in class terms are merely sketched, though the latter are supposed to determine the main lines of development.

(c) *Institutions and Forms of Consciousness*

I am uncertain how far we are supposed to distinguish between the institutional superstructure and the associated forms of consciousness. The 1859 Preface does not make it clear whether they are to be separated or identified. If they were to be separated, it would be the easier to establish (or at least give sense to) a relationship of determination between economic base and legal and political institutions, if only because of the prominence of the regulation of property in legal systems. But, the further one does separate them, the greater the danger that forms of consciousness will escape from economic determination.

I myself would welcome such a result. I do not see how to take literature, science, philosophy seriously without according to them a degree of autonomy and the possibility of lines of development internal to them. Some Marxist writers seem to manifest here the same sort of ambivalence as they do with regard to economic determination. In fact, I think they ought to welcome a firm distinction between the autonomous development of ideas, on the one hand, and the economic determination of their social acceptance, on the other. It is easier to make explanations of the social acceptance of ideas significant if autonomy is allowed to their internal development. If ideology is to be 'false' consciousness, we need a conception of 'true' consciousness as a point of contrast; and 'truth' must presumably be a matter of conformity with criteria integral to the field in question. Whatever may be the case with literature, or even with philosophy, this must I believe be the case with natural and social science, *and*—which is the currently relevant point—it seems that this is Marx's own position. The dominant tendency in his writings is to hold that there is the possibility of scientific objectivity: that the trouble with, for instance, bourgeois economics is less that it is bourgeois than that it is false. The class interests of the bourgeoisie come in only in order to explain how they come to accept false opinions. Comformably with this, Marx's own claims are offered as objectively true and addressed to all reasonable men; though, of course, he also thinks that some men are rendered unreasonable by class interest. (I welcome the similar interpretation of Marx's attitude to science in Chapter II of Cohen's book. It is regrettable that some latter day Marxists do not follow their master in this respect.)

(d) *Determinism*

I am conscious of having bandied about the word 'determination' without explaining it—I hope for the points I have been making so far it was not necessary. Some people see historical materialism as representing people as wholly passive in the grip of mindless social forces; and, believing as they do in human freedom and autonomy, are inclined to reject historical materialism on that account (e.g. Berlin in *Historical Inevitability*). I would not claim that the content of the belief in human freedom is wholly clear; but I do not think that historical materialists are obliged to deny at any rate the more obvious elements in it. It has often been pointed out (e.g. by Bober, Chap. IV) that the theory does not entail that people have no influence on what comes about, that history is, so to say, the *automatic* result of the workings of the economic system. People are allowed to have purposes and to act, in the light of their beliefs, in order to realize them. 'Men make their own history, but they do not make it just as they please' (Marx, 1852, p. 96). People choose to act; but much of what happens is not chosen, though it results from human choices. No doubt Marxists, like other people, have some determinism/freedom problems; but they do not seem to me to have specially difficult ones, nor to be committed any special degree to the freedom denying side.

One reason why this is not recognized may be the absence of a clear and accepted account in Marxist writings of the 'mechanism' by which the economic structure determines the other levels of social life. Psychological hypotheses tend to be repudiated as merely vulgar; the labour theory of value and the associated concept of exploitation are so much mystification and persuasive definition. Though there does not have to be a mechanism for the theory to be true—correlation would suffice—it is not altogether unnatural to think that there is a gap in the theory, and some consequent tendency to imagine a purely deterministic filling for it.

III. The Claim of Historical Materialism

I tried at the beginning to explain the point of view from which I proposed to consider historical materialism, namely, as a thesis in the analytical philosophy of history. I next outlined the view, and indicated the lines I was minded to take on certain disputed matters of interpretation—this, partly no doubt for the pleasure of saying what I think, but also with the thought that it was some contribution to the argument, or a help to the assessment of it, that I should put my interpretative cards on the table. I propose now to conclude by seeing how historical materialism does in the event fare as a thesis in the philosophy of history.

My first question is why it should appeal, as I think it does, to historians who are not for other reasons Marxists?

A large part of the answer seems to lie in the fact that historical materialism is so conspicuously opposed to superficial explanations in history. Marx, in his attack on Hugo's *Napoleon the Little*, made a great virtue of his unwillingness to explain events by reference to the desires and intentions of a single man. Much more important was it to explain the circumstances and relationships that enable so-called great men to cut the striking figures they do. I am not claiming that Marx was the first to hold the views he expressed so trenchantly. It would be a gross exaggeration to suggest that pre-Marxian history was typically a chronicle of the personal doings of individuals. All the same, historians, who would not agree that fundamental explanations must be in economic terms, are likely to share the historical materialist's conception of what is merely superficial.

Another, more positive, source of the appeal of historical materialism is its very firm recognition of the way people and institutions change through time. Marx puts great emphasis on the differences between apparently similar phenomena occurring in different periods and in different contexts. The similarities are superficial, the differences profound, between the class struggles of the ancient world and those of nineteenth-century Europe; between the English civil war of the seventeenth century and 1789, 1830 and 1848 in France. What comes later is always different in consequence of what has gone before. Even human nature does not remain the same throughout, as Hume seems to have maintained or assumed, for human nature is, at least largely, a social product and changes with changes in society. I am conscious that these observations must seem pretty banal; but this reaction only demonstrates recognition of their conspicuous truth. Marx exhibits to a high degree this feature of the (Marxist and non-Marxist) historical consciousness; he is also responsible to a considerable extent for fixing it there.

There are, then, at least two reasons for the appeal of the materialist conception of history to historians. I am supposing, in arguing in this way, that there is an historical attitude and practice, which are not, or not mainly, the result of the acceptance of historical materialism, with which historical materialism is in certain respects congenial. There is, however, much to be said on the other side. By the same token—appeal to entrenched historical attitude and practice—it cannot be the case that economic factors alone are important in history. In saying this I am not making such assertions as that it is false that the root explanations, say, of what came about in seventeenth-century England and nineteen-century France lie in the class situations of the contending parties. I have seen it denied by historians, at least in the former case; but essentially what we have here are historical questions to which I do not know the answers. It is unbecoming in a philosopher to attempt to adjudicate between historical claims about particular situations. What one can say, however, is that to hold economic factors fundamental to all historical enquiries would be untrue to historical attitudes and practice; that it would involve denying (even though historical reportage is inevitably selective) that objectivity and truth in history are relative to the enquiry in hand; denying too that causes as well as facts are relative to questions asked, and that historians have great, even if not unlimited, freedom in their choice of questions to ask. I do not deny that about a very wide variety of subject matters it is possible to ask Marxist questions, that is questions to which the answers will be in economic terms— *but* these are not the only *historical* questions it is possible to ask, nor, even when they are askable, are they certain to yield historically interesting answers. I am conscious that in a way all I am saying is that historical materialism is not built into our conception of history, which no doubt is truistic—but this means only that its denial would be a falsism. I suppose that my root conviction is that we have and will want to retain a more open conception of history than historical materialism really admits. I suspect too that historical materialists, who are also historians, will not in the end want to give up this conception of history either.

From this point on I can proceed, as I did in my book, only by illustration. I there referred first to the sort of case apparently most favourable to historical materialism, namely, the shifting pattern of allegiances in an apparently revolutionary situation. Even granted that explanations in terms of class positions were true and fundamental, it is surely still possible to be interested in matters not thus determined, in what, from the historical materialist point of view, are mere details. I have agreed that historians have a penchant for the fundamental; but it is also true that they interest themselves in the minutiae of motives and actions. Such minutiae may be historically important in that they fill gaps in historical knowledge. Evidences of them, in the shape of diaries, etc., seem to be welcomed when they come to light, and are apparently sought in pretty unlikely places by such acknowledged historians as R. C. Cobb; and are not, unless I am much mistaken, despised by Marxist social historians. My main claim is that the minutiae may reputably be held to be historically interesting. They are interesting too from an individualistic, humane value standpoint; but that is no more built into our conception of history than historical materialism is.

My second illustration was of what I called 'rather narrowly specialist history', say, of parliament or the law courts, where it seemed to me that much that was historically interesting might slip through the materialist net, in spite of the close involvement of the law with property relations. I thought that there would be many features of procedure which would have to be explained as responses to practical difficulties or as survivals from days when the institutions served different purposes. The explanations sought by the specialist historian will in many cases be internal to his narrow subject matter, which will to that extent constitute an autonomous field of study. Rigorous insistence on explanations being in economic terms would not illuminate the subject matter, but rather exclude it from history altogether. To the contention that it would follow that the subject matter was trivial, I was inclined to reply that this is so only from the value standpoint usually associated with the materialist conception of history, which standpoint is neither a necessary nor sufficient condition of historical importance. On reflection, however, I have come to think that some small qualifications might be in order here. Even in the most specialized history it may be illuminating occasionally to take a broader view—and historical materialism is one, but only one, such broader view. What is most illuminating is an alternation between wider and narrower perspectives.

I would make the same sort of qualification to what I said in my book about intellectual history. My contention was that, from the point of view of anyone interested in the history of philosophy or science *as* philosophy or science, changes are much more cogently and fundamentally explained as developments in accordance with the logic or method of the subject than they are in terms of the class situations of philosophers and scientists or in terms of social forces generally. Marxist approaches, I said, fail to engage with the broad outline, let alone the fine detail of developments in such subjects. (I allowed that Plekhanov made some concessions here, as also, evidently, does Lukács.)

I was staking a claim for the possibility of a sort of history of philosophy or of science which appeals mainly to considerations internal to those subjects. I tried to illustrate the possibility by reference to Berkeley's idealism, in my view most fundamentally explained as the result of more or less valid argument from the premises he started with, and by reference to Kant's doctrine of the good will—being provoked in the latter case by the remark in the *German Ideology* that Kant was the 'whitewashing spokesman' of the politically impotent German bourgeoisie. I still stand by this; but, as I have said, I do on reflection admit that it is enlightening on occasion to take a wider view. I think I have learned something from, for instance, Lucien Goldmann's writings on Kant. Once again, all I am saying is that some alternation of perspective is beneficial, not at all that the historical materialist perspective is uniquely so. And, as I have also said earlier, we have to have a conception of considerations internal to the subject matter, if we are to be able to discern developments not determined by them, and so get the most value from outside approaches. I restricted my illustrations to the history of philosophy because I thought I knew something about some of it. I simply asserted that I supposed the same would be true of the history of science. I am afraid that I cannot do any better here. Nor have I anything of consequence to say about art and literature, though here too I would expect there to be some interplay between internal and external considerations. I do not, it is true, feel quite so confident that in these areas there is room for clear talk of developments in accordance with internal criteria, but then I also feel that here biographical and psychological approaches are stronger competitors for Marxian ones than they are in regard to science and philosophy.

I said at the beginning that I would consider historical materialism, in abstraction from Marxist views about the course of history and from the revolutionary political commitment, solely as a thesis in the analytical philosophy of history, i.e. a claim about what historians may or should interest themselves in (what counts as historically important) and about what counts as an historical explanation. I have given reasons for rejecting historical materialism so understood. Marxist approaches may well be illuminating, but they are neither uniquely nor specially so. This negative conclusion derives largely from a view taken of historical enquiry, and is compatible with the truth of historical materialism interpreted as a thesis about the determination of the main lines of social development. I was surprised when a distinguished historical materialist appeared to say that the view should be conceived entirely in this latter way, without any implications for the conduct of historical enquiry. But with the likes of him, if there are any, I need not quarrel. I am agnostic rather than atheistic about historical materialism, so understood. It ought, I believe, to be expressible in significant form; but the truth value of a thesis of such scope is necessarily very uncertain. For the rest, I tried, in the middle part of this piece, to indicate my position on some disputed points of interpretation; but I remain of the opinion that my low opinion of historical materialism as a thesis in the philosophy of history would not be greatly affected if different interpretative decisions were taken.

University of Exeter

Principal References

Acton, H. B., *The Illusion of the Epoch* (London, 1955).
Atkinson, R. F., *Knowledge and Explanation in History* (London, 1978).
Berlin, I., *Historical Inevitability* (Oxford, 1954).
Bober, M. M., *Karl Marx's Interpretation of History* (Cambridge Mass., 1948).

Cohen, G. A., *Karl Marx's Theory of History* (Oxford, 1978).

Engels, F., *Anti-Dühring* (1878) (Eng. trans. Moscow, 1954).

Lukács, G., *History and Class Consciousness* (1922 and 1927) (Eng. trans. London, 1971).

Marx, K. *Wage Labour and Capital* (1849) in Marx & Engels, *Selected Works* (London, 1968).

Marx, K., *The Class Struggles in France* (1850) (Engl. trans. London, 1937).

Marx, K., *The Eighteenth Brumaire of Louis Bonaparte* (1852) in Marx and Engels *Selected Works* (London, 1968).

Marx, K., *Preface to the Critique of Political Economy* (1859) in Marx and Engels *Selected Works* (London, 1968).

Marx, K., *Capital*, I (1867) (Eng. trans. Moscow, 1954).

Marx, K. and Engels, F., *The German Ideology* (1846) (Eng. trans. Moscow, 1964).

Mešzáros, I., *Marx's Theory of Alienation*, 3rd edn (London, 1972).

Plamenatz, J., *Man and Society*, II (*London*, 1961).

Plekhanov, G., *The Development of the Monist View of History* (1895) (Eng. trans. Moscow, 1956).

Plekhanov, G., *The Materialist Conception of History* (1897) (Eng. trans. New York, 1940).

Plekhanov, G. *The Role of the Individual in History* (1898) (Eng. trans. New York, 1940).

Rader, M. *Marx's Interpretation of History* (New York, 1979).

Philosophy, Science and Myth in Marxism

JOHN N. GRAY

1. Introduction

'Feuerbach resolves the religious essence into the human essence. But the human essence is no abstraction inherent in each single individual. In its reality it is the ensemble of social relations.'[1]

It is a common belief, shared both by Marxists and by critics of Marxism, that differences in the interpretation of this statement have important implications for the assessment of Marx's system of ideas. How we read it will affect our view of the unity of Marx's thought and of the continuity of its development over his lifetime, and it will bear crucially on our appraisal of the epistemological status—metaphysical, scientific or mythopoeic —of the various elements of the Marxian system. Among Marxists, members of the Frankfurt School have emphasized the paternity of Marxian metaphysical humanism in Hegel's conception of man as a self-creating being, while Althusser and his disciples have seen in the extrusion from Marx's later work of any such 'anthropomorphic' notion a guarantee of the scientific character of his historical materialism. Among Marx's liberal critics, it is widely agreed that he espoused an essentialist view of man and, often enough, it is thought that this alone is sufficient to disqualify his system from scientific status. No consensus exists, however, as to the cognitive standing of the several components of Marx's thought. That agreement should be lacking as to the place in it of a conception of human nature is hardly surprising. Different construals of the role of a view of man will reflect divergent commitments, not only in the philosophy and methodology of social and historical inquiry, but in moral and political thought as well.

I do not aim to canvass systematically all the salient philosophical problems posed by Marx's assumptions about man. More modestly, I aim to offer an assessment of the epistemic status and mutual relations of the principal parts of Marx's system, but to do this indirectly and obliquely by way of a discussion of the contributions to Marxist thought of three important writers. Each of these writers is in a genuine Marxian tradition,

---

[1] 'Theses on Feuerbach', VI, in *Marx and Engels: Basic Writings on Politics and Philosophy*, Lewis S. Feuer (ed.) (London: Collins, Fontana Library, 1969), 285.

in that he develops a theme which is undeniably present in Marx himself, and each of them presents the Marxian system as a totality belonging to a different mode of discourse. Firstly, I shall consider some aspects of the writings of Herbert Marcuse. Against the attribution by Althusser of an epistemological rupture in the evolution of Marx's ideas, I shall contend that a definite metaphysical view of man runs consistently through all of Marx's writings. Not only does evidence from the body of Marx's later writings show that he never abandoned the philosophical anthropology he endorsed in the *Economic-Philosophic Manuscripts:* it can easily be shown that some such doctrine is presupposed by his materialist conception of history. But whereas Marx's historical materialism depends upon his metaphysic of human nature, the latter cannot adequately support the former. Indeed, Marcuse's writings suggest that emphasizing Marx's metaphysical humanism tends to undermine the claim of his system to be a theory of world history. In Marcuse's case, it yields an elegiac Marxism, from which class struggle has been all but eliminated, in which social revolution has the character almost of an improbable Pascalian wager, and whose primary uses seem to be those of a weapon in the armoury of cultural criticism. This result is to be accounted for, not by reference to the metaphysical status of the central postulate of Marcuse's system, but in terms of specific incoherences in its philosophical anthropology.

Secondly, I shall consider G. A. Cohen's recent defence of historical materialism in functionalist terms. Important weaknesses in Cohen's argument suggest the conclusion that, if Marx's system contains a theory of universal history and not just an explanatory model of capitalist development, it must trade on teleological explanations of a sort which social science cannot countenance. Thus Hegel's view that human history has an over-all intelligibility deriving from the fact that it has a telos or end-state, a view which Cohen expounds sympathetically in the first chapter of his book but whose bearing on Marx's historical materialism he does not systematically examine, is actually indispensable to it in so far as it contains a theory of the development of men's productive powers through successive economic systems. The collapse of historical materialism as a theory of world history carries with it the ruin of its central thesis about the primacy of productive forces in explaining social change. The upshot of my criticism of Cohen's book is that, whatever incidental contributions to social science it may contain, Marx's system does not in its main elements belong to the scientific mode of discourse.

Finally, I turn briefly to examine the interpretation of Marxism developed by Georges Sorel, a neglected Marxist thinker rightly described by Croce as the most original and important Marxist theorist after Marx himself. In Sorel we find a construction of Marx's system, in which Marx's own activist and Promethean conception of man and his doctrine of class struggle are fully preserved, but in which his historicist and scientistic pretensions have been decisively abandoned. In Sorel's writings, the mythopoeic character of Marxism as the ideology of proletarian class struggle is explicitly acknowledged and its source in a definite moral tradition identified. Sorel's Marxism is not without the difficulties connected with any form of relativism in social and political theory. It appears to be involved in paradoxes of self-reference, and I shall touch on a couple of these whose implications are serious for Sorel's idiosyncratic version of Marxism. I shall point to a tension in Sorel's thought between its mythopoeic and its scientific or diagnostic aspects and I shall suggest that developing a realist science of society involves abandoning some of the most distinctive claims of Sorel's Marxism.

The programmatic conclusion of the paper, whose cogency I do not aim to demonstrate but merely to support indirectly by way of a survey of three Marxian writers, is that Marx's is an explosively unstable system of ideas each of whose components has a distinct epistemological status and stands in need of a different kind of support. Elaborating each of these strands in Marx's thought produces such radically diverse varieties of Marxism that we are justified in regarding talk of Marx's 'system' as little more than a *façon de parler*.

2. Marxism as Metaphysics: Marx and Marcuse on Man as a Self-creating Being

The practical creation of an objective world, the fashioning of inorganic nature, is proof that man is a conscious species-being . . . It is true that the animals also produce. They build nests or dwellings, like the bee, the beaver, the ant, etc. But they produce only their own immediate needs or those of their young; they produce one-sidedly, while man produces universally; they produce only themselves, while man reproduces the whole of nature; their products belong immediately to their physical bodies, while man freely confronts his own product. Animals produce only according to the standards and needs of the species to which they belong, while man is capable of producing according to the standards of every species . . .

It is therefore in the fashioning of the objective world that man really proves himself to be a species-being. Such production is his active species-life. Through it nature appears as his work and his reality. The object of labour is therefore himself, not only intellectually, in his consciousness, but actively and actually, and he can therefore contemplate himself in a world he has himself created.'[2]

[2] In *Karl Marx: Early Writings*, Introduced by L. Colletti (Harmondsworth: Penguin Books, 1975), 328–329.

John N. Gray

It is clear from this and from other, similar passages, scattered throughout the corpus of Marx's writings, that when Marx asserts that man's nature is that of a maker, he intends his reader to understand far more than that man is a tool-using and a tool-fashioning animal. Certainly, that man's reliance on tools in the reproduction of his life-activity is part of what distinguishes him from other animals is never contested by Marx: it is a distinctive feature of human life to which he often refers. It may be supposed that when, in a well-known passage in *German Ideology*,[3] Marx observes that men may be distinguished from animals by their consciousness, their religion or anything else, but '(they) distinguish themselves as soon as they produce their means of subsistence', this is what he has in mind. The greater part of Marx's meaning is more plainly evident, however, when he returns to the question of man's *differentia specifica* in *Capital*,[4] declaring that 'what distinguishes the worst of architects from the best of bees is this: that the architect raises his structure in imagination before he erects it in reality'. In such statements Marx appears to be insisting on a sharp contrast between human life and that of the other animals: 'The animal is immediately one with its life-activity. It is not distinct from that activity; it *is* that activity. Man makes his life-activity itself an object of his will and consciousness. He has conscious life-activity. It is not a determination with which he directly merges. Conscious life-activity directly distinguishes man from animal life-activity. Only because of that is he a species-being.'[5] What separates the life of men from the life of other animals, it seems, is the element of Hegelian negativity, itself dependent on the capacity for abstract thought, which allows them to distance themselves from the behaviour, instinctual or conventional, which they inherit directly from nature or society. It is the negativity and critical reflexivity which forbids any inference from man's fixed characteristics as a biological species to his essential life-activity, and which licenses the claim that man's nature is that of a self-creative being.

It is only this understanding of the claim that man is the producer of himself and of his world which enables us to see how Marx could contrast his own standpoint with that of the old, 'contemplative' materialism. For, whereas he speaks of man as being a part of nature, Marx's standpoint is far from the caricature of German positivism preserved in the writings of Engels and Lenin. It is akin to the Hegelian and radically anti-naturalist standpoint, in which nature is given to man only as an artifact that he has himself produced. In this perspective, the relation between man and nature

[3] *The German Ideology*, S. Ryazanskaya (ed.) (Moscow: Progress Publishers, 1964), 31.
[4] *Capital*, I, trans. Samuel Moore and Edward Aveling, F. Engels (ed.) (Moscow: Progress Publishers, 1965), 179.
[5] *Economic-Philosophic Manuscripts*, in *Karl Marx: Early Writings*, 328.

is theorized, not as a process in which a domain of inert objects confronts a passive subject in whose consciousness it is reflected, but as a transaction in which it is their own practice which gives nature all those of its features which are recognizable by men. Far from subordinating men's lives and history to laws given independently of their purposes or self-interpretations, Marx tends to treat the whole domain of nature as a precipitate of human activities. So strong does this tendency become, so powerful the influence of the mystical idea (derived by Hegel from Böhme) of nature as man's larger body, that there is some basis for Kolakowski's imputation[6] to Marx of a species-relativism. In general, of course, Marx is far from an Idealist denial of the independent reality of the external world. Rather, in standard pragmatist fashion, he tends to regard the concepts and categories embodied in any view of nature as artifactual, useful fictions whose truth-value derives wholly from their contribution to the success of human struggles with the world. This is not to deny that man comes to self-consciousness to find himself situated in a natural order. It is to say that his picture of the world is not something given to him as a datum, but emerges in his practical struggles with it, which in their turn contribute to the progressive humanization of the world in an objective and factual sense. I shall call the thesis that man is in this radical respect his own maker and the shaper of his world Marx's *activist* thesis.

So far Marx's view of the nature of man would seem to be largely a development of some of the main preoccupations of German Idealism. Marx also picked out as among man's *differentiae specificae* another feature, owing more to the Romantic movement, according to which man is distinguished by a vital need for productive labour, going well beyond anything required in the struggle with brute scarcity. For Marx, the estrangement of labour in class and, above all, in capitalist society, consists, not only or primarily in the expropriation of its product, but in the fact that men's life-activity is governed by the autonomous power of the commodity. It is not just that men must work in order not to starve that constitutes labour's estrangement. After all, a rentier who does not have that necessity is judged by Marx to be no less disabled as a productive being than is a proletarian. Marx's view, rather, is that labour ceases to be estranged only when it is the direct expression of man's nature, only when its character is poetic or artistic. This aspect of Marx's view of man is *productivist*, not only in the sense that he acknowledges that men must secure the means of their survival before they can do anything else, but crucially in that self-expressive labour is conceived to be an endogenous imperative of man's nature. This feature of Marx's conception distinguishes his thought sharply from the outlook of the ancient world, in which human fulfilment was

<hr/>

[6] L. Kolakowski, *Main Currents of Marxism*, III, *The Breakdown* (Oxford: Clarendon Press, 1978), 277.

believed to lie in contemplative absorption in a natural or divine order. It separates him no less clearly from the Classical Economists, by whom labour was conceived typically as a distasteful incident *en route* to consumption, and whose social ideal is best epitomised in J. S. Mill's 'gospel of leisure'.

The expressive view of labour (which I have termed Marx's productivist thesis about man) is easily seen as a corollary or entailment of his activist view of man as in essence self-determining. Thus far Marx might seem little more than a radical individualist, a liberal humanist opposed to the fossilization of social life in oppressive institutions. To construe the Marxian system in this way, however, would be a grievous misunderstanding. For, in a drastic extension of the Hegelian tradition, Marx supposed that self-determination for man involves the suppression or dissolution of all distinct, autonomous spheres of social activity and modes of intellectual life. He states this view unambiguously in *Capital*:[7]

> The religious reflex of the real world can ... only then finally vanish when the practical relations of everyday life offer to man none but perfectly intelligible and rational relations to his fellowmen and to nature.
>
> The life-process of society, which is based on the process of material production, does not strip off its mystical veil until it is treated as production by freely associated men, and is consciously regulated by them in accordance with a settled plan.

Here Marx asserts than man's self-determination is inhibited just in so far as the objects and relationships of the social world have a life and laws of their own. It is not too much to say that, for Marx, social science withers away with the ending of alienation, precisely because its subject-matter—a densely textured ambience of autonomous institutions, conventions and practices—has ceased to exist. Similarly, it is only men's pre-history that can on this view be law-governed. To acknowledge that for men the social world must always remain a world that is not of their own making, that men's identities will always be constituted by the roles and activities in which they find themselves, would be for Marx to acquiesce in an utter loss of human freedom. It is not easy, all the same, to envisage what the end of estrangement would be like, given that so much that is constitutive of our lives as we know them would vanish. There is no doubt that the Marxian conception of a de-alienated community would have been resisted by Hegel himself as asocial and abstract to the point of virtual incoherence. However this may be, Marx's view that full human self-determination is incompatible with the survival of any independent spheres of social life

[7] *Capital*, I, 79–80.

yields an important clue to his central understanding of capitalism and of its dialectical negation. It is not in virtue of the distribution of income or the form of property that it involves that capitalism is regarded by Marx as the supremely dehumanizing mode of production. It is because capitalist production has the character of an impersonal process by which human subjects are constrained, and in which their transactions are frozen or crystallized into reified forms of the species-life, that Marx sees it as the radical loss or negation of the human essence. The alienation of labour cannot survive the end of commodity-production, just because estranged labour is *defined* as that which occurs whenever productive exchanges fail to be the direct expression of organized human will.

What defines socialism, accordingly, is the overcoming of commodity-production and its replacement by planned production for use. It is planned production for the direct satisfaction of human needs (including the vital need for expressive labour), production no longer mediated by monetary exchanges or by impersonal laws of supply and demand, which is definitive of the socialist order.[8] It was taken for granted by Marx, no doubt, and it is a natural implication of his account of self-determination, that economic planning in a socialist order would be democratic. (I leave to one side here difficult questions about the decision-procedures, majoritarian or otherwise, appropriate to the democratic planning of a whole economy, and I refrain from commenting on the Arrow-type logical dilemmas such procedures would certainly involve.) It is crucially important to grasp, however, that the self-regulation of a socialist economy is in every respect diametrically opposed to that which obtains in a market order or catallaxy.[9] For, whereas the order that emerges from a series of market exchanges, though it has its source in human actions, owes its most important properties to the fact that it is *not* the result of human design, the order of a socialist economy in the Marxian conception of it is supposed to embody only the intentions of its constituent subjects. It is a fundamental criticism of Marx's idea of a socialist economy that, even supposing human preferences and purposes could in the absence of class stratification attain a measure of compossibility sufficient to obviate serious conflicts over the allocation of resources, the suppression of market processes would deprive economic planners of much information useful to the rational implementation of agreed projects. Whatever its difficulties, it is in the idea of the subordination to collective human will of spontaneous economic processes that the thrust of Marxian socialism is contained, and it is this thesis about the economic consequences

[8] On this and other points in my analysis I have learnt much from *Marx's Theory of Exchange, Alienation and Crisis* by Paul Craig Roberts and Matthew A. Stephenson (Stanford: Hoover Institution Press, 1973).

[9] The term 'catallaxy' I borrow from F. A. Hayek's recent use of it. See his *Studies in Philosophy, Politics and Economics* (London: Routledge, 1967), 164.

of human self-determination that I propose to call Marx's *anti-autonomist* thesis.

Each of these three facets of Marx's conception of man is fully preserved in Herbert Marcuse's version of the critical theory of the Frankfurt School. The activist thesis is expressed in Marcuse's constant emphasis on the creative role of man as the subject of history, the agent of the creation and continuous transformation of the forms of his social life, and his rejection of any image of man's self-development which pictures it in terms of submission to the necessity of historical laws. Like Marx, Marcuse argues that it is the reduction of human relations to relations between things and, in particular, to relations between commodities, that constitutes the essential inhumanity of capitalist society, and which, in reducing proletarian life-activity to a commodity on the labour market, generates the 'determinate negation' of the capitalist order. In Marcuse, as in Marx himself, again, the conceptual foundation of historical materialism is a form of metaphysical humanism, which conceives of history as the progressive disclosure of man's defining species-powers, but which acknowledges that the activities of empirical social groups and individuals may conceal as much as they reveal of man's essential nature and possibilities. Marcuse is in Marx's own authentic tradition in his strong emphasis on the functions of ideological false consciousness in inhibiting men's reflection on their circumstance as alienated labourers and thus in reproducing an irrational social order. In elaborating an ambitious theory of ideology, Marcuse follows Marx in presupposing a set of species-powers whose flourishing it is precisely the role of false consciousness to prevent. Like Marx and Hegel, Marcuse takes for granted that these powers of critical reflection remain latent in most societies, and are manifestly present only in relatively highly complex societies; but he is in no doubt that some such account of man's species-being is presupposed by any theory of ideology. His work shows clearly enough that both the logic of historical materialism and its development as a theory of ideology require a philosophical anthropology of just the sort Althusser's disciples seek to suppress from Marxism. In Marcuse, too, finally, we find Marx's productivist emphasis on the intrinsic value of self-expressive labour, and the anti-autonomist conception of a rationally reconstructed and holistically administered economic order.

In laying emphasis on the metaphysical humanist aspect of the Marxian system, however, Marcuse retreats from its historicist claims and abandons some of its most distinctive theses about the role of proletarian class struggle in the transition to socialism. The dilemma in which Marcuse's abandonment of Marxian historicism places him is well illustrated in his characteristic combination of repeated emphatic statements of the invincibly totalitarian character of modern capitalism with frequent affirmations of the real possibility of total social revolution and reconstruction. On the one hand, Marcuse has declared that 'the vital need for revolution no longer prevails among those classes that as the "immediate producers" would be capable of stopping the capitalist production'.[10] 'Marx's conception of revolution', he continues 'was based on the existence of a class which is not only impoverished and dehumanized, but which is also free from any vested interest in the capitalistic system and therefore represents a new historical force with qualitatively different needs and aspirations'.[11] According to Marcuse, the emergence of such an 'internal negative force' is blocked in advanced industrial society—'not by violent suppression or by terroristic modes of government, but by a rather comfortable and scientific co-ordination and administration'.[12] As a result of contemporary society's 'highly effective scientific management of needs, demands and satisfaction',[13] 'the internal historical link between capitalism and socialism ... seems to be severed',[14] so that 'the idea of the available alternatives evaporate into an utterly utopian dimension in which they are at home'.[15] Here Marcuse is asserting that, owing to the success of modern techniques of demand management, in which even the unconscious needs and instincts of the population become liable to manipulation, the traditional oppositional class in capitalist society has become attached to the circumstances of its servitude. Thus alienated labour may, with the perfection of industrial relations techniques, come to be experienced as rewarding and fulfilling. On the other hand, social groups exist which will seek to exploit the utopian possibilities which Marcuse believes to be inherent in modern capitalism. In *One-Dimensional Man*, Marcuse discovered the last vestiges of revolutionary protest within 'the substratum of the outcasts and outsiders, the exploited and persecuted of other races and other colours, the unemployed and unemployable'.[16] In *An Essay on Liberation*, Marcuse opines that, as a result of the advance of automation, 'a general unstructured, unorganized and diffused process of disintegration may occur'.[17] Marcuse proposes that an intellectual vanguard exploit the new contradictions of late capitalist society by implementing a policy of discriminating tolerance toward conservative and reactionary forces and forge an alliance with other oppositional groups. The new society will be inaugurated by a government consisting of an educational dictatorship of free men which, guided by a radical transvaluation of values and inspired by a new sensibility, can take ad-

---

[10] 'The Obsolescence of Marxism', in *Marx and the Western World*, N. Lobkowicz (ed.) (Notre Dame: University of Notre Dame Press, 1967), 411.

[11] Ibid., 411.

[12] Ibid., 411.

[13] Ibid., 411.

[14] Ibid., 411.

[15] 'Repressive Tolerance' in *A Critique of Pure Tolerance* (with Barrington Moore and R. P. Wolff) (London: Cape, 1969), 93.

[16] *One-Dimensional Man* (London: Sphere Books, 1968), 200.

[17] *Essay on Liberation* (London: Allen Lane, 1969), 85.

vantage of the vast technological resources of modern society and avoid the repression which has disfigured all previous revolutions. In Marcuse's last writings, the social revolution powered by the entry into radical politics of a minority of powerless outsiders, which in *One-Dimensional Man* he had described as 'nothing but a chance',[18] is again treated as a utopian possibility against which virtually all existing institutions and social forces militate.

Marcuse's thought clearly illustrates the tensions inherent in any revision of the Marxian system in which metaphysical postulates are given epistemological priority over social theory and historical interpretation. Socialism becomes a free-floating possibility, an abstract and avowedly utopian prospect, grounded only in a speculative distillation of the human essence. Shorn of the Marxian theory of transition, in which the proletariat is acknowledged to be the class in which mankind's universal interests are embodied, Marcuse's Marxism resembles nothing so much as a Left Hegelian radical humanism. In detaching the transition to socialism from any sort of proletarian activity, again, Marcuse (like Stalin) revives a pre-Marxist Jacobin tradition in which workers become passive objects of their own liberation. The dilemma of Marcuse's thought results from his recognition of the superannuation of the Marxian system conceived as a theory of capitalist development and a scheme for the interpretation of history coupled with his refusal to regard any empirical development as constituting any sort of criticism of Marxism's metaphysical core. Against this criticism, no doubt, it will be urged that Marcuse is at once more and less authentically Marxian than I have pictured him as being. Thus he has always maintained that working-class activity and initiative are indispensable to socialist revolution, just as Marx did. On the other hand, his theory of human nature owes much to Freud, and his theory of a 'technological eros' is oriented around the concept of play rather than that of labour. In reply, I would point out that Marcuse's writings contain some of the same tensions that haunt Marx's work. Like Marx, Marcuse seems to vacillate between a conception of man as *Homo laborans* whose nature has been thwarted by millennial class exploitation and a view of man in which his possibilities are realized only by emancipation from labour into playful freedom. In the one case, the ending of economic alienation is seen as necessarily involving some sort of self-management and transformation of daily labour into an inherently valuable experience, while in the other the emphasis will be laid on the progressive reduction of labour time. Both strands of thought about work are authentically Marxian, and it is unnecessary to invoke Freud's influence on Marcuse to account for the latter's emphasis on the intrinsic virtues of playful activity.

[18] *One-Dimensional Man*, 201. See also Marcuse's *Counter-Revolution and Revolt* (London: Allen Lane, 1972).

With regard to Marcuse's insistence on the necessity of working-class initiative in the making of a socialist revolution, it must be said that this has never carried much credibility. If the working class has any active role in Marcuse's scenario, it is *after* the socialist revolution—in the period of socialist construction. In denying to the working class any important role in the earlier phases of socialist revolution, Marcuse is merely reasserting his conviction of the integration of working-class people in advanced capitalist society. Surely, however, even a sympathetic critic of Marcuse will feel that a more perceptive response to evidences of this integration would have been to undertake a revision of some of his most fundamental Marxian commitments.

Now I do not mean here to invoke any naive falsificationist criterion of the adequacy of Marcuse's (authentically Marxian) metaphysic of human nature. To call Marcuse's view of man a metaphysical view, after all, is to say that no criticism of it which appeals solely to experience can ever be decisive; it is to say that it is a view which structures experience and which gives a framework to empirical evidence. This is not to deny that empirical evidences can have salience to a criticism of Marx's view of man, which may be evaluated in Lakatosian fashion as being part of a progressive or a degenerating research programme. Such an evaluation will not be attempted here, but an outline of it is easily sketched. We will have reason to regard the conception of man expressed in Marx's writings, and in such of his followers as Marcuse, as being part of a degenerating research programme, if there are philosophical reasons for revising it which bear on available empirical evidence. To put the point dogmatically, Marx's view of man as in essence an unconditioned and self-determining agent brings with it all the confusion of Idealist logic and ontology. Kamenka's criticism of Marx on this point is worth quoting:

Man, as Marx in his metaphysical moments portrays him, is (potentially) the unconditioned being of the scholastics (i.e. God), whose unconditionedness is one of his perfections, essential to his (true) nature, and therefore to be deduced from it. It is from the scholastic view of God that Marx unconsciously derives the conception of man as (properly) always a subject and never a predicate. It is from scholastic logic that he gets the otherwise unsupported notion that the self-sufficient, the self-determined, the always active, is morally superior to the conditioned, the determined, the also passive.[19]

More plausibly, perhaps, Kolakowski has suggested[20] that Marx's view of man is bound up inextricably with a Platonist ontology in which the

[19] E. Kamenka, *Marxism and Ethics* (London: Macmillan, 1969), 26.
[20] L. Kolakowski, *The Socialist Idea* (London: Weidenfeld and Nicholson, 1974), Chap. 2, 'The Myth of Human Self-Identity'.

world is conceived as a great chain of being, in which degrees of reality are recognized and are conflated with degrees of goodness, and in which the human species recapitulates in an historical theodicy the return to an undifferentiated unity pictured as the destination of Spirit in Neo-Platonic and Hegelian writings. The objection to Marx's view of man, then, is not the crass empiricist objection that its content has an essentialist or metaphysical aspect, but rather a philosophical objection of a substantive sort. It is not one that can be defended here, and I will not try to defend it. Perhaps it will suffice to say that the claim that Marxism constitutes a degenerate research programme rests on a conjunction of philosophical criticism of its underlying logic and ontology with evidences and reasonings about political life which suggest the incoherence of the Marxian idea of a return to a lost unity in a conflict-free union of civil and political society. The crucial objection here has been well put by Kolakowski in his critique of the myth of human self-identity as foundational in the Marxian project of a post-political society. This is a criticism which need not draw directly on philosophical reasonings, since it may be argued that the transcendence of self-division, which is the project of Marx no less than of Rousseau, is unachievable except at a price which Rousseau acknowledged but Marx did not—namely, a retreat to much lower levels of critical self-awareness in a far simpler social order. This suggests an ironical criticism of Marx's system, which is that it is disqualified from being a successful scheme of historical interpretation in virtue of its failing to take seriously the irreversibility of cumulative conceptual enrichment through the increasing moral complexity and cross-cultural sensibility of human society. There is a further strand of criticism salient here too, one which draws on the writings of Durkheim and Weber, in which it would be argued that role-occupancy of the constraining sort Marx condemns is not merely functionally indispensable to industrial societies, but actually largely constitutive of human self-identity in any conceivable society. Despite their abstractness, these are quasi-empirical rather than straightforwardly philosophical propositions and ones we are in a better position to evaluate than Marx was. This is to say merely that, if we are correct in judging Marx's system to embody a degenerate research programme in our own context, nothing follows directly as to its credentials in Marx's own time.

3. Marxism as Social Science and Theoretical History: Cohen on Historical Materialism as a Species of Functionalism

In G. A. Cohen's recent restatement of Marx's historical materialism in functionalist terms, the dependency of Marx's system on a view of human nature is explicitly acknowledged, though its metaphysical content is largely suppressed. Cohen notes that there is 'a Marxist tradition to deny that there exists an historically invariant human nature', but insists that there are 'enduring facts of human nature'[21]—facts which Marx's system depends upon, and which are not controverted by the insistence on the partial self-transformation of man in history. As Cohen puts it, 'man is a mammal, with a definite biological constitution, which evolves hardly at all in some central respects throughout millennia of history'.[22] How does Cohen construe the place of a view of human nature in Marx? He states as the central claim of historical materialism what he calls the *primacy* thesis, which asserts that 'the nature of a set of productive relations is explained by the level of development of the productive forces embraced by it (to a far greater extent than vice versa)'.[23] He tells us that the primacy thesis is associated with a second thesis, which he calls the development thesis and which he states as follows: 'The productive forces tend to develop throughout history'.[24] He specifies this as entailing more than that productive forces *have* developed. For, whereas this might have happened 'for a miscellany of unco-ordinated reasons',[25] the development thesis asserts a universal tendency to development of the productive forces. It does not entail that the forces *always* develop, since, as Cohen notes, citing the decline of imperial Rome as an example, there are 'exceptions to the generalization that the productive forces, though indeed capable of stagnation, do not, barring natural disaster, go into reverse'. Thus, as Cohen puts it succinctly, the development thesis 'predicate(s) a perennial tendency to productive progress, arising out of rationality and intelligence in the context of the inclemency of nature'.[26] As to apparent counter-examples, a theory of history is not answerable to abnormal occurrences, Cohen tells us, though he admits that there is an as yet unsatisfied need for criteria of normalcy for human societies.

Cohen tells us that the development thesis, for which criteria for abnormality in society or history seem to be indispensable, is itself a necessary support for the primacy thesis. What then supports the development thesis? Cohen declares that 'we put it as a reason for affirming the development thesis that its falsehood would offend human rationality'.[27] The development thesis gains plausibility, he says,[28] if we note three facts about men: that they are somewhat rational; that their general historical situation is one of scarcity; and that they possess intelligence of a kind and

[21] G. A. Cohen, *Karl Marx's Theory of History: A Defence* (Oxford: Clarendon Press, 1978), 151.
[22] Op. cit., 151.
[23] Op. cit., 134.
[24] Op. cit., 134.
[25] Op. cit., 135.
[26] Op. cit., 156, 155 respectively.
[27] Op. cit., 153.
[28] Op. cit., 152.

degree which enables them to improve their lot. Cohen observes that the thesis that men are irrational if they fail to exploit the opportunity to expand productive forces whenever the growth of knowledge allows this has two difficulties. We do not know 'the relative magnitude of man's material problem and consequent interest in its solution, by comparison with other human problems and interests . . . Whether the falsehood of the development thesis would offend rationality demands a judgment of the comparative importance of potentially competing interests'.[29] Cohen identifies a second difficulty when he observes that 'it is not evident that societies are disposed to bring about what rationality would lead men to choose. There is some shadow between what reason suggests and what society does'.[30]

Cohen says of his defence of the development thesis that it is 'not conclusive, but it may have some substance'.[31] This modest disclaimer fails to do justice to the difficulties in which Cohen puts himself. They all arise from the fact that the conception of rationality with which Cohen works, though it is intended by him to have a universal application, has the content he needs only if the values of some elements of our own culture are fed into it. Otherwise, it is an almost completely empty, indeterminate and programmatic conception, and the thesis that productive relations tend to alter to allow for the most efficient use of productive forces becomes vacuous rather than contingently false. The notion of more or less efficient uses of productive forces makes sense only when, as in problems of engineering, there is agreement on objectives. Even within our own culture, it is a salient feature of social problems, including problems of production, that typically they arise from conflicts of ways of life rather than from the kind of technical disagreement that might occur between engineers charged with the completion of a common project.[32] Consider in this regard current controversy about factory farming and about the elimination and replacement of small family farms by large agricultural corporations.[33] To suppose that discussion of the merits of rival forms of agricultural enterprise can proceed by reference to some common standard of efficiency is to suppose, what is patently false, that farming has a single undisputed purpose. Understanding current controversy in this area involves recognizing that rival conceptions of farming are at issue, each of which is bound up with the defence of a broader way of life. An appeal to some over-arching standard of efficiency in satisfying express preferences could settle such dispute

[29] Op. cit., 153.

[30] Op. cit., 153.

[31] Op. cit., 151.

[32] See on this R. Rhees, *Without Answers* (London: Routledge, 1969), 23–49, for a critique of Marxism from which I have learnt much.

[33] I owe this example to D. Z. Philipps and H. O. Mounce, *Moral Practices* (London: Routledge, 1970).

only if there were a common market to which all demands could be brought and a reasonable bargain struck.[34] No criterion of efficiency could be at the same time neutral in a conflict of this sort and yet authoritative for all parties to it. For, while contending social movements and ways of life often come to a working compromise, such a settlement is wholly different in character from a marketplace bargain, since it often represents only an abatement in the struggle between incommensurable claims.

These difficulties are even more formidable when an appeal to efficiency is made, not to settle practical conflicts within a given culture, but to help to explain transitions from one social order or historical epoch to another. When capitalist enterprise emerged from feudal societies in Europe, protagonists of the rival forms of economic life did not self-evidently share objectives and problems for which capitalism proved to be the most cost-effective solution. Those who think that human history as a whole can be understood as a movement from less to more efficient uses of expanding productive forces take for granted a common standard of efficiency where one is not even conceivable. None of this is to suggest that immanent criticism of a culture or a way of life cannot proceed by invoking efficiency. It is not to endorse some quasi-Parsonian view in which the rationality of any social arrangement is indistinguishable from its sheer persistence. It is to say that a standard of efficiency is lacking which can be applied cross-culturally or even (within a single society) between ways of life expressive of incommensurable values.

These difficulties are not met by Cohen's observation that the development thesis depends on a judgment about the relative importance in men's lives of material and other interests. A sharp distinction between material and other interests is apt only in a secular and post-traditional society of just the sort in which capitalist enterprise is dominant. Even within a society of this sort, applying such a distinction presents problems, not of imprecision or of open texture, but of sheer indeterminacy. If an affluent but harassed businessman relinquishes a high income for a more relaxed and leisurely life in the country, is he settling a conflict between his material and his non-material interests in favour of the latter? If workers object to the introduction of Taylorian techniques of time-management into the life of the factory, and their opposition is not dampened by a credible offer of higher wages, is this a case where material interests are foregone for the sake of other goods? And are we to understand that the path of rationality lies in always favouring material interests, supposing a rough and ready demarcation criterion between these interests and others is available? If not, what sense is there in the claim that the falsity of the development thesis would be an impeachment of human rationality? Invoking criteria

---

[34] I a indebted to the writings of John Anderson, and especially to his *Marxist Ethics*, in *Studies in Empirical Philosophy* (Sydney, 1962), for these points.

of normalcy in history or in society (there is a disturbing slippage here) is unhelpful, since we lack criteria which satisfy Cohen's requirement of yielding the development thesis without question-beggingly presupposing it. Finally, even if a workable classification of human interests existed, and it were true that men always tended to favour their material interests over others, still the development thesis would not follow. Cohen alludes to Marx's apparent belief that it was population growth which, in disrupting the balance between needs and natural resources distinctive of primitive communism,[35] spurred the adoption of what he calls 'a more aggressive technology'. An equally effective way of remedying the imbalance caused by demographic growth, and a way which has been favoured by the overwhelming majority of traditional societies, is the institution of population controls. Unless a parochially European preoccupation with human mastery of the natural environment is written into the conception of rationality with which Cohen works, I do not see how such a response can be disqualified as irrational. The conception of *Homo economicus* which Cohen's conception of rationality comprehends has, in fact, no tendency to support Marxian productivism.

That Cohen works with an ahistorical, unMarxian and almost Benthamite conception of rationality emerges from his cursory consideration of the problematic aspects of any criterion for the assessment of productive power. Productive power, he tells us, is 'the amount of surplus production the forces (of production) enable', where surplus production is understood in this context to signify 'production beyond what is necessary to satisfy the indispensable physical needs of the immediate producers, to reproduce the labouring class'. Thus, he declares, 'the development of the productive forces may be identified with the growth of the surplus they make possible, and this in turn may be identified with the amount of the day which remains after the labouring time required to maintain the producers has been subtracted'.[36] Now it is no news to Cohen, any more than it was to Marx, that criteria for 'subsistence' inescapably contain cultural elements: for, apart from anything else, differing forms of social life will make differing demands on men's bodies, and so necessitate differences in diet and so on. Further, it is not obvious on the face of it what time-span is to be used in assessing a productivity increase. These are problems of which Cohen is clearly aware, and which might be thought to pose no fatal threat to his proposed criterion. The real difficulties lie elsewhere. First of all, the efficiency or productivity criterion he suggests needs to be argued for: why adopt this criterion rather than any other? It is not a criterion whose salience is *self-evident*. Men have nowhere consistently regarded a shortening of the working day, or an increase in their capability to support ever

[35] Cohen, 24.
[36] All of the preceding quotations occur on p. 60 of Cohen.

larger numbers of human beings, as constitutive of their welfare. How could the priority of such goals over others—over goals to do with national grandeur, spiritual development and the preservation of ancient traditions, for example—possibly be constitutive of rationality? Secondly, in presupposing our ability to make on-balance aggregative judgments about socially necessary labour time, Cohen's proposed productivity criterion arguably involves just that weighing of incommensurables which it was its purpose to circumvent.[37] The key point, however, is that, even if Cohen's productivity criterion can be coherently spelt out, he has said nothing to show that increasing productivity is always (or paradigmatically) rational. He needs to do this, given the distance between the productivity criterion and ordinary (culturally and historically variant) conceptions of rationality, if his proposal is to have any intuitive forcefulness.

It may be from an awareness of these difficulties that Cohen affirms that 'the fact that capitalism did not arise spontaneously outside of Europe is a serious problem for historical materialism'.[38] Unless we begin by ascribing to human history an end-state for which capitalism is an indispensable condition, there seems no reason why capitalism should not be regarded as a unique episode. This view of the matter is given added plausibility when we recall that Marx himself regarded the expansionist and productivist imperatives which Cohen deploys in an attempt to develop a scheme of universal historical interpretation as distinctive of and peculiar to the capitalist system.[39] The dynamism which capitalism displays as a system cannot be used to account for its emergence in the first place, given what Marx describes[40] as the essential conservatism of all pre-capitalist modes of production. On one occasion, indeed, Marx apparently disavows any generalization of an explanatory model which is in place when it is applied to the workings of the capitalist system to the domain of human history as a whole. If this statement of Marx's[41] is taken as an authoritative evidence of his intentions, we have reason to regard historical materialism as a theory of capitalism rather than a scheme of historical interpretation.

If the development thesis lacks rational support, what of the primacy thesis which Cohen rightly takes to be the corner-stone of Marx's historical materialism? Cohen specifies the explanatory relation postulated in historical materialism as holding between productive forces and productive relations as being a functional father than a causal relation. In part this

[37] On p. 353 Cohen asserts that the theses of the labour theory of value are not presupposed or entailed by any of the arguments he advances in the book. The productivity criterion may presuppose some elements of the labour theory of value; but I am not concerned to argue this here.

[38] Cohen, 248.

[39] Cohen, 155.

[40] Cohen, 169.

[41] Cohen,

claim, along with the construal of the Marxian model of society as tri-partite rather than bipartite in which it is embedded, is intended as a rebuttal of some criticisms of historical materialism. Cohen aims to answer, especially, writers such as Acton, Plamenatz and Nozick, who maintain that historical materialism's explanatory pretensions are nullified by the conceptual impossibility of making the sorts of distinctions it pre-supposes. Thus he maintains against such critics that a characterization of production relations is available which is *rechtfrei* in that it does not contain those very things (normative or superstructural aspects of social life) that it purports to explain. It is still unclear, I think, that Cohen's description of the rights and powers of proletarians in a capitalist order, for example, is *rechtfrei* in the sense he needs if capitalist production rela-tions are to be describable independently of the legal and ideological forms in which they are found. Cohen is probably right, then, when he contrasts his own account of production relations with that which Engels stigmatized as the 'force theory' in *Anti-Dühring*,[42] but it may be doubted if the force theory (whose absurdity is manifest when it is assessed as an account of the production relations characteristic of a whole epoch or mode of production) can be avoided without embracing an account which remains open to the criticisms Cohen is concerned to rebut. I do not want to pursue these questions here, however, since nothing in my argument turns on how they are answered, but merely to look more closely at the functionalist reformu-lation of the primacy thesis which Cohen advances.

To say that production relations and legal and political institutions have a functional connection with productive forces is to say that they allow the latter to develop and expand according to their potential powers. This is a technological reformulation of Marx's materialism which captures at least a part of Marx's meaning, and which allows for critical discussion. It does not treat technological innovation as explanatory of all great social changes but as itself beyond explanation, but asserts that, once the dis-position of human beings to conquer natural scarcity has brought about a new set of productive forces, production relations and the rest of society will adjust so as to permit their most efficient deployment. What is lacking in the account so far is any elaboration of the mechanism whereby this is supposed to occur. Cohen tries to supply this with an Engels-type argu-ment that the explanatory form of Marx's materialism is akin to that of Darwin's evolutionary theory,[43] but the argument has two crippling dis-abilities. One of them has been noticed by Peter Singer,[44] when he points

[42] Cohen, 223

[43] Cohen, 160–166.

[44] Singer, *New York Review of Books*, 20 December 1979, 46–47. In reply to Singer, Cohen has insisted that Darwinian theory has a functionalist aspect. I am not persuaded by his claims, but their cogency would not affect the main line of my argument.

to the misconception of Darwin's theory contained in Cohen's statement of it. Darwin did not (as Cohen suggests) explain the long necks of giraffes by saying that long necks have the function of enabling giraffes to survive, for to say that would be to say nothing. Darwin's explanation of the long necks of giraffes was in terms of the action of natural selection on giraffes with necks of varying lengths—an explanation which displaces any functional explanation. Contrary to Cohen, a theory of evolution by the natural selection of the products of random genetic mutations renders any functional explanation otiose in these domains.

More fundamentally, Cohen's reformulation identifies no mechanism, akin to that of natural selection of genetic accidents in Darwinian theory, whereby more efficient uses of productive forces replace less efficient ones. To be sure, such a mechanism exists within capitalist economies in which firms behave as Marx, following the Classical Economists, thought they would behave. In a competitive capitalist environment, it may well be true (as Cohen observes) that adopting more efficient methods for the exploitation of available productive forces may be a condition of a firm's survival. The same competitive pressure may indeed account for technological innovation and the spread of new technologies throughout the economy as well as for firms seeking to make the best use of existing technology. (This latter is a point Cohen does not make.) Where the mechanism of market competition is lacking, we have no reason to expect that productive forces will gravitate to their most efficient uses. Cohen tells us that this might take place in the absence of market competition if, for example, the central planners of a socialist economy were to decide to take advantage of economies yielded by increases in the scale of production. That this *could* happen cannot be disputed, but—as the complaints of dissenting Soviet-bloc economists confirm—socialist economies contain no mechanism in virtue of which it is bound to happen, or which generates any persisting tendency in favour of such a development. When Cohen speaks of this, the only case he mentions of a move to more efficient uses of productive forces happening in the absence of competitive pressure, he gives the game away by calling it *a purposive* elaboration of a functional explanation. It clinches the suspicion that, except when its subject-matter is purposive behaviour and its cybernetic simulations, functional explanation is out of place in social science. A Darwinian (but not a functional) explanation may be given for technological innovation and for productive efficiency in the context of the pressures of a capitalist economy, but no such explanation can be given for the replacement of one mode of production by another which is more efficient. The productive efficiency of a metropolitan capitalist economy may enable it to overwhelm less efficient peripheral economies by a variety of means, including military force, but that is another matter. Considerations of productive efficiency cannot account for the emergence of the capitalist mode in the first place, and it would be fanciful to suppose that they explain its extension into hitherto traditional economies. More unblinkingly than Marx himself, Cohen mistakes an imperative of the capitalist system for a universal tendency. There is nothing in Cohen's argument which adequately supports his claim that Marxian functionalism lacks the conservative complications of functionalism's non-Marxian variants.

I do not claim that the corpus of Marx's writings contains nothing of interest or importance in the way of scientific analysis of the capitalist system. Marxian trade-cycle theory, for example, though it remains eminently controversial, is part of a theory of capitalist crisis and breakdown which is still well worth studying, but nothing in it warrants the belief that capitalism's successor will be a more efficient mode of production. Even the full validity of the Marxian theory of capitalist crisis would not guarantee the development thesis. All this suggests that, quite apart from any of the difficulties I have mentioned in specifying the exact content of Cohen's functionalist statement of Marx's historical materialism, the scientistic and positivistic version of the Marxian system which Cohen develops cannot support its role as a theory of history. It might be replied that the weakness of Cohen's defence lies in the view of human nature with which he works—a view which he admits[45] is not be be found elaborated in Marx's writings, though he claims they contain much that is consonant with it. It might be thought, in other words, that Cohen's failure is to write into his view of human nature a strong endogenous productivist imperative. Even if this were done, however, it would not yield anything like an historical law, or even a persisting tendency, unless other, competing human dispositions were reliably defeated. This could be thought to be so, I suggest, only if the expansion of human productive powers were an end-state ascribed to human history as a whole. Unless human history has an immanent goal or purpose, unless teleological explanation is appropriate in respect of vast multi-generational changes, the Marxian theory of history fails. The conclusion is irresistible that historical materialism has the character of an historical theodicy and not of a contribution to a science of society.

4. Marxism as the Ideology of Proletarian Class Struggle: Sorel on Myth and Moral Regeneration in the Social Revolution

In Sorel's Marxism we find a species of revolutionary socialist ideology which, as Isaiah Berlin has observed in a luminously perspicuous essay,[46] breaks with two of the most fundamental beliefs of the Western intellectual

[45] Cohen, 159.
[46] In *Against the Current: Essays in the History of Ideas* (London: Hogarth Press, 1979), 296–322.

tradition—the Greco-Roman belief that knowledge liberates and the Judaeo-Christian belief in an historical theodicy—which inform and shape Marx's own thought to its very foundations. Yet Sorel's claim to be a follower of Marx was neither fanciful nor perverse. In at least two important respects, Sorel develops distinctive and valuable features of Marx's thought.

First, Sorel expounds in a sharp and clear form the metaphysical conception of man as a creative and self-creative being which I have claimed is a logical presupposition of historical materialism. Against the thinkers of the French Enlightenment, against Bentham and his followers among the Philosophic Radicals, Sorel affirmed a view of man as active rather than passive, struggling rather than enjoying, doing and making rather than contemplating or absorbing sense-data. Human action he seems to have conceived as erupting from an inner necessity to imprint a unique mark on the world. Nothing could be further removed from the inertial conception of human action as a response to external stimulus or internal deprivation, which we find in Hobbes, Bentham or Holbach. Sorel greatly valued natural science, which he pictured in Marxian pragmatist fashion as a weapon in which human order is imposed on an inherently formless natural world, but he had nothing but disdain for projects for a social science wherein human conduct would be subsumed under the intelligibility of impersonal and abstract laws. Sorel takes from Marx, then, his view of man as a creature standing apart from the objects of the natural order, as distinct from other animals in that his life is, first and foremost, an expression of a primordial creative impulse.

Sorel takes from Marx, secondly, what I might call an agonistic view of society. It is viewed, not as a perpetual motion machine in which a rational harmony of interests produces continuous progress in the satisfaction of wants, but as an arena of conflicting classes, moralities and world-views. One implication of the pluralistic and conflictual model of social development Sorel derived from Marx is that, for Sorel as for Marx, socialist revolution has a social rather than a political character. It is not a *coup d'état* or a putsch, the fruit of a conspiracy of *déraciné* intellectuals, but the culmination of a long period of class struggle. More radically than Marx, Sorel attributed an anti-political character to the social revolution. It was not just that revolutionary syndicalism, as Sorel imagined it, repudiated the prudent and temporizing politics of the Third Republic, but that social revolution was construed as an expressive and not a purposive act, a gesture of independence and solidarity to the assessment of which its consequences were almost irrelevant. In his strong emphasis on the internal moral qualities of class struggle, Sorel is doubtless influenced by Proudhon, but his anti-utopian indifference to blueprints for a future socialist order is authentically Marxian. More decisively than either of the two Marxist writers I have discussed, Sorel grasps Marx's distinctive insight that social development is the story of conflict between distinct social groupings, with different places in society's productive apparatus and having contending moral outlooks and views of the world. He develops Marx's accent on class struggle—an aspect of the Marxian system which tends to fall out of Marcuse's and Cohen's reformulation of it.

So far, I have maintained that Sorel adopts Marx's activist view of man and the pragmatist view of knowledge that goes with it in Marx. He develops Marx's doctrine of class struggle into an anti-utopian critique of ideas of social unity and rational harmony among men which goes well beyond Marx's own intentions. He shares with Marx an anti-instrumental and expressive interpretation of human action and, above all, of human labour, whose centrality in men's lives he doubted as little as Marx did. Where Sorel departs from Marx he is, in my view, on his strongest ground. He relinquishes any historiosophical pretensions for his conception of class struggle and goes so far as to condemn Marx for an excessively determinist account of social development. Sorel's voluntarism is related to a deeper difference from Marx, namely the primacy he gave to will over intellect in human affairs. In insisting on the importance of myth as a non-rational moving force in society and history, and in belittling the role of prudence and of rational calculation of self-interest, Sorel broke decisively with the intellectualist psychology Marx inherited from the Enlightenment and which he attempted (somewhat incongruously) to marry with the expressive conception of action he borrowed from Hegel. Sorel is influenced by Schopenhauer and by Nietzsche in treating the conceptions men form of their social circumstance as being moulded primarily, not by disinterested reflection on an available body of evidence which is neutral as regards conflicting purposes, but by their hopes and needs. Sorel's conception of myth is akin to Marx's conception of ideology and to Freud's notion of illusion in that the truth content of beliefs, images and symbols so characterized is not denied but regarded as irrelevant to their function in the economy of human activity. Sorel's departures from the intellectualist psychology of the Enlightenment, however, lead him to view myth in a fashion radically divergent from anything that can be teased out of Marx's writings on ideology. In Marx, one of the criteria whereby a belief or conception is judged to have an ideological function is that, apart from its supportive role in rationalizing men's interests, it is typically distortive of their real circumstances and conceals from them the true character of their activities. A distinction between appearance and reality in society is the hinge on which any authentically Marxian theory of ideology turns. In Sorel's thought, on the contrary, the idea that there is a true or essential state of society to knowledge of which men can attain, if it is present at all, is extremely subdued. Sorel comes close to the view that men's social relations are so constituted by their ideas and beliefs, and especially by myths which make an appeal to the will, that any idea of a science of society must be rejected as incoherent. Revolutionary socialism could not then be a part of such a science: it must be viewed rather as a moral outlook and a conception of the social world, evolved obscurely (like its rivals) from the unknowable depths of the minds of men sharing a common lot.

Sorel's construal of socialist thought as the conceptual form of proletarian class struggle was, of course, a direct influence on Lukács' *History and Class-Consciousness*, where (as in Sorel) it gives rise to well-known difficulties and paradoxes. All these problems turn on a paradox of self-reference. For the claim that socialism, like all other ideologies, is a perspective on society generated at a specific vantage-point, and serving specific interests, seems itself to have the aspect of a cognitively absolute claim formulated at a point of neutrality between competing interests and their associated world-views, whose very possibility the general theory of ideology denies. Another way of stating the difficulty is to say that judgments that such-and-such a belief is ideological in character are always theory-dependent. Further, the theory presupposed by any such judgment must itself be given a privileged immunity from the relativization which it confers on its subject matter if it is not to have a self-defeating effect. These difficulties are, if anything, more prominent in Sorel's theory of myth than in Marx's account of ideology.

I do not propose to comment directly here on these questions, but one observation is worth making about the way in which Sorel's successors developed his thought. It is in the writings of Michels and his school that we find both a continuation of Sorel's work and a resolution of some of its difficulties which at the same time embodies an incisive criticism of some of Sorel's excesses. The substantive burden of Michels' criticism of Sorel is, of course, contained in his denial that the revolutionary syndicates could reasonably be supposed to be agents of the moral regeneration or *ricorso*, the renewal or recursion from decadence, that Sorel hoped for. In so far as the syndicates acted as organs of genuine class struggle, with intermediate as well as long-term aims demanding a consideration of strategic and tactical advantage, their anti-instrumental and anti-political integrity was inevitably compromised. The pressure of a quasi-military struggle itself generates élitism and an oligarchy with interests distinct from those of the proletarian majority. In short, Michels saw that there was no reason to think the revolutionary trade unions were exempt from the fate that had befallen the social-democratic parties.

Michels' criticism exposes an epistemological tension in Sorel's thought as much as it exposes its practical weakness. The tension is between those areas of his writings in which Sorel acts merely as the exponent of a proletarian world-view and morality and those in which he is the theorist of its emergence and conditions. The latter role is arguably presupposed by much of what Sorel says in the former capacity. Further, its culmination is precisely a realist science of power and of social movements of just the sort Sorel despised. Since these aspects of Sorel's thought, the diagnostic and the prophetic, were never clearly distinguished, the one frequently corrupted the other. Thus we find nowhere in Sorel any theoretical recognition of the historical limitation of the proletarian outlook whose governing myths he had poetically explored. Nowhere does Sorel acknowledge that the outlook he is expounding is that of certain social groupings at a certain stage of their development, in a specific (and soon transformed) economic and political environment. This is the price of Sorel's abstention from grand theories of history—that his account of the working-class movement and its morality is hopelessly unhistorical. If the delusive character of Sorel's hopes for the proletariat is ever conceded by him, it is only implicitly in his late flirtation with radical nationalist groups whose anti-bourgeois stance seemed to him to offer some prospect of the *ricorso* and cultural renaissance which to the end of his days he continued to conceive in political (if highly idiosyncratic) terms.

5. Conclusion

Each of the three Marxian thinkers I have discussed and criticized recalls elements of Marx's thought and develops them in a legitimate and in some respects a fruitful direction. Like Marx's thought as a whole, each of these thinkers elaborates upon an aspect of Marx's contributions, and it turns out under pressure to disintegrate into several categorially distinct segments. The upshot of my criticism of each of these writers is that the epistemological instability of the Marxian system of ideas is such as to ruin it as a contribution to rational inquiry. It liberates thought from some forms of absolutist limitation, but creates new obstacles to unfettered inquiry in their place.

It may be asked, at this point, what conclusion may be reached as to the place in the Marxian scheme of a conception of human nature? Much that I have said might seem to support a view akin to Alasdair MacIntyre's,[47] when he denies that social and moral conflicts can ever be arbitrated by appeal to a view of man. No view of man can have practical authority, he suggests, because each moral tradition carries with it its own view of man. Each man will see himself in terms of the moral practices in which he stands, and his conception of human nature will itself be constituted by the moral practices to which he belongs. This radical sceptical view, though it may seem to be supported by what I have said in criticism of Cohen about the incommensurability of different cultures, is not entailed by it. It would be Idealism of just the sort against which Marx struggled to suppose that man can be whatever he tries to make himself become,

[47] *A Short History of Ethics* by Alasdair MacIntyre (London: Routledge, 1968), 268–269.

and this is a view neither entailed by Marx's system nor ever expressed by him. Certainly, it is an important task to establish what are the biological constraints on the possible variety of human nature, and the theorists of socio-biology are making a contribution to this question even if all their positive conjectures are in error. Even a well-founded theory of man's biological limitations, however, is not social theory, or any part of it. For, if a conception of human nature is indeed indispensable to social theory, it is as its prelude and not as its foundation.

MacIntyre is on the right track, however, in that he is denying that a conception of human nature (or a social theory embodying or presupposing a view of man) can have practical or moral authority. This is a conclusion profoundly subversive of Marxism in whatever epistemological mode its propositions are framed. For, whether metaphysical, scientific or mytho-poeic in character, the central notions and theses of Marxism have always been supposed by its exponents to be capable, not merely of illuminating conduct, but of guiding and inspiring it.[48] The running together of theory and practice in this way has led to a disastrous confusion of categories in modern thought from which we are only lately recovering. But that is another story, and one that cannot be told here.[49]

Jesus College, Oxford

[48] I have not forgotten those neo-Kantian Marxian thinkers who treat Marxist social theory as purely explanatory. I would contend that their writings sacrifice that unity of theory and practice which is distinctive of the Marxian standpoint.

[49] I am particularly grateful to Gerry Cohen, David Miller, Bhikhu Parekh and Bill Weinstein for their comments on previous versions of this paper.

Historical Explanation in 'The Critique of Dialectical Reason'

MARY WARNOCK

The Critique of Dialectical Reason was first published in France twenty years ago, in 1960. The book, we know from Simone de Beauvoir, was flung together in a hurry, written virtually without correction during the height of the Algerian war, a period, for Sartre, of stress and anxious stock-taking of his position as a Marxist and a long-term non-joiner of the Communist Party. The whole sense in which, in 1960, Sartre was a Marxist, the question of precisely how eccentric his kind of Marxism was, is centred on his theory of historical explanation. I do not propose to raise many detailed questions about the relation of Sartre's views on history to those of Marx himself, still less to those of other Marxists. Ignorance alone would rule out such a course. I would like if I can, however, to consider Sartre's own view of historical explanation as it appears in the *Critique*, and leave it to others if they wish to fit it into the Marxist tradition, or exclude it. In order to perform this relatively modest expository task, it will be necessary for me to refer, from time to time, to Sartre's earlier philosophical views. But this will come in incidentally.

It would be a simplification, but not, perhaps, too much of an exaggeration, to say that Sartre's purpose in embarking on the *Critique of Dialectical Reason* (he published only Volume One, and never wrote more than a few paragraphs of Volume Two) was to justify a certain way of looking at history, in order in turn to justify the pursuit of certain broadly *political* goals for the future. Like Marx, he believed that one could base a political programme only on a full understanding of the history of man up to the present time, whatever that present time might be. But he held that Marx, and, in particular, Marxists, though they worked in the light of this belief, had failed to prove it, or even seriously to examine the particular form in which they held it. He proposed to assert a dialectical interpretation of history; to demonstrate that things in the world being what they are, and men being what they are, no other interpretation of history is possible; and finally to expound, largely by means of examples, in what sense his dialectical interpretation was to be understood. This was the tripartite aim of the *Critique*.

History *must* be dialectical, because of the peculiar nature of man, and his relation both to other men and to his environment. It is our task to try to understand what such a proposition means. One could take as a text for an exegetical sermon on the *Critique* the words of Marx in the *Eighteenth*

Brumaire of Louis Bonaparte, which Sartre quotes in his introduction: 'Men make their own history, but under circumstances given and transmitted from the past'. Sartre comments thus: 'If this statement is true, then both determinism and analytical reason must be categorically rejected as the method and law of human history. Dialectical rationality, the whole of which is contained in this sentence, must be seen as the permanent unity of freedom and necessity. In other words . . . the universe becomes a dream, if the dialectic controls man from outside, as his unconditioned law. But if we imagine that everyone simply follows his inclinations and that these molecular collisions produce large-scale effects we will discover *average* or statistical results, but not a historical development. So in a sense man submits to the dialectic as to an enemy power; in another sense he creates it; and if dialectical reason is the reason of history this contradiction must itself be lived dialectically, which means that man must be controlled by the dialectic in so far as he creates it, and create it in so far as he is controlled by it. Furthermore it must be understood that there is no such thing as man; there are people, wholly defined by their society and by the historical movement which carries them along; we do not wish the dialectic to become a divine law again, a metaphysical fate. It must proceed from individuals and not from some kind of supra-individual ensemble.' We must, that is, understand history, if at all, as a developing dialectic, and understanding will itself be the exercise of dialectical reason, through which we recognize the mutual relations between men and things, between the creators and the created objects. Analytical reason would be the kind of thinking which treats the history of man as capable of being understood by treating individual units, separate human beings, as intelligible in themselves (or this is what Sartre appears to mean). Determinism, on the other hand, would be that form of theory which supposed men's conduct, and therefore the whole course of human history, to be explicable through causal laws . . . given certain material circumstances, certain events were inevitably bound to occur. Neither method will do for the understanding of history. And it is when this is fully grasped, and only then, that the future can be properly planned, and man's future relation to his world properly determined.

So far, perhaps, so good. But the middle way between what Sartre calls the analytic mode of thought and determinism, between the belief, to put it shortly, in freedom and in necessity, is not all that easy to understand. We may approach understanding by raising a further question which arises from Sartre's comment that I have just quoted. To what extent does he want to insist on the primacy of the individual ('there is no such thing as man; there are people')? What does he think is the relation between believing that people (individuals) make history, and believing in non-determinism? What, most crucially, is the relation between the belief in the primacy of the individual and the notion of *intelligibility* which lies at the heart of the *Critique of Dialectical Reason*, and which it is my present task to explain?

According to Sartre, *intelligible* history, that is history within which explanations can be given and can be understood, is the same as *the historical dialectic*. If from time to time one suddenly finds oneself asking *why* a critique of dialectical reason seemed necessary, why *dialectical*, what is dialectical reason supposed to *be*, one has to remember that for him it was quite obvious that you cannot understand man and his place in nature, you cannot raise or answer philosophical or political questions at all, except in a historical dimension; and to think historically *is* to employ dialectical reason. This conviction is simply what Sartre had taken over from his first introduction to Hegel (through Kojève's Paris lectures in the mid-thirties) his frantic reading of early Marx during the German occupation of Paris in the 1940s and his knowledge of Heidegger, whose approach to the problem of Being was through the consideration of human reality, necessarily in *time*. And according to Heidegger, too, to understand man you have to understand him as equally operating on his material environment and operated on by it, creator and created, in the true dialectical style. Moreover, in Sartre's view, the dialectic *demonstrates itself*, each individual becomes aware of it inevitably, as he exercises his reason in thinking about history. For it has often been pointed out that a Critique of Dialectical (or any other sort) of Reason cannot be a true critique, since it must use itself to criticize itself (an objection raised by Nietzsche against Kant). Sartre would entirely agree that in thinking about history or anthropology I am partly a product of the time at which I live and the circumstances and tastes and beliefs which I have as a result of living at that particular time; and therefore that my theory of history or anthropology will *itself* be, in part, a creation of my circumstances. But it will also affect the future. For what I write is new. It is *my* work, *my* project, and *my* praxis. So it, in turn, will, by being written and read, be the creator of future history, and thus of future theories. *Reflecting on this* is itself proof of the dialectical nature of such thought. And it is only by reflecting on it that I shall understand what is happening, or, therefore, be able intelligently to see what should happen next.

So each individual can see for himself the nature of the dialectic of his own grasp of the world, part caused by his past, yet part cause of the future. But even if this is taken to prove that dialectical reason exists, and is used in our thinking of the past and the future, it does not yet answer the question of the nature of *historical explanation, nor of the relation of that to the individuals who are the actors on the historical stage*. To come nearer to an answer, we must consider two passages from the *Critique*. The first is perhaps the only part of the *Critique* that has become at all well known. It comes in Book 1 and, in Rée's translation, it is headed *Duality and the Third Party*. I shall quote it in an abbreviated form: 'From my window, I can see a roadmender on the road and a gardener working in the garden. Between them there is a wall with bits of broken glass on top protecting the bourgeois property where the gardener is working. Thus they have no knowledge at all of each other's presence; absorbed as they are in their work, neither of them even bothers to wonder whether there is anybody on the other side. Meanwhile, I can see them without being seen, and this passive view of them at work situates me in relation to them: I am taking a holiday in a hotel; and in my inertia as witness I realize myself as a petty bourgeois intellectual; my perception is only a moment of an undertaking (such as trying to get some rest after a bout of overwork . . .) and this undertaking refers to possibilities and needs, appropriate to my profession and milieu . . . My present perception functions as a means in a complex process which expresses the whole of my life. Hence my initial relation to the two workers is negative. I do not belong to their class, I do not know their trades, I would not know how to do what they are doing, I cannot share their worries.' And so the scene is set. What are we to make of the story? First, like so much in Sartre's earlier work, it is a narrative with a meaning. It is not an allegory (like the cave in Plato's republic). It is more like the plot, or rather the realistic photography, in a film with a moral. It is by the details that we grasp Sartre's meaning. He sees in the details what he wants us to understand as their sense. It is his uniquely successful way of deploying his imagination to make us see the universal in the particular . . . his version of romanticism.

So we must raise the question, why are the details as they are? Why, for instance, is the bourgeois gentleman observing *two* workers, not just one? In the first place, though neither is aware of the other, the gentleman is aware of both, and even in saying to himself that their ends are not his, he has recognized them as ends. He sees that quite independently of each other they are pursuing purposes, which can be identified as such. Secondly, in discovering himself looking at them, identifying himself as an idle holiday-maker, he identifies *them* in their relation to their work. He cannot, if he tries, see them as ants or robots, but like himself as members of a particular society 'which' (I quote) 'determines everyone's opportunities and aims. And so beyond their present activity, I rediscover their life itself, the relation between needs and wages, and, further still, social division and class struggles.' Thirdly, in looking at these two people, the gentleman is bound to grasp the difference between looking at *things*, which are indifferent to him, which are totally composed by their histories (the wall, for example, nothing *but* a wall, which was once built, needs mending, and so on), and looking at people, who, though their purposes are different, both escape from him and affect him, just because they are pursuing their own goals, and working with their own ends in view. Sartre says, in this passage, 'The Other affects me in the depth of my being to the extent that it is not *my* reality'. We are inevitably reminded of *Being and Nothingness* where the perception of the Other is seen as a scandal and an outrage, because the Other drains away from me through his own consciousness of the world. The man seen reading in the park is reading with his own eyes and thinking his thoughts, not mine, and collecting a whole world around his awareness, in which I feature, if at all, only as an *object*. So here Sartre says that the two workers are seen as two centrifugal and divergent '*glisse-ments*' within the same world. But, and here at last we come to the real point of there being two of them, 'Since it *is* the same world', Sartre says, 'they are united by my personal perception within the universe as a whole, and in so far as *each* deprives the *other* of it'. I shall return to this deprivation in a moment.

For the time being there are two final points to be made about the bourgeois gentleman's observation. First, what he is observing and what he is doing *in* observing, both constitute *praxis*. Praxis is impossible without there being other people, impossible except in a world inhabited by other people, a world handed down to one by others, with institutions already defined by others and classes consisting of other individuals. In Sartre's words, praxis is 'the dialectic, as the development of living action in everyone, as it is pluralized by the multiplicity of men within a single material zone. Every existent integrates the other into the developing totalization and thereby even if he never sees him and in spite of barriers, obstacles and distance defines himself in relation to the actual totalization which the other is performing.' Secondly, it would be impossible to think of the two workers as ignorant of each other, if they were not being seen in that light by the observer. Each by himself would, by the very nature of ignorance, be simply related to the world through his work, and to nothing else. But once they are both *thought of* by the observer as separated by a wall yet both working, they are brought into relationship with each other through the medium of his perception, even though it is a negative relation. Moreover, being thought of as both workers, both working in ignorance of the other, a kind of unity is bestowed on them, 'They differ from one another less than they differ from me', Sartre says, 'and in the last analysis their reciprocal negation is for me a kind of complicity. A complicity against me.' At three levels, then, we have proof of the dialectical reason, which we must use even in the simplest narrative. (1) The men working are themselves part of 'totalization', that is the developing change which makes history. (2) The bourgeois observer is 'totalizing' in so far as he is understanding his role in relation to theirs, and therefore is himself *developing* and *understanding* history. And (3) Sartre, in telling the story, in getting us to understand it, is equally part of a totalization, a developing of the understanding of history.

The second passage to consider comes a bit further on in the *Critique* and is where Sartre first clarifies the statement, in the passage just quoted that the two workers both inhabit the same world and *deprive each other of it*.

The paragraph I want to quote now is headed in Rée's translation *Scarcity and Marxism*. Sartre quotes, with modified approval, a passage from the correspondence of Marx (the 'Reply to Nicholas Mikhailovski' written in 1877) in which he describes the transformation of the precapitalist Roman society into a more advanced state, the development of classes and the ultimate outbreak of the class war within it. He praises Marx for seeing as he puts it, that 'the past is not over and done with', and that it is necessay to study past societies and compare them with one another and with modern society. But, he says, although the story as Marx tells it may be correct, it lacks *genuine intelligibility*. And one cannot hope to render it intelligible simply by means of analogies with other stories of other societies. If a part of history is to be intelligible, the sources of intelligibility must come from *within that part itself*. The dissolution of Roman society may have come about just as Marx says it did; but *why*? Both Marx and Engels are guilty of assuming that a particular series of events occurred, and occurred as a result of some scientific law of necessity, which is in fact an assumption merely of observed regularity. It has no inner intelligibility at all. Sartre proposes to provide such intelligibility by a greater emphasis than either Marx or Engels give on the concept of *scarcity*. Dühring, who Sartre says was in other respects a fool, at least saw this: that violence is necessary to history. 'The historical process' (I quote from Sartre), 'cannot be understood without the permanent element of negativity, both exterior and interior to man. This is the perpetual possibility in man's very *existence* of being the one who sends others to their deaths or whom others send to his ... in other words of scarcity.' Scarcity is what makes people see one another as enemies. It is also both a material fact, and one which dictates a mental attitude. Thus it is not only the source of our understanding of human interrelations, but it is also the very type or paradigm case of dialectical understanding. For material facts determine mental attitudes, but equally the mental attitude itself determines how people *work on* the material world, how they produce, how they earn and how it is that the effects of scarcity are shifting and unstable. So one can *understand*, for example, the development of precapitalist Roman society only by both investigating what happened and reducing it to order (as Marx did) and *also* seeing it as a result of human behaviour, itself to be explained by scarcity. It is important to make it absolutely clear that Sartre thinks of scarcity as a causal factor *only* in so far as it is *mediated through human grasp of it*, only as far as it is *felt* to affect each person who lives with it. Indeed it is to be thought of as a cause only in the *sort* of sense in which one might say that the presence of something absurd is the cause of laughter in the observers, or the presence of tragic circumstances the cause of grief. It is *not* a cause in the sense that shortage of food causes hunger, unless hunger itself is interpreted as something to which people have a natural and an inevitable *attitude*, of disliking it, and wishing to satisfy it, and of fearing its recurrence. Sartre says, 'No one has the right to regard the fear of famine which is so striking in under-developed societies or the Great Fear of peasants under feudalism confronting the spectre of starvation, as *mere* subjective feelings. On the contrary, they represent the interiorization of objective conditions and are in themselves the origin of *praxis*.' Scarcity, then, provides the foundation for intelligibility. Whatever we do or make becomes part of the material world which then in its turn oppresses us by the need to go further, to compete still more with our natural enemy, the other man, who may deprive us of what we thought we had possessed. Sartre says, 'If one grants Marx and Engels the idea of class struggles, that is of the *negation* of classes by one another; in other words, if one grants them a *negation*, then they are able to comprehend history. But then we still have to explain negation in the first place. And we have just seen that under the rule of scarcity the negation of man by man, adopted and interiorized in praxis, is also the negation of man by matter, in so far as matter is the organization of his being, outside him, in nature.'

Sartre is very unclear about whether he holds that scarcity is a necessary and inevitable feature of the world, or whether it is a contingent feature, one which we can imagine absent in at least a possible or foreseeable world. He speaks of it as 'fundamental but contingent'. But in any case, there is no doubt that just as in *Being and Nothingness* he defined the nature of man in the Hegelian terms of the For Itself, who, being conscious, was aware of the possibilities of questioning the world and grasping in answer to his question what is *not* the case, as well as what is (and on this ability, all imagination and therefore all possibility of changing the world was founded), so in the *Critique* it is because people *want* to satisfy the need which is caused by scarcity in the world that they can be understood as human. Wilfred Desan in his book *The Marxism of Jean-Paul Sartre* quotes a snatch of conversation between Sartre and Castro. 'Man's need is his fundamental right over all others', said Castro. 'And if they ask you for the moon?' asked Sartre. 'It would be because someone needed it' was Castro's reply. And Desan comments 'In a sense the entire *Critique* is a philosophy of those who, in the words of Castro, "have the courage to understand their suffering, and to demand that it be ended: in short who are men".'

Scarcity is the phenomenon, then, against the background of which alone history is intelligible. For it is that alone which, when perceived by the individual man, the gardener and the roadmender each side of the wall, renders their actual work intelligibly purposeful. And even though they are in ignorance of one another, we, the bourgeois intellectual observers, can see that they are each other's enemy. In *Being and Nothingness* Sartre set out to demonstrate the gloomy inevitability of man's hostility to man, but starting from a different sort of premise. Despite his insistence that there is no such thing as 'human nature' and that each man makes himself what he does or chooses, he did in fact argue from a Nietschze-like belief in the universal will to dominate. Going with this will to power was the individual fear, necessarily experienced by everyone, of being reduced to thing-like status by the paralysing, fixing look of the Other. All was Hegelian in those days (Marx had not yet been read, or not properly understood). But it was a version of Hegel without hope, a dialectic of conflict with no resolution. Though historical examples are used and analysed in *Being and Nothingness*, the position of the individuals involved is presented as static. A permanent relation was defined which held between Beings-for-themselves and Being-in-itself, between Beings-for-themselves and one another, between consciousness and the world, no more *truly* historical than the relation defined by Descartes. In the *Critique*, however, the concern, as we have seen, is *essentially* and not merely *accidentally* with history. And though Sartre talks grandly of founding any possible future anthropology, there is no sharp distinction between anthropology and history; for both equally will be based on dialectical understanding of the relation between man and matter, the world in which his history unfolds.

For the great lesson of Marx which, Sartre tells us, he did not learn until the 1940s, was that you cannot just *read* Marx like other philosophers. To read him and understand is to recognize the dynamic nature of your understanding. Merely expounding Marx is already an activity which will change the world. So understanding Marx is understanding *and* contributing to history, like it or not. It follows from this that Sartre has now to look at men, not merely as individual centres of consciousness, but as they actually are embedded in a society at a particular time, which is subject to change. And of course in society men are not isolated individuals, or not that alone. For one thing they inhabit a *common* world, made and handed down to them by their ancestors and constantly being made by their contemporaries (as Heidegger had insisted, they wear ready-made suits; as Sartre knew, they listen to the same radio stations and are all manipulated together by the record companies). More importantly, their relations with each other may change and develop under the influence of, perhaps temporary, common purposes. They may form themselves into groups or into other more ossified institutions.

Now my subject is the nature of historical explanation in the *Critique*, and I cannot therefore expound in detail the different kinds of relationship which Sartre enumerates through his lengthy historical accounts, the series, the group in fusion, the fused group (or group under oath) and the institution. I must take it as understood that these are the four kinds of human relations, or types of unity which he exposes to our view. But I will briefly distinguish them.

(1) *The series* is the unity which is essentially imposed from without, a

unity like that of a bus queue, where any member of the queue can be substituted for any other, where the persons in the queue have the *same* purpose, to get on to the bus, but it is in no sense a *common* purpose, for each wants it for himself alone, if necessary at the expense of the others, and where each regards the other with enmity, as a competitor, but otherwise with indifference. (2) The *group in fusion* is the unity of common purpose where, because of a shared goal, the individuals who form the group act as one. Sartre's example here is the Parisian uprising of 14 July 1789, culminating in the storming of the Bastille. (3) The third social form is the *group-under-oath*, where the immediate danger which drew people into unity has passed, and in order to maintain the possibility of joint action, the members have to be sworn to loyalty, and penalties attached to the breach of the oath. The acknowledged aim of such a group is its own preservation; the oath is taken, and the terror submitted to, in order, to use Hume's words, 'that society may be preserved'. (4) The last social form is that wherein the fused group becomes fixed and *institutionalized*, where sovereignty is propped up by law, the legitimacy of the institutions preserves them, and where change necessarily becomes revolution.

Such is a general sketch of the different social forms. And in order to come to understand Sartre's view of historical explanation it is necessary to ask to what extent he believed that the four stages of social unity had been accurately described, to what extent they were an account of the *necessary* development of societies, to what extent one is supposed to think that the stages will necessarily follow one another and be recognized as they do. There is no doubt that each is described by Sartre as arising out of the one before, and it is tempting therefore to see them as a linear progression. But this would, in my view, be a mistake. It is true that the different forms are presented as changing, and indeed as changing into the *next* form. But, as we have seen, Sartre now thought that it was impossible to describe human nature at all, except historically, and this meant describing men as working on their surroundings, with the presumptions inherited by them, to produce that which would in turn become such surroundings or give rise to such presumptions for the next people, chronologically.

Nevertheless, and this cannot be too often stressed, to *see oneself* as a member of a group with a common purpose, or as committed to and bound by certain institutions, is already to see the future *as containing different possibilities*. The imagination by which one can distance oneself from one's own situation and *describe oneself and one's neighbour in particular terms* is still, as it was in *Being and Nothingness*, the necessary condition for choice, the ground of human freedom. The progress from one social form of unity to another is *not* inevitable, nor does just one and only one form of unity exist at any one time, even within a compact geographical area. While the revolutionaries were storming the Bastille, doubtless other

Frenchmen were existing in the impotent unity of seriality, not many miles outside Paris. Sartre says, 'It is no part of our project [that is, in writing the *Critique*] to determine whether series precede groups or vice versa, either originally or in a particular moment of history. On the contrary ... the only thing which matters to us is to display the transition from series to groups and from groups to series as constant incarnations of our practical multiplicity, and to test the dialectical intelligibility of these reversible processes.' He praised Marx, you will remember, for realizing that the history of early societies is 'not over and done with'. The point is that the different forms of association may be seen in society at any time, or co-existing at the same time; but whatever form is detected it has emerged *as new* from its surrounding society, by reason of the actual projects and ends pursued by the individuals making up the association.

Only so understood can the history of the associations be understood. To take a different example; if Sartre had written the *Critique* after 1968 he could have described the student revolution of May in terms of the emergence of a group out of hitherto impotent seriality: but it is also the case, according to his theory of dialectical reason, that if the students had then seen themselves as a group in fusion they might have organized themselves differently, been clearer about their common bonds, and not relied, as they did, on allies who were not in Sartrean terms truly a part of the group. A genuine explanation of such a part of history as 1968 would be in terms of the reciprocal relation between the individual revolutionaries and the recalcitrant world against which the attempted revolution took place, the inert mass of previously man-made institutions, whether abstract entities like 'the university' or concrete objects like particular buildings, streets and gates.

One of the chief ways of rendering history intelligible, according to such a theory, would be biography. In his belief in the importance of biography, Sartre is nearer to Dilthey than to Marx. For Dilthey conceived of history as ultimately the history of individuals, of whom it was possible to achieve *understanding*, because of shared attitudes, but more because of a common concept of purpose. And so we may be reminded of Sartre's bourgeois gentleman who understood that the observed workers had purpose and intentions in doing what he saw them doing, even though he did not himself have any of the same aims or needs as they had. But Dilthey equally thought of an individual as giving meaning to his own life in terms of his own particular experiences and beliefs, his own upbringing, his religion, literary tastes and so on. Thus, to write a proper biography would be to express the purposiveness of such an agent, placed on the particular *field* that he was; it would be to see the world through his eyes, and thus to understand a whole course of historical events. Here we have a theory, never fully put into practice by Dilthey (whose *magnum opus*, a great biography of Schleiermacher, was never completed) which is very close to

Sartre's own, and may well have influenced his. This similarity can be best demonstrated by an examination of the essay entitled *A Question of Method*, which was published at the beginning of the *Critique* in 1960, though written earlier and intended originally for separate publication. Sartre was not particularly happy about placing it at the beginning of the *Critique*, and in many ways it would serve better as a postscript than an introduction to the longer work; for it is a summary, not of the *Critique* as a whole, but of its hoped-for outcome, namely to cure Marxism of some of its doctrinaire rigidities, by marrying on to it the 'ideology' of Existentialism.

The accusation against Marxists was that they insisted on imposing a general pattern, a framework of abstract ideas, on history, and, in attempting to make history scientific, they failed to make it intelligible. The aim of the Existentialist/Marxist on the other hand would be to 'interiorize' history. This amounts to a recognition that there is no complete whole which is the universe and which can be categorized once and for all. There is no totality, only endless 'totalization', the attempt of individuals to make and to understand history, which has no completion, because the world has not come to an end. My way of working on the material of the world and organizing it is not yours, though they are inextricably bound up together. History is the way in which different totalizations have interacted. It is of no use therefore simply to clamp down the category 'bourgeois idealism' and explain works of literature as expressions of this. The work of Valéry, which is the example Sartre takes, cannot be so explained. 'Valéry', he says, 'is an intellectual petit bourgeois, but not every petit bourgeois is a Valéry.' What we want is 'to grasp the process which produces the person and his product inside a class and inside a given society at a given moment of history'. Even when the course of history turns on actions and decisions of certain groups, we can understand these actions and decisions only by understanding what it would be to be a member of the group, how the group came to identify its enemy as it did, how scarcity gave rise to just *such* a need and no other.

In the end what Sartre insists is that materialism alone cannot provide us with historical explanations. We cannot understand history in the material mode alone. As so often in the case of Sartre, after thousands and thousands of words we end with what looks no better than a cliché. For if history is the history of humans, or if anthropology is our ultimate interest, then it is not surprising to find that the history of matter alone will not do. Man is after all a composite being. There is no sharp way to distinguish mind from body. We are all of us both. And this leads us straight back to Dilthey: 'Mankind, if apprehanded only by perception and perceptual knowledge would be for us a physical fact and as such would be accessible only to natural scientific knowledge. It becomes an object for human studies only in so far as they find expression in living utterances and in so far as these expressions are understood. Of course this relationship of life, expression and understanding embraces not only the gestures, looks and words by which men communicate. The mind-body unit of life is known to itself through the same double relations of lived experience and understanding.' I doubt if Sartre would dissent from these words. If he would not and if they do express something very like his concept of historical explanation, then it can be made a question whether he was not almost as bad a Marxist as he was a bad, non-joining, Communist. But this I leave others to decide.

St Hugh's College, Oxford

Marx, Engels and Russian Marxism

W. J. REES

Russian Marxism is the outcome of two distinct traditions, namely, nineteenth-century Russian radicalism and Western European Marxism. In this paper I shall briefly trace its descent from these traditions and try to distinguish those features of it which differentiate it both from the older radicalism and from the Marxism of Marx and Engels. I shall deal in turn with three main topics, the nineteenth-century radical tradition, early Russian Marxism, and finally, Leninism.

I

Radicalism was almost an inevitable product of Russian society in the nineteenth century. The century witnessed two simultaneous developments; one of growth, the other of decay. On the one side was the growth of the empire, the growth of industry, especially towards the end of the century, and the growth of higher learning which in turn was accompanied by a magnificent flowering of Russian literature. On the other side was the decay of autocracy, the spiritual decline of the Orthodox Church, and the economic decline of a nobility which had dominated social and public life since the reign of Peter the Great. In these circumstances there came into being a long and bitter conflict between radicals and conservatives, the one for the most part attacking, the other for the most part defending, the autocracy, the Church and the nobility. The conservative outlook was well summarized in 1832 by Count Uvarov, Minister of Education under Nicholas I (from 1833 to 1849), in his slogan 'Orthodoxy, Autocracy and Nationality'.

Radicalism of a serious nature first appeared in Russia towards the end of the eighteenth century in the form of attacks on serfdom, the censorship and autocracy. Its most distinguished representative at that time was Alexander Radishchev (1759–1802) whose revolutionary tract, *A Journey from St Petersburg to Moscow*, was published in 1790. Radicalism as an organized political movement appeared towards the end of the Napoleonic wars. On returning to Russia a number of army officers who had had experience of life in Western Europe began to form revolutionary societies and to lay plans for the transformation of Russian institutions. It was a group of these officers in St Petersburg who tried in December 1825 to enforce the succession to the throne of the second Imperial brother, Constantin. The attempt failed and the ensuing reign of Nicholas I became one of the most oppressive in the country's history.

From the mid-thirties onwards the radical movement re-emerged as a movement of the intelligentsia. The ranks of the intelligentsia had been strengthened largely as a result of the establishment of new universities at Dorpat (1802), Kazan (1804), Kharkov (1804) and St Petersburg (1819). Excluded from any share in political power, the new intelligentsia was highly critical of the whole of the existing social order. Among the leading critics of the regime were Peter Chaadaev (1794–1856), Vissarion Belinsky (1811–48), Alexander Herzen (1812–70), Michael Bakunin (1814–76), the two brothers Ivan Kireyevsky (1806–56) and Peter Kireyevsky (1808–56), the two brothers Constantin Aksakov (1817–60) and Ivan Aksakov (1823–86), and the theologian A. S. Khomyakov (1804–60). These men were fairly united in what they opposed; they opposed autocracy, censorship, serfdom, the servitude of the peasantry, the privileges of the nobility, and the subservience of the Church. But they were far from united in their positive proposals for reform. One group, usually known as the Slavophiles (the Kireyevskys, Aksakovs, Khomyakov) wanted to separate the Church from the state and to reform Russian life around the village commune and a liberated Orthodox Church. Another group, usually known as the Western-izers (Herzen, Bakunin, Belinsky in his later years) was more radical. Belinsky sought the abolition of serfdom, the abolition of censorship and the reform of the judiciary. Herzen and Bakunin looked to a form of agrarian socialism built on the foundation of the village commune and to the replace-ment of autocracy by a federation of rural communes and co-operative organizations in trade and industry. Bakunin's attitude towards the Church was one of frank and open hostility. He regarded religion as a superstition which had to be destroyed in the interests of social progress.

The main sources of revolutionary ideas during this period were the two journals *Kolokol* (The Bell) and *Poliarnaia Zvezda* (The Pole Star) which were published by Herzen in London. Herzen's long-term objective was a socialist agrarian society, but in the journals he treated the practical issues of the day for the most part in a pragmatic and realistic manner. The more immediately urgent reforms in his view were the abolition of serfdom and a drastic relaxation of censorship. He advocated 'emancipation with land', that is, an emancipation which would provide the emancipated serfs with sufficient land to enable them to earn their own livelihood. In general, he tried to weld together a body of support for a twofold programme of land for the peasants and freedom for the intelligentsia. He appealed to the intelligentsia and the enlightened nobility, rather than to the peasantry, since the peasants were mainly illiterate and unable to read what he had to say. His programme had a growing appeal during the years following the Crimean War, and from the end of the war until emancipation in 1861 Herzen was a considerable influence on the course of Russian events.

It is difficult to over-emphasize the importance of the Crimean War in nineteenth-century Russian political history. The war revealed grave weaknesses in transport and communications as well as in basic industrial production. The government and the more enlightened among the conservatives came around to the view that reforms were desirable provided these were not such as to endanger the autocracy, the Church or the status of the nobility. Serfdom was abolished by a decree of 1861 and this was followed in 1864 by reforms in local government and in the legal system. These reforms did nothing to endanger the autocracy, the Church or the status of the nobility, but the abolition of serfdom did have one far-reaching consequence; it cleared the way for a rapid development of industrial capitalism.

These events had a dramatic effect on the radical movement. From the point of view of the intelligentsia the main enemy was the autocracy and its supports in the shape of the Church and the nobility. From their point of view a new capitalism which preserved these institutions intact was hardly an improvement on the old serfdom. The hatred of the old serfdom was accordingly replaced by a hatred for the new capitalism. In these circumstances many of them adopted without reservations Herzen's ideal of agrarian socialism. They advocated socialism not as a means of solving economic problems but as a means of achieving political results, results which the abolition of serfdom had failed to bring about. Moreover, agrarian socialism, hitherto a long-term aspiration, became an immediate objective. It was necessary to establish socialism *before* capitalism could secure a firm hold on the economic life of the country. In order to achieve this it was necessary to form direct contacts with the peasantry, to learn about the peasants' needs, to bring to them the rudiments of education, and to spread among them the ideas of socialism. The main literary representatives of these standpoints were Nicolai Chernyshevsky (1828–89), Peter Lavrov (1823–1900), Nicolai Mikhailovsky (1842–1904), and to some extent the avant-garde realist, Dmitri Pisarev (1840–68).

A division arose among the radicals between those who wanted to proceed by means of propaganda and peaceful persuasion, and those who wanted to adopt more forceful measures. The former were at first the stronger element. They adopted Herzen's slogan *V Narod* (To the People) and the movement as a whole acquired the name *Narodnichestvo*, which is usually translated into English as Populism. In 1873 and 1874 some two and a half thousand students went out of the towns to the countryside to mingle with the peasants and to carry out propaganda. They discovered that the peasantry wanted not socialism but more land, and that, in some confused way, they regarded the monarchy as their best ally against the nobility. Large numbers of the students were arrested. In 1877, 243 were put on trial (50 in one trial, 193 in another). Some were imprisoned, others exiled.

The failure of the movement *V Narod*, and the arrest of so many of its members, gave the material and psychological advantage to those who wanted to pursue more forceful measures. In 1876 these formed the organization *Zemlia i Volia* (Land and Liberty). This was, in effect, a political party, and the first of the kind in Russia. The aims were now to overthrow autocracy and the class domination of the nobility and to redistribute the land. The movement was able to incite a few local peasant risings, but was soon weakened by internal dissension in its own ranks. Many members wanted still more forceful measures. In 1879 there was formed within *Zemlia i Volia* the revolutionary terrorist organization *Narodnaia Volia*. The name meant The People's Will or The People's Liberty: '*volia*' in Russian can mean either 'will' or 'liberty'. The organization was led by A. I. Zheliabov (1851–81), A. D. Mikhailov (1855–84), Vera Figner (1852–1942), and Sofia Perovskaia (1853–81). Its aim was to enforce the surrender of the government by the assassination of its leading members, including more especially that of the Emperor himself. Other members of *Zemlia i Volia*, led by Plekhanov, formed a rival group entitled *Cherny Peredel* (Black Repartition) committed to redistributing the land but renouncing terrorism. *Cherny Peredel* made little headway. *Narodnaia Volia* went on with plans to assassinate the Tsar and finally achieved that objective on 1 March 1881. The only immediate result of the assassination was to create a more oppressive political climate in the country. The radical movement was largely stifled for about a decade after the event, and the reign of Alexander III was one of extreme repression.

When the radical movement re-emerged in the nineties it was no longer a predominantly Populist movement. Radical Liberalism and Marxism were gaining ground very rapidly. From the point of view of material and human resources, Liberalism had most of the initial advantages. But it had internal weaknesses which made it an ineffectual instrument in any battle with the nobility or the autocracy. Its strength represented the growth of the entrepreneurial class. While the entrepreneurial class was growing rapidly at the end of the century, its prosperity depended very much on general economic stability, which in turn depended on maintaining the existing regime in the countryside. It tended to side with the nobility, who were the *de facto* custodians of law and order. The entrepreneurs were also generally short of capital and their prosperity was heavily dependent on the ability of the state to attract capital from abroad. Since foreign governments and financial institutions were usually prepared to grant loans only if they were guaranteed by the state, entrepreneurial prosperity was closely bound up with the credit-worthiness of the state itself and hence with the stability of the monarchy. While the Liberals and the entrepreneurial class certainly disliked autocracy and wished to have more say in government, they usually had more to lose than to gain from a collision with the monarchy. These weaknesses, in the end, proved disastrous to the cause of Russian Liberalism, and allowed revolutionary initiatives to fall into other hands. The hands most competent to receive them became very soon those of the Marxists.

II

The growth of Marxism, like that of Liberalism, reflected the growth of a social class, in this case, that of the industrial working class. The earliest converts to Marxism were Populists. Before looking at the details of that conversion, there are certain general aspects of it which need to be borne in mind.

There were a number of similarities between Populism and Marxism which made the transition from the one to the other easier than it would otherwise have been. In the first place, both were socialist in their objectives and revolutionary in their methods. The Populist and Marxist ideals of socialism were different, but the move from the Populist ideal or an agrarian socialism to the Marxist ideal of an industrial socialism was a natural one to make in a period of rapid industrial growth. Both Populism and Marxism were also much concerned with social class and class conflict. In the case of the Populists this concern arose partly out of a concern for the peasantry and partly out of a revulsion for the legal estates into which Russian society was divided. The estates were not classes in the sense understood by Marx and Engels; nevertheless the Marxist doctrines, which placed great weight on the class origins of human motivations, lent support to some of the most fundamental of Populist beliefs. Again, many Populists, under the influence of Bakunin or Pisarev, were atheists or philosophical materialists who regarded religion as a superstition and an enemy of science and material progress. Their materialism was seldom coherent and was in any case different from that of Marx; nevertheless they found in Marxist materialism a philosophical outlook in many ways akin to their own. Many Populists were also, like Marx and Engels, deeply concerned about history and about the nature of historical processes. Many of them held the view that history proceeds through certain stages of development and that human progress is possible only by proceeding through those stages. This aspect of Marxist thought exercised and eventually agitated the Populist movement probably more than any other.

Leaving aside these similarities, Marxism had a further attraction to radicals of the second half of the century. It appeared to be an advanced element in Western European culture. An attraction towards Western scientific and philosophical ideas was a frequent feature of Russian radical thought. Herzen, Belinsky (at one time) and Bakunin tried to fashion out of Hegelianism and French socialism a system of thought original to themselves. Chernyshevsky did similarly with English Utilitarianism and the materialism of Feuerbach, and Mikhailovsky did likewise with Comte's positivism and the evolutionary theories of Herbert Spencer. Marx's theories were studied and discussed as part of the continuing attempt to keep abreast with the most advanced and up-to-date Western thinking. Even had there been no important similarities between Populism and Marxism, the Populists would still have reacted to Marxism in one way or another. The similarities between them ensured that the reaction was in many cases a positive rather than a negative one.

Naturally, not all Populists found the new Marxist doctrines acceptable. Many, especially among the followers of Lavrov and Mikhailovsky, were unable to accept atheism and philosophical materialism. Others, especially among the anarchist followers of Bakunin, were unable to accept the Marxist doctrine of the dictatorship of the proletariat. There were many Populists of every following who believed that their primary allegiance was not to the industrial workers but to the peasantry. To them, the adoption of the Marxist doctrines seemed tantamount to a betrayal of the peasantry whom they had so often encouraged to rebel and whose cause they had championed for so long. Towards 1900 or thereabouts these various groups of Populists coalesced to form the Party of the Socialist Revolutionaries, usually referred to as the SRs. The SRs and the Marxists had an ambivalent attitude towards each other up to and beyond the Revolution of 1917. In 1918 the SRs split into Left SRs supporting the Bolsheviks and Right SRs opposing the Bolsheviks. They split further in 1919. In 1922, after the end of the Civil War and the adoption of the New Economic Policy, most of them either accepted the Bolshevik supremacy or else went into prison or exile, and the Party disintegrated.

What we see, then, is the gradual erosion of the Populist movement under the impact of Marxist ideas. During the period from 1840 to 1900 or thereabouts it is possible to distinguish three main stages in this process.

During the twenty years from 1840 to 1860 Marxist ideas were slowly becoming known to Russian radicals, but they did not yet have an appreciable influence on radical thinking. The earliest Russian contacts with Marx came through the intelligentsia in exile. Bakunin left Russia for Western Europe in 1840 and he and other Russian exiles and expatriates had frequent contacts with Marx while Marx was in Paris from October 1843 to February 1845. Bakunin later had serious conflicts with Marx, but the two were not far removed from each other in outlook at this period. The man who did most to carry impressions of Marx and Marxism back to Russia during this period was P. V. Annenkov (1813–87). Annenkov was a member of Belinsky's circle, he lived abroad from 1846 to 1848, and he was an associate of both Herzen and Bakunin. There exist two early letters which Marx wrote to Annenkov while the latter was in Paris.

One of these, written in December 1846, gives a fairly lengthy account of Marx's views about Proudhon's book, *The Philosophy of Poverty*.

During the next twenty years, from 1860 to 1880, Marxist ideas began to influence Populist thinking in a fundamental way, but not yet in such a way as to cause a break-away Marxist movement. With the emancipation of the serfs in Russia and the subsequent growth of industry, leading Populists turned to Marx in search of ammunition against capitalism. In 1862 Bakunin translated *The Communist Manifesto* into Russian. In 1872, the first volume of *Capital* was translated. The translation was begun by Lopatin and completed by Danielson, both of whom were well-known Populists. This was the first translation of *Capital* into any foreign language, and it was completed only five years after the appearance of the orginal work. The second volume was translated in 1885 by Danielson and the third in 1896, again by Danielson. Marx himself also showed an increasing interest in Russian affairs. He corresponded regularly with Danielson from 1868 onwards and with Lavrov from 1871 onwards. Engels corresponded regularly with Lavrov after 1871, and with Danielson and Vera Zasulich after Marx's death in 1883. Much the most important part of this correspondence centred on the issue which came to be known as 'exceptionalism'. The Populists wanted to know whether or not Russia was subject to the same law of economic development as Western Europe, whether or not she had to go through a progression from feudalism to capitalism, and from capitalism to socialism, whether or not Russia could, exceptionally, skip the capitalist era altogether.

On the question of 'exceptionalism' both Marx and Engels gave an uncertain answer. In 1875, during a controversy with the Russian Jacobin, Peter Nikitich Tkachef (1844–85), Engels tried not to raise any false hopes that the Russian peasantry could skip the bourgeois stage of development; but he was prepared to concede that this could happen if it were accompanied by a socialist revolution in some of the more economically advanced states of Western Europe.

> It is clear (he wrote) that communal ownership in Russia is long past its flourishing period and to all appearances is moving towards its dissolution. Nevertheless, the possibility undeniably exists of transforming this social form into a higher one. . . . This, however, can happen only if, before the complete breakup of communal ownership, a proletarian revolution is successfully carried out in Western Europe, creating for the Russian peasant the preconditions necessary for such a transformation, in particular, the material conditions which he needs in order to carry through the reconstruction of his whole agricultural system. . . .

In 1877, Marx himself was somewhat more encouraging, and also less dogmatic. In a letter intended for the Editorial Board of the Russian journal

Otechestvenye Zapiski (Annals of the Fatherland), he takes the editors to task for elevating his views about the transition from feudalism to capitalism in Western Europe to a historico-philosophical theory about the path which all peoples are destined to tread. The relevance of his analysis to Russian conditions, he wrote, was

> Only this: if Russia seeks to become a capitalist nation after the example of the West European countries . . . she will not succeed without having first transformed a good part of her peasants into proletarians; and after that, once taken into the bosom of the capitalist regime, she will experience its pitiless laws like other profane peoples. That is all.

Nevertheless, he implies that this path is not historically predetermined, and adds:

> I have arrived at this conclusion: if Russia continues to pursue the path she has followed since 1861, she will lose the finest chance ever offered by history to a people, and undergo all the fatal vicissitudes of the capitalist regime.

The passage does not make anything abundantly clear, but the implication seems plainly to be that Russia could proceed more or less directly to a socialist form of society, even in the absence of a proletarian revolution in the West. There are indications in the letter that he was led to this conclusion as a result of a growing respect for the economic judgment of Chernyshevsky.

While these enquiries and speculations were engaging the minds of the Populist intellectuals, there was also developing an indigenous working class movement in the towns. The first organization of working men was the *Union of Workers of South Russia* which was formed in 1873 or 1874. This was led by Zazlavsky and was based on Odessa. On 6 December 1876 there was a workers' demonstration on the square of Kazan Cathedral in St Petersburg at which Plekhanov played a leading part and was arrested. In December 1878 the *Northern Union of Russian Workers* was formed in St Petersburg and in 1879 the *Workers' Union of South Russia* was formed in Kiev by Akselrod. These organizations lasted for no more than a year or two, after which time they were broken up by the police, but they were symptomatic of new developments in Russian society. Although they were led by Populists, they presented the Populists with a dilemma. Some Populists saw in them a new and welcome source of support for the Populists' peasant policy. Others saw in them ominous signs of the spread of capitalism in Russia and confirmation that Russia was following the same pattern of economic development as Western Europe. Yet others began to see in them the possibility of proceeding towards socialism through proletarian revolution rather than through peasant insurrection. With that last thought, Populism was on the way out and Marxism was on the way in.

During the two decades between 1880 and 1900, Marxism became established as an independent and indigenous element in Russian radicalism. The man mostly reponsible for bringing about that result was Georgi Valentinovich Plekhanov (1856–1918). Plekhanov had dissociated himself from the terrorist movement in 1879. After the assassination of the Emperor in 1881 he progressively dissociated himself from the Populist movement as a whole. In 1883, together with Akselrod, Zasulich, Deutsch and Ignatov, he founded in Geneva the Group for the Emancipation of Labour. He proceeded to apply the Marxist doctrines to Russian conditions in two works: *Socialism and the Political Struggle* (1883) and *Our Differences* (1885).

The basic thoughts underlying these two works were the rejection of 'exceptionalism' and hence of Populism, and the identification of the industrial working class as the only vehicle for the advancement of socialism. The detailed defence of these positions was also not unreasonable. 'Exceptionalism' he regarded as an erroneous deduction from the fact that capitalist *accumulation* in Russia happened to coincide with capitalist *production* in the West. It was but a muddled appraisal of Russian economic backwardness. But if 'exceptionalism' was false it was unreasonable to expect that the overthrow of autocracy and the socialist revolution could be made to coincide historically. To achieve the first it would be necessary to strengthen the urban bourgeoisie as well as the urban working class for a battle with the monarchy and the nobility, and that was politically incompatible with the objective of an immediate socialist revolution. To achieve the second it would be necessary to strengthen the working class for a battle with the bourgeoisie and to establish a dictatorship of the proletariat, but that would be historically possible only after capitalism had created a working class far more powerful than that which already existed. Plekhanov looked therefore to two distinct revolutions, first a middle class revolution which would overthrow autocracy and the supremacy of the nobility, and which would be supported by the industrial workers, and, secondly, after a further period of capitalist development, a proletarian revolution which would overthrow the supremacy of the bourgeoisie and initiate the era of industrial socialism. The aim of all socialists should be to try to bring about the first of these revolutions more or less immediately and to try to shorten the time-span between the first and the second as far as possible.

In the history of Russian radicalism Plekhanov's conversion to Marxism was a major turning-point comparable in importance with Herzen's conversion to agrarian socialism half a century earlier. His analyses and strategies were also more realistic and better founded in economic theory than anything previously achieved by the Populists. Even so, they were not without weaknesses. The more important weaknesses were exposed by Lenin from 1900 onwards. During the nineties Plekhanov had to contend with other tendencies in the labour movement, tendencies which, with the aid of Lenin, he succeeded on the whole in defeating.

One such tendency came to be known as Legal Marxism. The censorship permitted attacks on the Populists and on industrialists but prohibited attacks on the nobility and on the autocracy. Some Marxists saw in this a loophole whereby they could express some part of their own case, and they soon found themselves free to attack the Populists and the liberal bourgeoisie provided they remained silent about the nobility and the autocracy. Books began to appear exploiting these possiblities, the more important being Peter Struve's *Critical Remarks on the Question of Russia's Economic Development* (1894), and Tugan-Baranovsky's *The Russian Factory, Past and Present* (1898).

The Legal Marxists did some valuable work in economic studies. Both Plekhanov and Lenin were initially disposed to regard their work favourably, but after a while they parted company with them and launched an attack on them. From a radical standpoint the tactic of the Legal Marxists had one serious weakness: it was more helpful to the autocracy than to the radical movement. What else, indeed, was to be expected from a tactic the success of which depended on attacking only the enemies of the autocracy, namely the Populists and the Liberals. The tactic was self-defeating and it soon disappeared. The whole episode revealed, however, as Lenin was quick to realize, that Plekhanov himself had gone too far in his attack on the Populists and that some reappraisal of his general theory was needed.

Another tendency came to be known as Economism. The nineties were boom years in Russian industry. Stoppages in production were often more costly to employers than judicious and timely concessions to workers' demands, and many workers' leaders felt that their objectives could be achieved by action on economic issues alone. The standpoint was perhaps best expressed by the journal *Rabochaia Mysl* (Workers' Thought) which began publication in St Petersburg in 1897.

Economism was more a spontaneous reaction to current economic conditions than a fully considered body of theory. This gave Plekhanov and Lenin the opportunity to launch an offensive against it. The political and economic aspects of society, they argued in effect, were interrelated, economic gains which were not matched by gains in political power were insecure, only a well-organized political movement could give working men long-term economic protection, and, in any case, working men had political as well as economic interests and to sacrifice the one for the sake of the other was the classic mark of subjection and servitude. Partly as a result of this offensive and partly as a result of a change in the economic climate, Economism soon lost much of its influence, although some of it remained in the form of working class suspicions of the aims of the intelligentsia.

A more serious challenge to Plekhanov's general theory and strategy came not from Russia but from Germany. This came about with the publication of Eduard Bernstein's articles in *Die Neue Zeit* in 1898 and with the publication of his book *The Premises of Socialism and the Tasks of Social Democracy* in 1899. While claiming to be a Marxist in other respects, Bernstein argued that class conflict was diminishing with the development of capitalism, and that it was becoming possible to advance from a capitalist to a socialist economic system by gradual and non-violent means, that is, without resort to the proletarian revolution and the dictatorship of the proletariat as prescribed by Marx. In orthodox Marxist circles the doctrine came to be known as Marxist Revisionism.

Plekhanov, supported by Lenin, attacked Revisionism from the outset. The attack was initially uncertain and unconvincing. Both Plekhanov and Lenin were tempted to treat Revisionism as a form of Economism, but although there were similarities between the two, there was one basic difference; Bernstein was not opposed to political action or to the organization of a workers' political party. Strictly, therefore, the case against Economism did not apply to Revisionism. Yet the fact that both Plekhanov and Lenin felt a need to destroy Revisionism indicated that *something* was beginning to divide Russian from German Marxists. Nor is it difficult to see what that was; it was the Russian autocracy. In Russia there was no prospect of establishing a socialist democracy without first destroying autocracy, and there was nearly a century of radical tradition to show that that could not be done without a considerable revolutionary upheaval. In the circumstances, Russian Marxists simply disowned Revisionism, and Revisionism made no headway.

With Legal Marxism, Economism and Revisionism defeated, Russian Marxism was an established and, to all outward appearances, a reasonably united movement. Its organization, however, was still primitive, its theory was still derivative, and both were largely untested in the fire of Russian political practice. Before the first major test could be made in the revolutionary upheaval of 1905, the movement split irretrievably. Out of that split arose Leninism.

III

At the Second Congress of the Russian Social Democratic Labour Party in 1903, Lenin broke the unity of the Marxist and labour movement over two issues. One issue was how to deal with the problem of the peasantry. The other was how to respond to the political methods of the autocracy. At the Congress the group led by Lenin had a slight majority and came to be known as *Bolsheviki* or Majority Men; the other, led by Iuli Martov, came to be known as *Mensheviki* or Minority Men. Until 1914, neither group could be said to be Revisionist in the sense in which Bernstein was a Revisionist. After August 1914, however, the disputes between them became complicated by the further question of the attitude to be taken towards the Great War. On this question the Bolsheviks adopted a position which was in line with that of orthodox Marxism, while the Mensheviks adopted a position more in line with that of German Revisionism and of Western Social Democracy.

Russian Marxists at the turn of the century had one very solid reason for paying greater attention to the peasantry; some 80 per cent of the population of the Empire consisted of peasants. Lenin's fundamental attitude towards the peasantry was formulated in his work *The Development of Capitalism in Russia* which was published in 1899. The general thesis which he tried to prove was that rural capitalism was the foundation for the urban capitalism which was then coming into being. Russian capitalism, in his view, was predominantly a rural phenomenon. The new textile, coal, iron, steel and oil industries were not, metaphorically speaking, islands of capitalism in a sea of feudal agriculture; they were more like the peaks of mountain ranges which had their foothills in the capitalistic Russian countryside. Consistently with this, he did not regard the Russian peasantry as a homogeneous social class. It consisted partly of an embryonic bourgeoisie and partly of an embryonic proletariat; the one being a class of relatively wealthy peasants who were acquiring more land, employing labour to till the land, and selling an increasing amount of their produce on the market; the other being a class of poor peasants who were falling into debt, having to sell their lands to pay their debts, and finally having to sell their labour as a means of earning a livelihood. It consisted also partly of a group of 'middle peasants', whose economic and social fate was as yet undetermined, but was likely to be progressively determined by the advance of rural capitalism. According to Lenin's calculations at least a half of the total number of peasant 'households' fell into his category of 'the rural proletariat'.

From this economic analysis Lenin drew two major consequences. These were drawn not in the same work but in other and illegal writings.

In the first place, he conceived of a revolution in two stages, but the stages were different from those envisaged by Plekhanov. The aim of the first stage should be to organize the urban proletariat and the peasantry so as to bring about the downfall of the autocracy and the nobility. The aim of the second stage should be to organize the urban and rural proletariat (that is, the industrial workers and the poor peasantry) so as to bring about the downfall of the urban and rural bourgeoisie (the downfall, that is, of the industrialists in the towns and of the wealthier peasantry in the countryside). In both stages, what was essential to success was an alliance between the urban working class and the poor peasantry. An important feature of Lenin's strategy was that it avoided the necessity of going through an era of capitalism before embarking on the second stage of the revolution. An alliance between the urban and rural proletariat made it unnecessary to wait until the urban proletariat could carry through a revolution on their own.

The second consequence was that the Russian labour movement would need to express not only the demands of the urban workers but also those of the peasantry and especially those of the poor peasantry. The peasantry were mostly illiterate and dispersed over a vast countryside; they could not be organized and assembled in the same way as workers in factories or in mines. A political party which expressed their interests would need to be a paternalist party, ready to guide them and not simply to follow them, ready to articulate their grievances without waiting for them to do it themselves, and ready to act and to make sacrifices on their behalf. In short, such a political party would need to act as 'the vanguard of the proletariat' in both town and country.

Lenin's main concern in *The Development of Capitalism in Russia* was with the old question of 'exceptionalism'. He rejected 'exceptionalism' as an economic thesis but he rejected it in such a way as to preserve many of its political consequences. As against Populism he was arguing that the leading revolutionary force in Russia was the urban working class; but as against earlier Russian Marxism he was also arguing that it was possible to carry through a socialist revolution, even in his own generation, with the support of a substantial part of the peasantry. The net political result was a partial return to earlier Populist standpoints. Once more, the support of the peasantry was seen as central to a realistic revolutionary strategy. The need for peasant support led back to older Populist conceptions about political work among the peasants, to the need to formulate and express their legitimate grievances.

The strength and weakness of this strategy depended in the last resort on the correctness or otherwise of the underlying belief about class differentiation among the peasantry. Historians, relying on the same official statistics as Lenin used, confirm the tendency to differentiation, and, allowing for differences of opinion about the speed at which differentiation was taking place, there is not much doubt that Lenin was, in the main, right. It was a further question whether or not he had drawn the correct political conclusions from the economic facts. The Mensheviks remained sceptical about that, especially after the introduction of the Stolypin land reforms from 1907 onwards. The reforms were designed to create in the countryside a class of independent land-owning farmers who would provide additional political support for the regime. The fact that they were thought necessary for that purpose confirmed Lenin's own analysis of the revolutionary potential of the peasantry, but it was also clear that in the long-term the success of the reforms would undermine Lenin's strategy. In the event, the reforms never proceeded far enough to make much difference. On the whole, their effect was merely to speed up the differentiation which was already taking place. There is not much doubt that this differentiation was one of the prime factors in the tangle of circumstances which led to the Revolution and that Lenin's understanding of it accounts in some considerable measure for his ability to control the events of the period.

Lenin's tactics for dealing with autocracy were laid down in his pamphlet *What is to be Done?* which he published in 1902. The problem with which he was concerned may seem to us to be somewhat exaggerated, but it was one which had exercised the minds of Russian radicals for some two generations. It was the practice of the autocracy to place police spies in the revolutionary organizations. Clandestine though the organizations were, the police had seldom found much difficulty in breaking them up. *Narodnaia Volia*, however, did have some success in countering police tactics. This was partly because the organization consisted of a very small group of highly dedicated, disciplined and determined individuals, and partly because one of their leading members, A. D. Mikhailov, succeeded in placing one of his own counter-spies in the police force. Although *Narodnaia Volia* squandered its political capital on assassinations and terrorist activity, it nevertheless taught the radical movement some lessons in political organization. Lenin's solution to the problem presented by police tactics was to return to the organizational methods of *Narodnaia Volia* and to try to improve on them.

In his famous pamphlet he argued, among other things, the following: that a political organization which was wide and open enough to be accessible to the working men generally would be accessible also to the police and would be destroyed by them; that it was necessary to separate economic and social organizations of working men from their political organizations; that while the former should be based on a trade or craft and be as widely based as possible, the latter should consist of professional revolutionaries, chosen for their disciplined revolutionary consciousness, regardless of trade or craft, and regardless of whether they were working men or intellectuals. Above all, it was necessary that every member of the political organization should undertake to do, and be required to do, illegal work. This latter provision was the crucial one. Its purpose was to place the police in a quandary. By that provision, police spies would be required to co-operate with other party members in doing illegal work, in which case the police would find it difficult to arrest *bona fide* party members without also arresting their own spies. Alternatively, if the police chose not to arrest their own spies, they would be handicapped in arresting other party workers, and the spies themselves would have to contribute to the party's revolutionary work.

The Mensheviks disliked these tactics and opposed them, not so much on the ground that they disliked illegality—although after the establishment of the *Duma* in 1906 this was to some extent also true—as on the ground that they fostered autocratic and bureaucratic methods. Lenin's reply was to advocate, in addition, what he called 'democratic centralism'. 'Democratic centralism' was a name for a number of procedures among which the essential ones were the following: full discussion within the organization before deciding on any major course of action, the acceptance by all the members of the organization of any decision finally reached by a majority, the execution without reservations, and by all members, of the course of action then decided upon, and full and frank criticism and self-criticism when the consequences of the action were known. The real purpose of these procedures was to ensure, as far as possible, maximum freedom of discussion with maximum unity in action. The procedures were accepted by both the Bolsheviks and the Mensheviks at the Stockholm Congress of 1906.

From a revolutionary point of view, Lenin's tactics had some real merits. They did effectively place the police in a dilemma. The police responded by keeping their spies in the Bolshevik groups and by using them to try to gain control over the groups. By 1910 four of the 'leaders' of the Bolsheviks in Moscow were police spies, and one of them, Roman Malinovsky, was elected a Bolshevik deputy to the Fourth *Duma* in St Petersburg. Ironically, the Bolsheviks were gaining strength at the expense of the Mensheviks, at least partly as a result of the revolutionary activity of police spies. Tactics which were defensible before the revolution did not, however, have the same merits once the revolution had succeeded. In the post-revolutionary period, Lenin's tactics fostered autocracy and bureaucracy within the Bolshevik party—precisely the consequences which the Mensheviks had feared. Lenin himself saw the dangers and tried to find ways of safeguarding the Party against them. But in that he failed. His failure was the failure to impress upon the Party the need for a greatly strengthened judiciary and legal system. It was not at any time his intention to replace one autocracy with another, yet, given the legal system and the legal resources which the Bolsheviks inherited, that was almost bound to happen. In those circumstances, autocracy and bureaucracy on a large scale were essential in order to govern the country. That would have been so no matter whether Russia was feudal, capitalist or socialist, and would be the more so if it was also socialist. With greater reliance on law and legal procedure, Bolshevism in authority would have been less oppressive than in practice it turned out to be.

The outbreak of the war in 1914 affected Russian Marxism and its historical destiny very profoundly. The attitude of Lenin and the Bolsheviks towards the war stemmed partly from the historical experience of Russian radicalism and partly from Marxist first principles. As far as Russian radicalism was concerned, Russian military disaster had always been its best ally. It was Russian failures in the Crimean War which led to the abolition of serfdom, and it was Russian defeats in the war with Japan which led to the upheaval of 1905 and to the first serious breach in the system of autocracy. It was not unreasonable to expect that further defeats in war would initiate further revolutionary changes. The Marxist view on the war was that any war fought in contemporary conditions would be fought in capitalist interests, that working class parties should oppose it and try to bring it to an end without reparations or annexations. With all these considerations in mind, Lenin and the Bolsheviks announced their policy of revolutionary defeatism. They declared that the war was a war to redivide the world among the capitalist powers, that the proper course for a socialist party was to convert the predatory imperialist war into a revolutionary civil war, to work for the defeat of one's own capitalist government and for its replacement by a socialist government. This policy was enormously unpopular in Russia during the early stages of the war, but it brought Lenin and the Bolsheviks enormous political gains as Russian military disasters accumulated and the country's economic and military weakness became clear for all to see. It made them rulers of the land and set Marx–Leninism on a course of historical expansion which is still continuing.

In all this, Lenin had no doubt that Bolshevik policy was straight and clear and wholly justified. Nevertheless, the whole business of the war raised grave theoretical issues for him. With the exception of the Bolsheviks, the socialist and workers' parties all over Europe rallied to the support of their own governments and undertook to prosecute the war until final victory. From Lenin's point of view, this represented a degree of collaboration between capital and labour hitherto unthinkable among socialists. It was also the logical outcome of the revision of Marxist doctrines which had been initiated by Bernstein. The question was therefore inescapable; was Bernstein right in his assessment of the long-term course of the conflict between capital and labour and had Marx been wrong? Lenin was too serious and fundamental a thinker to leave a question of this magnitude unsettled in his own mind. The result of his struggle with it was his theory of imperialism.

The economic side of Lenin's theory was developed in his pamphlet *Imperialism, as the Highest Stage of Capitalism*, which was written in 1916. The main contentions of this work may be summarized briefly as follows: Marx had taken for granted a freely competitive capitalism in domestic markets and free-trade in the international market, and, on these assumptions, his prediction that class conflict would intensify under capitalism was justified; but after 1870 or thereabouts there occurred three interrelated developments unforeseen by Marx, the growth of monopolies, the growth of finance capital and the export of capital; finance capital was mainly held by the banks and, as a result of co-operation between the banks and the monopolies, was progressively being invested in foreign countries; the risks to which this practice was subject created a need for political control over the territories in which capital was invested; as a result of co-operation between governments, banks and monopolies, this control was achieved either by conquest and annexation, that is, by overt colonialism, or by one-sided agreements enforced upon nominally sovereign governments, that is, by a form of semi-colonialism; the result of all this was a parasitic system the success of which depended upon the exploitation by the metropolitan countries of the human and material resources of the dependent or semi-dependent territories; the 'scramble for Africa' at the end of the century, was the clearest example of the scramble by capitalist powers to participate in this method of exploitation.

The political consequences of these economic developments were described by Lenin in other writings. One consequence, in his view, was an increasing collaboration between capital and labour in the major capitalist countries. In those countries, he argued, the spoils of imperialism were distributed throughout the whole of society by means of the price system and state welfare services and in the form of increased profits, rents, interest and wages. This led, on the side of capital, to a measure of tolerance for trade unions and working class political parties and, on the side of labour, to the growth of conforming trade unions and reformist, that is, Social Democratic, labour parties. It led those same Social Democratic labour parties to co-operate with capitalist governments in imperialist adventures and in waging predatory wars.

Another consequence was the appearance of new sources of revolutionary energies in colonial territories. Imperialism had the effect of transferring some part of the conflict between capital and labour from the major capitalist countries to the colonial and semi-dependent territories. In the colonial territories this conflict appeared in the form of a conflict between foreign capital and native labour; the revolutionary struggle took the form of a struggle both for national liberation and for the overthrow of colonial capitalism. Even if the prospects of a socialist revolution were receding in some of the main capitalist countries of Europe, they were for that very reason slowly maturing in colonial territories. The weight of Marxist political endeavour should be placed accordingly at the service of anti-imperialist movements in those territories.

This has been a powerful theory. In the Marxist tradition, it has a somewhat different status from that of Lenin's other theories. While his views about capitalism in Russia and about tactics in dealing with autocracy had little relevance outside Russia, his theory of imperialism had a world-wide significance. While the other theories remained peripheral, this one soon became central to basic Marxist doctrine. From the point of view of theoretical consistency there was every justification for that. Essentially the thesis is not about imperialism. Lenin knew well enough that history has record of many forms of imperialism, but he was not concerned with its past or possible future varieties. Basically he was concerned with capitalism. He saw contemporary imperialism as an episode in the history of a declining capitalism: had he seen it as an episode in the history of anything else his attitude towards it would almost certainly have been different and could well have been much more favourable. Anyone who searches in the writings of Lenin for ammunition against other forms of imperialism, or for what some now call 'Soviet imperialism', is well advised to search elsewhere. All he will find in the end is ammunition against what is supposed to be a decaying capitalism.

Regarded as a thesis about capitalism, it is designed primarily to counter Marxist Revisionism. The antagonists are Karl Kautsky and, behind Kautsky, Eduard Bernstein. Implicitly, the thesis is a recognition that Lenin's earlier arguments against Bernstein were weak and ineffective. The outcome of the thesis, though this is not actually stated, turns out to be this: if we restrict our attention to certain local, that is to say national, circumstances, Bernstein's predictions about the probable course of the conflict between capital and labour were defensible, but if we adopt an internationalist standpoint and direct our attention to world conditions as a whole, Marx's predictions remain valid and Bernstein's were mistaken.

Leaving aside the significance of the thesis for the development of Marxist doctrine, it was also an important thesis from the standpoint of Western political thought in general, and it is important to try to distinguish what is true from what is false in it.

On the economic side, it must, I think, be admitted that it was roughly true in what it said, although it left some important things unsaid. The element of exploitation in the colonial economies of the period, which Lenin was more particularly interested in, is well authenticated and too well known by now to be seriously contested. It was known to many economists at the time. Lenin, in fact, expressed his debt to the English economist, John Hobson, and used for his own purposes the statistics of many others. Even so, the thesis was weak in at least one respect. It was well known that colonial exploitation was more marked in some imperial possessions than in others, and that it was usually more marked in the territories of the less advanced rather than in those of the more advanced capitalist powers. This seemed to indicate that where capitalism was more successful the less it needed to resort to imperial exploitation.

This, in turn, has implications for the political side of the doctrine. It weakens the argument for the view that imperial exploitation alone accounted for the increasing collaboration between capital and labour in the more advanced capitalist countries. Lenin did not sufficiently acknowledge that such collaboration could arise from more than one source. In particular, he did not sufficiently acknowledge that it could also arise from advances in the techniques of production. Marx himself held that the application of new technological discoveries tended to increase profits and to counteract a long-term tendency for the rate of profit to fall. But as long as profits increase, no matter for what reason, both capital and labour can secure some share of the increment, provided that labour is well organized. This provides some incentive both for greater organization of labour and for some measure of collaboration between capital and labour. On the whole, Lenin did not sufficiently enquire how much of the class collaboration which he saw under capitalism was the result of colonial exploitation and how much was the result of continuing improvements in technology. This handicapped his attempt to give a satisfactory account of Social Democracy, as also his attempt to give realistic estimates of the prospects for the survival of capitalism in individual states other than Russia. We now know that over the past fifty years Social Democracy has flourished in Scandinavian countries with little damage to capitalism (as Lenin would have expected) but also without benefit of imperialism (which he would not have expected), but we must bear in mind, of course, that he was not in a position to take this important experience into his account.

Having said all that, however, there remains in Lenin's doctrine an important core of truth. If my criticisms are sound, then, by implication, he was right in holding that Social Democracy looks to a continuation of capitalism rather than to the establishment of socialism, and that doctrines like those of Social Democracy and Marxist Revisionism are not forms of Marxism. There can be little doubt that in capitalist lands imperial exploitation, where it existed, weakened any revolutionary tendencies which might exist among working men (it does not follow that it strengthened Social Democracy, for it may have weakened that also by strengthening other and more conservative tendencies), and there can be little doubt that in colonial territories it fostered a revolutionary consciousness which could readily be given a Marxist theoretical content. In any case, in colonial territories Lenin's doctrine often met genuine human needs. Colonial exploitation has diminished in the last thirty years or so, but it has diminished at least partly as a result of the influence which Leninism has acquired in many old colonial territories. It is not surprising that in these territories the spread of Leninism is still continuing.

How should we now assess Lenin's doctrines ?

From a comparative and historical standpoint it is fairly clear that they form a more distinctly Russian form of Marxism than that adopted by either Plekhanov or the Mensheviks. Their effect, broadly speaking, was to move the doctrinal content of Russian Marxism a number of steps nearer to that of the older Populism. Lenin accepted from Western Marxism the belief in industrial development and the belief in an industrial rather than an agrarian socialism; and he accepted the view that the industrial proletariat was the social class most capable of leading the rest of society towards socialism. In these respects he did not differ from other Russian Marxists. But he also took from the Populist tradition a belief in the revolutionary potential of a guided peasantry, and he took over from it, and further perfected, a technique of revolutionary organization which carried within it many of the marks of the autocracy which he sought to destroy. In these respects he differed from Plekhanov and the Mensheviks, no less, of course, than from Western European Marxists.

As to the consistency of this body of theory it would be unreasonable to claim consistency for it in every detail, but if we take it in its broad outlines it is, without much doubt, reasonably self-consistent. It is also consistent with the basic doctrines of Marx and Engels and can be seen to follow from them if we add the two further premises for which Lenin contended, namely the premise about the nature of Russian capitalism and the premise about imperial exploitation. One could contest both of these premises and still remain a Marxist, but that would be at the price of having to propose a revolutionary strategy very different from that proposed by Lenin. Many like Plekhanov, Martov, Trotsky, Rosa Luxemburg did that. That Lenin's strategy proved more successful than theirs is no proof of the correctness of the premises. Nevertheless, there was much truth in the premises, and probably enough truth to account for what turned out to be the decisive superiority of his strategy over theirs, within the conditions of the time.

As to Lenin's originality one has to allow a large measure of originality to his analysis of Russian capitalism; and something of the mark of genius also, since he had reached his underlying ideas at the age of twenty-three. One must also allow some originality, though much less, to his theory of imperialism. But the originality of his thought as a whole lies, I think, not in the novelty of individual doctrines so much as in the synthesis which he achieved of Russian revolutionary practice and Marxist revolutionary theory. He brought together an existing revolutionary practice and a body of revolutionary theory which had arisen independently of that practice, and he adjusted the one to the other in a remarkably short space of time. This was not his achievement alone; others including Plekhanov, Trotsky, Bukharin and Stalin contributed to it. But his was by far the major contribution. The result was both a different revolutionary practice and a modified revolutionary theory. Both were vital factors in bringing about the October Revolution of 1917 and the many far-reaching consequences of that event.

The Marxist Theory of the State

GRAEME DUNCAN

Marx did not approach the state in answer to some such broad and abstract philosophical question as: What is the state? Nor did he offer a full sociological or historical or analytic account of state institutions and functions, and there are hence clear and substantial dangers in extrapolating to all or most conditions an account which is, in large part, specific to bourgeois society. Failing a comprehensive and formal treatise on politics and the state, Marx's own discussion consists of a number of scattered and not altogether consistent general observations and some detailed investigation of the role and character of the state in particular historical situations. It seems sensible, then, to begin an elucidation of his account of the state with a comment on the nature of his interest in the subject. Why did he need a theory of the state? At what points does it become important to his explanatory and his revolutionary doctrines?

A theory of the state is inevitably also a theory of society, a theory of the ways in which economic and social structures, groups and circumstances express themselves politically—ways which may be strongly influenced by the forms of political mediation themselves. Given that the causal connections are likely to be both complex and far-reaching, the state in Marxism (and in anything else) cannot be treated in isolation or independence. Analysis is pushed outwards to related concepts and ultimately to the total social theory of which it is part. But to pursue the enquiry more narrowly, with that crucial proviso in mind: the argument about politics and the state is an argument about the relations between class and state power, i.e. the relationship of political institutions, processes and personnel to the class struggle which is the motor or dynamic of historical change. Marx sought to explain how the ruling class or the bourgeoisie—whatever these might be—maintains a position of dominance through consent and coercion, both of which are expressed or mediated in and through the state. As the force for political coercion the state might limit, control or divert class struggle, and hence contribute to stability, but as an arena of conflict both within and between classes, it could be the focus of new fissures, contradictions and crises. And it was these which political action was to clarify and exacerbate. The state rests upon a volcano, dormant at times but subject to heavy murmuring and explosive outburst. Given steady changes in historical conditions and the varying incidence and form of the class struggle, it is not surprising that Marx and Engels should have presented several distinct if not contradictory pictures of the state. Nor is it surprising that this should be a growth point in the flourishing industry of Marxist exegesis, especially within the broad area of modern political economy.

It is important to note, by way of introductory clarification, that within—though not exclusively within—the Marxist tradition there is a narrower and a broader sense of the political, which has both substantive and formal significance. Slides or shifts from one to the other, within or outside a particular tradition, easily obfuscate discussion. For example, the state may be seen as merely a political mechanism or set of coercive arrangements, or as a national community or even a partnership in all virtue. We face, not merely different evaluations of similar things, but essentially different characterizations of political phenomena, closely associated with diverse valuations. Within nineteenth-century social theory, a distinction was made commonly between state or political arrangements and society or civil society. To many of those studied by Marx, society was portrayed as solid and substantial, decisive in the explanation of why groups of men co-operated, and moral or potentially moral: it represented man's communal needs and desires—perhaps distorted owing to political or other artificial interventions, but which could in the right circumstances produce all necessary social coherence (at a higher level to what passed as coherence in the present, of course). The state, as the badge of lost innocence, a symbol and a source of imperfection, would wither with the emergence of a new stage of advanced or highly developed simplicity. There were, of course, great differences over the character of the new post-political or post-state bodies and formations, and over the social conditions and arrangements which was their appropriate setting. But the general distinction remains: administration was presented commonly as impartial, non-coercive, rational, pure, while government, the whole arena of politics, was seen as partial, coercive, irrational and corrupt. Free men gather in society, whereas the state is an organization or apparatus of power, helping keep some—if not all—men in subjection. Hence the subject was not the reform or improvement of political institutions, but something as grand as the transcendence of politics. The evil lay, as Marx was to declare in commenting upon the deficiencies of the French revolutionaries, not in defective political institutions but in political institutions themselves, not in a particular form of the state but in the state itself. Given a characterization of the state as narrow and nasty—a body of coercive institutions and arrangements—its withering away will seem neither unlikely nor undesirable, and attention can be focused, as it was by Lenin in *The State and Revolution*, on the strategic and organizational tasks necessary to demolish it.

But at the same time, the roots of the state spread wide and deep, and a broader, more excavating, sense of the political becomes vital to the Marxist revolutionary. He cannot accept the liberal view that the state, the political organization, constitutes—or may constitute—the framework for private, voluntary action: both the private and the voluntary character of such action are denied. The broader sense of the political emerges in answer to such questions as: What is politically relevant or significant? What affects or determines the entrance or non-entrance of people to the so-called formal political arena, and the form and substance of their entry? The answers are likely to suggest a great range of institutional and ideological influences making man what he is, or preventing man/woman from becoming fully human. The range of phenomena seen as political is much wider than is the case with liberalism: indeed, politics may be discerned everywhere, in a complex and vibrant totality within which the artificial and arbitrary divisions of liberalism are seen for what they are— reflections and defences of the world of elites, of classes, of barely bridled economic power. According to such views, the public–private and political– personal dichotomies of liberalism help maintain the existing order by limiting the area within which political action is deemed appropriate. To the revolutionary—cutting through the surface pluralism to the real power structures, perhaps the real totalitarianism, behind—no area of man's formation can be accepted as apolitical, purely personal or private. Things must be seen for what they are. Many places, some still unacknow- ledged, are vital spheres of political reproduction and political action. This may amount to a simultaneous assertion of the width or range of politically relevant institutions and influences and the narrowness of the actual state or political apparatus—e.g. the case of Gramsci, who concentra- ted upon the formation of consciousness, or cultural hegemony, which must be challenged and overcome if radical social change is to occur. Clearly a strong perception of the weight of popular culture and conscious- ness may lead to a view of the revolutionary process as a protracted and difficult one, as the state—the concentration of political power—has many outposts, defensive trenches and so on. It is one arena of struggle, but it will fall only when new collective feeling has penetrated its pores, so to speak, in a variety of counter-hegemonic institutions and arrange- ments. Whether we incorporate these institutions and areas into the state, as Althusser does with his Ideological State Apparatuses—the educational ISA, the religious ISA, the family ISA—is another question: my own preference is for a narrower, more rigorous definition of the state combined with a recognition that the power to make, and to avoid making, political decisions, and the inability to do either, are underpinned by various institutions, arrangements and ideologies, that class power is diverse and diffuse (dominant classes have many resources), and that class conflict occurs within a number of arenas. The arena of state power is not co- terminous with the arena of class power. And only rarely and temporarily are societies held together primarily through state repression.

It is time to return to Marx's own account of the state. It is clear that the classical Marxian account is neither static, consistent nor complete, nor did Marx try to make it so. The basic, crude Marxist theory of the state—the stuff of a thousand polemical pamphlets—is that it is the instrument of class purposes, the mechanical expression and servant of dominant economic interests. But there are complexities, concerning the state and its relative autonomy, and the nature of those deeper arrangements and relationships which it allegedly seeks to maintain or strengthen. In the mature writings, the state appears, in some specific historical conjunctures, as the apex or expression of a rough equilibrium or equality between contending class forces, none of which is in a position to assert itself decisively in the political realm. The assumed class role is then taken over in essence by others. Yet again, the state develops characteristic institutions, procedures and personnel which give its growth a certain independent momentum. Both of these apparently uncharacteristic views imply some separation or remoteness of the state from the class struggle, though the explanations and the expected outcomes are different— in the one case, whatever independence the state has arises from the unclarity, muddle or formlessness of the class struggle, and in the other from internal movement which suggests a process of separate development, along with its general subservience to class purposes or interests. In the first case we would expect a reversion to type once class domination returns, whereas in the second, a fat and weighty state, pressing in its own direction, may feed off the dominant as well as other classes. But there might also be complex historical connections, e.g. a tendency towards bureaucratization might be strengthened by the absence of a single dominant class.

Marx's early theory of the state—as alienated social power—need not detain us much here, though it will call for further comment in the concluding remarks on the withering away of the state. The essence of the early view is that the political community, the state, into which man projects his image of himself as communal being, as distinct from the private individual of civil society, is a fiction or illusion, resting upon the contradiction between public and private life, general and particular interests: it is an idealized representation and an expression of genuine human need. Man's 'political lion-skin' is empty. The illusion or idealization is politically useful, however, in that men's equality in 'the heaven of their political world' blinds them to real earthly inequality. But the view of the state is not at this point attached to a theory of class domination, and the resolution does not lie in the abolition of classes. The revolutionary point lies in the fact that what man has put into this fantastic and deformed creation must be reclaimed, drawn back into himself, so that the process of human self-affirmation or emancipation necessarily evaporates the state.

In the early writings we do find Marx elaborating a crucial and persisting claim about the state: its dependence upon civil society. 'The material life of individuals ... their mode of production and form of intercourse, which mutually determine each other—this is the real basis of the state and remains so at all stages at which division of labour and private property are still necessary, quite independent of the will of individuals. These actual relations are in no way created by the state power; on the contrary, they are the power creating it.'[1] Civil society is a system of 'complete interdependence, the division of labour and exchange'. Natural necessity and interest 'hold the members of civil society together: civil not political life is their real tie ... only political superstition imagines that social life must be held together by the state whereas in reality the state is held together by civil society'.[2] Now of course Marx was to give the state some role in holding social life together, through coercion and ideological control and befuddlement. But what is important here is that Marx appears to be presenting a straight-forwardly reductionist and materialist theory: the state is not autonomous and creative, but is dependent upon civil society—or, later, it is 'conditioned' by the mode of production of material life,[3] of which it is in some way the expression or outcome. Political explanations of social change, assuming the weight of political institutions, are denied. They rest upon a romantic exaggeration of the will, of the kind which erupts in the useless violence of Jacobinism. These comments support a false view of Marx as a systematic and firm materialist and determinist.

On my reading of Marx, he did not commit himself to an extreme or hard version of technological determinism, according to which the forces of production determine everything else. Such a theory would hold, not merely that the forces of production are the key causal factors in social change, but that they produce a particular form of the division of labour and particular social relations, which in turn produce a particular ideological superstructure. The secondary elements correspond to the productive forces and are dependent upon them. The relationship is presented as functional in a technical sense—variables are correlated in such a way that changes in one can be systematically related to changes in the other, with the productive forces being, in this case, the independent variable. Some of Marx's statements—rejected by soft interpreters, such as myself, as crude and simplistic—suggest that he believed this.[4] Yet he clearly

[1] Marx and Engels, *The German Ideology* (Moscow, 1964), 357.

[2] Marx and Engels, *The Holy Family* (Moscow, 1956), 163.

[3] Marx, Preface to *A Contribution to the Critique of Political Economy*, in K. Marx and F. Engels, *Selected Works*, I (Moscow, 1958), 363.

[4] For a determined defence of a hard technological version of Marx's historical materialism, see G. A. Cohen's *Karl Marx's Theory of History: A Defence* (London, 1978).

recognized what are often presented as serious objections to his view of social causation—that technology must itself be caused, that much more than productive forces determine social change, and that political and socio-economic relations are necessary for the very existence of technological activity. The materialism of Marx and Engels remains uncertain or—more positively—open. And that brings problems.

The key problem, in general terms, is whether Marx's modified materialism can be given a precise and firm meaning. For the classical theory asserts a close relationship between two kinds of phenomena—material or economic and ideological—but is unclear as to their precise composition and the (varied) connections between them. The notion of economic conditions is already a spongy one and, as soon as interaction is admitted, those conditions are partly made up of those things (ideas, etc.) which they are supposedly determining. Once there is a complex totality, the parts of which interact dialectically, it becomes extremely difficult to fix limits to the role of ideology, the state and so on, which are interwoven with economic phenomena as a whole. The necessary prevarications, e.g. 'in the last analysis decisive', multiply. One can aim at the best of both worlds—a continuous process of mutual interaction, as opposed to any sharp, mechanical, abstract separation of two elements or parts of social existence, and some notion of 'basic' or 'most significant' or 'primary' causes or forces, but it naturally becomes difficult to separate out their weight and their effects in general. It may involve an extremely complex account of causal connections, as the causal chain is lengthened from the remaining material basis, or the admission of non-material causes.

At this point the problems become, not philosophical—though they have sometimes been construed as simply such, and it is true that clear conceptualization is vital—but historical and empirical: it is a question of pursuing, on the assumption of the primacy of the 'economic base', the concrete study of particular societies and social institutions. Marx himself pointed out the danger of using 'as one's master-key a general historico-philosophical theory', whose greatest virtue consisted in being 'super-historical'.[5] The invocation is towards undogmatic historical research along with a recognition of the primacy of the mode of production: 'in all forms of society it is a determinate production and its relations which assign every other production and its relations their rank and influence. It is a general illumination in which all other colours are plunged and which modifies their specific tonalities. It is special ether which defines the specific gravity of everything found in it.'[6]

[5] K. Marx to the Editorial Board of the 'Otechestvenniye Zapiski', November 1877, in Marx and Engels, *Selected Correspondence* (Moscow, undated), 329.

[6] Marx, *Grundrisse*, quoted by Perry Anderson, *Passages from Antiquity to Feudalism* (London: New Left Books, 1975), 27.

The secret of the state is to be found in the mode of production, but it is a secret which has to be unravelled. The general claim that 'political forms' can only be understood when related to the 'anatomy of civil society', and the specific historical assertion that they serve, more or less precisely, the demands of the capitalist system, namely accumulation and exploitation, do not necessarily imply a rigorous form of economic determinism. Political institutions and arrangements grow out of production but react back upon it as determining elements, conditions produce them but they are necessary to sustain or maintain those conditions and hence the state is credited with significance: it helps to hold a particular form of civil society together. According to Engels, the state develops a movement of its own at a certain stage, although this need not reduce or remove its class character.

Marx himself posed a specific question to Kugelmann, concerning 'the relations of different state forms to different economic structures of society'.[7] The facts that the state is not independent from society, and that it commonly fulfils the same function as government machine, i.e. that it is an instrument of class rule, are compatible with the belief that there is a plurality of state forms, resting on a plurality of underlying economic conditions. The same type of economy will exhibit endless variations and gradations, such variations being due to 'innumerable empirical circumstances—natural environment, racial composition, effects of external historical influences, and so on'.[8] There are significant variations in the configurations, class and otherwise, upon which the state depends. There is no single state form appropriate to capitalism in all its phases and areas of development, and hence the development of the state is neither uniform nor unilinear. In capitalist societies, the state forms include the bourgeois republic, the constitutional monarchy, the Bismarckian and Bonapartist states. The capitalist state is not submerged in one type. Thus the perception that the dominant mode of production conditions the form of the state is the starting point of analysis and not its end result. The configuration of class forces in particular societies at particular times, the form of the state, and the exact way in which it is related to class configurations, are matters of empirical investigation. Given the variety of state forms in capitalist societies and the power of the state in certain circumstances to create specific economic conditions or structures one can only establish the general correspondence between state forms and modes of production in abstract or formal terms. A recognition that there are real differences between capitalist states will be significant politically as well, in view of their relevance to the form

---

[7] 28 December 1862.

[8] *Capital*, Vol. III, extract in Bottomore and Rubel (eds), *Selected Writings in Sociology and Social Philosophy* (London, 1961), 99–100.

and possible extent of proletarian class activity. For example, Marx thought that the bourgeois republic offered unusual opportunities to the class to organize itself and advance its own interests, perhaps gaining materially in the short run at least, although there were limits to its possible progress within the capitalist system.[9] My view of Marx, then, is that he was neither *politicist*, conceding the independence of institutions, nor *economist* or *economic reductionist*, treating political institutions as merely dependent variables.[10] But to define Marx's position between these two extremes, to identify the areas of creativity or free play or relative autonomy is extremely complex, and different judgements here underly basically different political perspectives, e.g. between revolutionary and reformist thinking.

These comments are intended to alert us to the dynamism and diversity of Marx's discussion of the state. Against that interpretative background, we can return to what is sometimes seen as *the* Marxist theory of the state. And without doubt there is at times a strong mechanistic or instrumental flavour to classical Marxist views of the state, both in brisk definitions of its general character, and in historical accounts of its connections with dominant classes and fractions thereof. Marx and particularly Engels tell a supposedly historical story—no logical or hypothetical account, as in Social Contract doctrine. In that half-history, the state appears at a certain stage of development: precisely, when class antagonisms threaten to tear society apart, and it is a response to these conditions, with the function of controlling, managing or changing them, to the primary advantage of certain groups. The structure of this crude acount of the state is that

(1) it emerges to manage or resolve the conflict of classes or, a more complex formulation, it arises from—as part of—the functional division of labour, which arises out of the development of common into private property, and which is associated with the emergence of class division and class conflict,

(2) it becomes a clear-cut instrument of class rule,

(3) it will disappear with the disappearance of classes and of class rule.

[9] There are difficulties in defining these limits in general, as an objective definition, e.g. what is necessary to the survival of capital, itself raises contentious issues and may not be accepted by particular groups of capitalists, while a subjective one, in terms of what particular groups of capitalists or particular capitalist states want, may be lost in diversity and confusion. It is, on the other hand, easy to demonstrate various interventions designed to protect capitalist interests against working class (and other) threats and challenges. The limits to working class progress are, presumably, both material or economic and moral (concerning the possible development of their human capacities.)

[10] See Holloway and Picciotto, *State and Capital*: *A Marxist Debate* (London, 1978), Introduction.

Thus we have a preliminary or basic account of what the state exists to do: it is to preserve or expand those relationships—essentially class relationships, which are relations of domination and subordination—which serve the interests of the ruling class. This rough account, which is applied above all to capitalist or bourgeois society, and which cannot simply be treated as *the* Marxist theory of the state, portrays the state as both product of class conflict and the supreme instrument in its control or management. It is 'the active, conscious and official expression' of the structure of society, and it acts as an instrument or partisan body of institutions; i.e. according to this sharp and simple vision, the state is the instrument of the ruling class, concerned with facilitating the processes of exploitation, it is 'a special repressive force', 'the organized collective power of the possessing classes' (Engels, *The Housing Question*) or, in the historically narrower context which most concerned Marx, 'a committee for managing the common affairs of the whole bourgeoisie' (*Communist Manifesto*). The state is a separate entity, but 'it is nothing more than the form of organization which the bourgeoisie necessarily adopt . . . for the mutual guarantee of their property and interests'.[11] During the June days in Paris, the Republic appeared 'in its *pure form* as the state whose admitted object it is to perpetuate the rule of capital, the slavery of labour'.[12] Its general purpose is that of 'forcibly keeping the exploited classes in the condition of oppression corresponding with the given mode of production (slavery, serfdom, wage-labour)'.[13] There are three apparently clear but in fact complex claims contained within these statements—the state is an instrument (a force, a power, a committee, a form or organization) of a particular kind (repressive, consisting of armed men and of 'material appendages, prisons and coercive institutions of all kinds', as Engels put it) serving a particular group (the possessing classes, the whole bourgeoisie, the bourgeoisie). Each of these claims might collapse upon analysis or empirical investigation.

It should be observed that this popular if vulgar view of the state is common to Marx and Engels. Avineri, seeking to free Marx of the incubus of Engelsism, points a very sharp contrast between the two on the state, claiming that Marx conceived the modern state as 'a perpetual tension between the idea of universality, ideally a bulwark against the particularist interests of civil society, and these antagonistic interests themselves', whereas for Engels, allegedly, it was 'nothing more than an external organization for coercion mechanistically directed by the dominant economic powers.[14] This, I think, both exaggerates the differences between

11 *The German Ideology*, quoted M. Evans, *Karl Marx* (London, 1975), 113.
12 Karl Marx, 'The Class Struggles in France', *Selected Works*, I, 162.
13 Engels, 'Socialism: Utopian and Scientific', *Selected Works*, II, 150.
14 S. Avineri, *The Social and Political Thought of Karl Marx* (Cambridge, 1970), 203.

the two, largely because of a concentration on Marx's early writing, and underrates the complexity of what we can loosely call the 'mature Marxian theory of the state'.

Let me say at once I have no difficulty in accepting a weakened version of the Marxian class instument view of the state. It is easy to demonstrate, historically and in the present, the lean towards the interests of capital, or capitalists, in a great range of pieces of legislation and institutions of state, including constitutions and voting systems. 'Legislation, whether political or civil', claimed Marx, 'never does more than proclaim, express in words, the will of economic relations.'[15] Heavy penalties for offences against property, labour statutes, poor laws, were examples in Marx's own day. He himself had strong doubts about even good laws, e.g. the Factory Acts—in that case because the interpretation of an increasingly complex body of law was a skilled task beyond the competence or resources of ordinary men, because interpretation offered escape routes which were picked out by 'the lynx eye of capital', and because the masters sat in judgment on themselves. There are common sense explanations of the bias, systematic or random, to be found in any state system. These have been summarized neatly by Ralph Miliband.[16] The first is in terms of the personnel of the state system who, through source of recruitment and the definition and character of bureaucratic roles, develop conservative class interests. The second is simply that economic strength expresses itself politically. The third, a structuralist view, focuses on the structural constraints exercised by the mode of production. The state is a class instrument because 'given its insertion in the capitalist mode of production, it cannot be anything else'.[17] There is plenty of support, from detailed empirical investigation and from general argumentation (what we should expect or what must be the case), for the view that the state, as governmental machine, has been and is a class instrument, though it may not be that alone. It is not a neutral instrument or umpire, the servant of society as a whole or of the general interest, as some liberals and pluralists have argued. The state machine is manifestly not neutral.

However, to deny that the state as we know it is—or can be—objective and impartial is not the same thing as accepting a strong Marxian class instrument view. One reason for this is that the state appears capable of at least some manipulation by subjected groups. Marx found it difficult to evaluate the democratic state and the possibilities of social reform which it opened up. Given the politico-legal regulation of English capitalism, Marx responded by denying that parliament was the creative force— it simply responded to outside pressures—and characterized reform as the

---

[15] Marx, *The Poverty of Philosophy* (Moscow, undated), 93.
[16] R. Miliband, *Marxism and Politics* (Oxford, 1978), 71–74.
[17] Ibid., 72.

product, not of humanitarianism and reforming zeal, but of prudence or 'frightened avarice'. Calculated or enlightened conservatism stabilized the capitalist system by reducing its greatest or most blatant evils. And presumably such responses could continually take the initiative away from radical movements, if not civilize the system. Our own reactions to this account of the necessary limitations on the state, and of the related incapacities of reformism, will hinge partly on the assumptions which we make about the nature and the limits of capitalism, e.g. whether we find real and significant institutional and moral differences between different capitalist states, or whether all capitalisms are put on one side of a fundamental divide, with a truly new order—communism—on the other. This limitation of the state to class or, more broadly, capitalist purposes, is not something which can be confirmed or disconfirmed simply by empirical research. It is not just a matter of what the French Civil Service or the British Conservative Party happen to do. The assumption is a structuralist one: the logic of capitalist production, the logic or force of the economy which is more powerful than that of the polity, requires certain political mechanisms, and these political mechanisms—the various appearances or forms of the bourgeois state—will intervene in accordance with the needs of capital. Presumably this necessary fact is also capable of empirical demonstration, though it may be that in the course of such demonstration or elaboration, the notions of capitalism, the needs of capital, the ruling class and so on, will change and will probably become looser. But that steady challenge from within may be met by a retreat to abstraction and essentialism, proclaiming the temporary or ultimate irrelevance of developments in the real world.

Marx's own wrestling with the possibly problematic relationship between class, class interest and state is contained in *The Eighteenth Brumaire of Louis Bonaparte*. This provides an instance of a state which does not rest upon and express an exclusive class domination. According to Marx's historical analysis, the internal divisions of the bourgeoisie constituted the class basis for the apparently independent Bonapartist state which emerged from the collapse of the Second Republic. Despite a common interest in profit maximization, through exploitation of the proletariat, the class split into factions, on hostile terms as competitors. As Marx had commented earlier, the members of the modern bourgeoisie have common class interests, but they also have 'opposite antagonistic interests inasmuch as they stand face to face with one another. This opposition of interests results from the economic conditions of their bourgeois life.'[18] Parliamentary government was a temporary compromise between the 'finance aristocracy', industrial bourgeoisie, landed proprietors, savants or 'so-called men of talent', and the Bonapartists. It broke up,

---

[18] *The Poverty of Philosophy*, 137–138.

over both material interests and ideological differences (prejudices, illusions, convictions, principles). There is some tension between theory or assumption and empirical analysis—on the one hand the parliamentary republic represented the common interest of the bourgeoisie as a whole, overriding, in principle anyhow, those more specific interests which fragmented the class, but that class in fact revealed great and disastrous heterogeneity, which lost it political power and enabled a 'grotesque mediocrity' to rule and to perfect the state power as an 'appalling parasitic body'. The extra-parliamentary bourgeoisie declared unequivocally that it 'longed to get rid of its own political rule in order to get rid of the troubles and dangers of ruling'. And so parliament, 'left in the lurch by its own class', succumbed to the executive power.[19]

This analysis and its theoretical underpinning are instructive. Marx's underlying assumption was that in normal circumstances the bourgeoisie would take political power in the parliamentary republic, in a fairly open and undisguised way (though some shrouding of the naked reality was politically necessary), thereby constituting itself the ruling class. But in this case the peculiar balance of social forces, with the potentially dominant class divided and even conflict-ridden, produced an unusual gap between civil society and the state, which was expressed in the domination or separate authority of the executive power. And yet, beneath the authoritarian government of the detached executive, industry and trade prospered in 'hot-house fashion'. The implications are that in certain circumstances the state can assert its independence and that, in so doing, it may serve the interests of classes better than they themselves could by taking power in their own name. This suggests that a certain freedom or relative autonomy on the part of the state—normally meaning the executive authority—is necessary if the state is to protect the bourgeois class against 'its members taken individually' as well as against the exploited class. In this vein, some Marxist political economists, observing the contemporary 'capitalist' state, have concluded that, owing to the serious divisions within the capitalist class, and perhaps also to the irrationality of certain sectors of it, the state must act in support of the logic of capitalist production or the needs of the system, independently of and in some cases against the wishes of particular groups of capitalists. These groups presumably suffer from false consciousness or have economic interests which are regressive or otherwise incompatible with the existing system. In these circumstances the state may function as an 'ideal collective capitalist'.

My final piece of attempted exegesis concerns the withering away of the state, which is one of the basic items of the speculative Marxist agenda of the future. Communism is characterized by the absence of a state,

[19] 'The Eighteenth Brumaire', *Selected Works*, I, 329.

while the intermediate period between the breakdown, collapse, disintegration or takeover of capitalism and the emergence of a truly human society is characterized by the appearance of democratic, proletarian political institutions which are necessary both to rationalize the economy and to defeat the enemies of revolution. Marx and Engels insisted on the need for political mediation at this stage, and on the fact that it would be more democratic than any previous regime. There would be no standing army or police or bureaucracy, delegates were immediately revocable by the people, communes were working assemblies and differentials were abolished, with all state servants on working men's wages. The transitional period, over whose character and circumstances Marxists have differed significantly, was conceived by Marx as a new revolutionary form of democracy, and not simply the occupation and use of the bourgeois state by the proletariat. Though he later had second thoughts, Marx did affirm, in *The Civil War in France*, that the Paris Commune was 'the political form at last discovered under which to work out the economic emancipation of labour'.[20] Engels indicated clearly the nature of the transitional process in a Preface to that work, saying that the state was at best 'an evil inherited by the proletariat after its victorious struggle for class supremacy, whose worst sides the victorious proletariat will have to lop off as speedily as possible, just as the Commune had to, until a generation reared in new, free social conditions is able to discard the entire lumber of the state'.[21] And in that remoter future? Human emancipation cannot be consummated within the state: the 'free state' is a contradiction in terms. The future of political institutions is described in various ways— so various, indeed, that the substance or content of the assertions appears to be different in different formulations. The most familiar of these claim that the government of persons will be replaced by the administration of things and the conduct of the processes of production, that public power will lose its political character, that there will be no state in the 'current political sense', that human emancipation will end alienation and the institutions and structures which are related systematically to it (as expressions or symptoms rather than causes). Civil society will no longer be smothered, alienated social power will disappear. The implication clearly is that in no sense will a class or partisan state survive in a communist society, although the need for some authority, regulatory agency, planning bodies, is affirmed. *The Critique of the Gotha Programme* indicates that state functions are not confined to class repression: they include means 'for performing the common operations arising from the nature of all communities'. The survival of state-like functions, even though these are

---

[20] Marx, 'The Civil War in France', *Selected Works*, I, 522.
[21] Engels, 1891 Introduction to 'The Civil War in France', *Selected Works*, I, 485 (different translation).

separate from class or repressive or exploitative functions, suggests that in some respects the transformation may be more apparent than real, in that a new form of communal political (or public) apparatus will emerge. If authority has a rational core, regardless of its particular historical manifestations, we may have difficulty in both separating out its tolerable aspect and relating this to a theory of its real abolition. But the differences with a typical liberal-pluralist account of the state remain decisive: a combination of alienation and class theory suggests, logically, that with an end to alienation and to classes, their issue—alienated social power and class institutions—will also come to an end, while Marxian optimism about human capacities implies a new basis to all human arrangements. Man's creativity and communality will underly social institutions, and external direction and control will be replaced by something intimate and ultimately spontaneous. Executive functions, demythologized, become routine and straightforward. To critics, impressed more by social complexity and diversity, if not bowed down by the weight of man's sinful nature, this will seem a barren or a highly dangerous utopia.[22]

Marx's account of the state, and my own presentation of that account, leave many questions unanswered. There is clearly plenty of evidence to support the narrow Marxist view of the state—systematic and class bias in the legal and political systems of capitalist (and other) states, class interests of the ruling personnel, etc. There is also a lot to be said for the general Marxian approach, that of analysing the structure and functions of historical states in the context of underlying economic and social structures: while conceding a certain and variable independence to political institutions, Marx placed them in their totality, i.e. capitalist economic and social relationships, but recognized that the connections could be contradictory as well as harmonious. Problems, both conceptual and empirical, emerge over the manner, detail and fullness of the state's expression of the interests of capital, given the diversity of capitals, and the lack of rationality and information. What political institutions and instruments are most appropriate to the needs of capital now? There is no universally appropriate form, of course—nor did Marx pretend that there was one. What is needed, in circumstances very different from those familiar to Marx, is a general model of capitalist states, including some indication of the limits within which the variable significance of the political can emerge, an account of the nature of the world capitalist system (how it impinges upon, influences and is influenced by particular national states) and of the specific features of any particular national state. Its own culture,

[22] For some typical assaults on the dangerous side of Marx's utopianism, see R. Tucker, *Philosophy and Myth in Karl Marx* (Cambridge, 1964), C. Rossiter, *Marxism: The View From America* (New York, 1960) and H. B. Parkes, *Marxism: An Autopsy* (Boston, 1939).

resources and history will lead to a mixture of unique or exceptional and shared or common features, with uneven development and perhaps different limiting factors and different political options. In relation to the options perceived by some, one important issue is what it is that would enable, or what is it that emphatically prevents, reformists from bursting through to a new society. There are incoherences in the Marxian account. It is not internally consistent (or, alternatively, there are several theories of the state), there are problems when the state is separated from its ostensible class base, the degree of amenability of the bourgeois state to social reform is uncertain, precision and firmness weaken once political and other ideological variables are given some independence, and the withering away of the state at once seems to go further than it in fact does, and leaves the tough questions of diversity, conflict and power not only unresolved, but unconsidered.

University of East Anglia

Macherey and Marxist Literary Theory

TERRY EAGLETON

A resurgence of interest in the materialist aesthetics of Walter Benjamin and Bertolt Brecht has helped to free Marxist criticism from the neo-Hegelian forms within which it has long been imprisoned. Yet the central category of those materialist aesthetics—the 'author as producer'—remains a *transitional* concept, potently demystificatory but politically indeterminate. And crucial though the analysis of the relations between 'base' and 'superstructure' *within* art itself clearly is, its historical explanatory power is not yet fully evident. The moment of Brecht, for example, is not easily translatable to English literary culture. Donne's *Songs and Sonnets* and George Herbert's *The Temple* belong to different modes of literary production, but inhabit alternative areas of the same ideological formation; Defoe and Fielding practise the same mode of literary production, but it is their ideological antagonism which claims our attention. *Henry Esmond* was the only novel of Thackerary to be published complete, rather than in monthly serialized parts; but though this difference of productive mode undoubtedly impresses itself on the novel's form, it leaves the 'Thackerayan ideology' essentially intact. No one expects modes of literary production and literary 'superstructures' to form a symmetrical relationship, dancing a harmonious minuet hand-in-hand throughout history; yet even if we allow for disjunction and uneven development, it seems true that the 'author as producer' concept is one which must, as it were, lie dormant over certain spans of literary history. The aesthetic redefinition of fiction as 'organic form' which develops in late nineteenth-century England, to discover its major ideologue in Henry James, is doubtless related to those shifts in literary production (from serialization and the 'three-decker' novel to the single volume) determined by the economic demands of the monopolist private lending libraries; yet it is not clear how such material mutations become an *active* element in the reconstruction of fictional ideologies.

This is not the kind of question which the work of Pierre Macherey proposes to answer, despite the title of his major work.[1] Like Lukács and unlike Benjamin, Macherey moves almost wholly within the terrain of a work's 'superstructures'. 'Production' refers not to the material apparatus, technological infrastructures, and social relations of an artefact, but to its

[1] *Pour une théorie de la production littéraire* (Paris, Maspéro, 1966).

self-production as a chain of significations. Yet if Macherey's work resembles that of the neo-Hegelians in its dissolution of the text's materiality to a set of mental significances, it resembles it in little else. Indeed the thrust of Macherey's project is nothing less than the liberation of Marxist criticism from every taint of Hegelianism and empiricism; and to say that amounts to saying that he is, effectively, the first Althusserian critic. His intention is to inaugurate a radical 'epistemological break' with what has come before, to construct an entirely distinct problematic; and since he is therefore, in my view, one of the most challenging, genuinely innovatory of contemporary Marxist critics, the rest of this article will be mainly given over to an exposition of his as yet little publicized positions.

Macherey begins with a bold application of Althusserian epistemology to critical enquiry. Criticism and its object—the literary text—are to be radically distinguished: science is not the reduplication of an object but a form of knowledge of it which displaces it outside of itself, knows it as it cannot know itself. Criticism is not merely the elaboration of the text's self-knowledge; it establishes a decisive rupture between itself and the object, distancing itself from that object in order to produce a new knowledge of it. To know the text is not to listen to, and translate, a pre-existent discourse: it is to produce a *new* discourse which 'makes speak' the text's silences. Such an operation, however, is not to be misconceived as the hermeneutical recovery of a sense or structure hidden in the work, a sense which it possesses but conceals; it is rather to establish a new knowledge discontinuous with the work itself, disjunct from it as science is disjunct from ideology. Scientific criticism is in this sense the antagonist of empiricist critical 'knowledge', which ends effectively by abolishing itself, allowing itself to be reabsorbed into a literary object which it has left essentially unchanged. Criticism is not an 'instrument' or 'passage' to the truth of a text, but a transformative labour which makes its object appear other than it is.

Scientific criticism, then, produces a new object, refusing the empiricist illusion of the text as a 'given' which offers itself spontaneously to the inspecting glance. Such empiricism merely *redoubles* the artefact: it succeeds in saying less in saying more. But this empiricist illusion is coupled with what might seem its opposite: the 'normative' illusion, which measures the text against a ghostly model of what it might be. The normative illusion constitutes a refusal of the object as it is: it 'corrects' it against an independent, pre-existent model of which the empirical text is an imperfect copy, an inessential appearance. Grasping the text as the mere fictive rehearsal of an ideal object which precedes it, an ideal present within the text as the abiding truth or essence from which it may lapse and deviate, the typical gesture of normative criticism is to inscribe a 'Could do better' in the text's margin. The determinateness of the work is radically denied: normative criticism assumes that it could have been different from what it is.

As such, the normative illusion is merely a displacement of the empiricist fallacy: it treats and modifies the object so that it can be better consumed. To attribute the text's empirical characteristics to an ultimate, always pre-given model which is the truth of the text's phenomenality is merely an epistemological variant of the naive empiricism which 'receives' the work as a spontaneous consumable given.

For Macherey, the literary object is determinate, and so can be the object of rational study. It is the effect of a specific labour, the product of a writer who does not fabricate the materials with which he works. (This is why it is mere mystification to speak of the author as a 'creator'.) Those materials are not neutral, and so spontaneously assimilable to a unity imposed upon them by the writer; they preserve, rather, a specific weight and autonomy of their own. The 'necessity' of the text is not the reflection of the author's sustaining, unifying intention; the writer's 'choice' of how to construct his narrative is the mere illusion of a choice, since his 'decisions' are already determined by the exigencies of the narrative itself. (The hero, in a given fictional *genre*, cannot disappear in the first few pages.) The writer 'discovers' rather than 'invents' his narrative, 'encounters' rather than 'creates' his solutions; he is the first reader of his own work. The true necessity of the text manifests itself in the fact that not a word of it can be changed and nothing can be added, even though it appears at each moment as though a new topic could be chosen, an alternative narrative selected. But it is precisely this ceaseless shadowy presence of other possible phrases which could be pronounced, this ineradicable sense that things could have been other than they are, which enforces the constraining necessity of the text we actually have before us. There is, after all, only one text; each of its moments is 'free', surprising, but each is definitive too. The work is at once achieved and changing, presenting itself as a contradictory combination of arbitrariness and necessity; and the task of criticism is to theorize the *necessity of this diversity*. The work's 'necessity' is not an initial 'given' but a product—a product which presents itself as the meeting-place of several diverse 'lines of necessity', several distinct and conflictual chains of meaning. The determinateness of the artefact, then, inheres not in its achieved 'unity' but in the necessity of its internal ruptures and contradictions—although it is important not to reduce contradiction itself, in Hegelian fashion, to the mere moment of an underlying unity, the self-divided appearance of a single abiding sense. The question which literature poses to criticism is that of the 'organization of a multiple', the laws of a form of necessity which preserves the real diversity by which the work is constructed. Such diversity characterizes every text, and the 'adventure story' is its image: for every work is constituted by an interior 'rupture' or 'decentrement' worked upon its initial situation, as the adventure story operates by surprise and reversal. The work, then, is neither improvised nor *pre*-determined; it works, instead, by a sort of 'free necessity', in which we continually discover the ineluctable beneath the form of the unforeseen, and vice versa.

The form of that 'free necessity' is nothing less than literary language itself. Literature institutes a new relationship between word and object which cancels the distinction between 'true' and 'false'; rather than conforming to an independent order of things, it confers its own truth on itself, suggests itself the order of truth on which it is founded. It is the source of its own sense, having nothing, it seems, either before or behind it, apparently free from the hauntings of any alien presence. It is autonomous to the degree that it lacks depth: everything is unrolled on the surface, a surface which is, however, mutliple and diverse. Literary language confronts nothing exterior to itself: its units signify only in their internal interrelations. It is, in effect, a kind of tautology, endlessly repeating, prolonging and reproducing itself. It is language 'reduced to its thinness', reflecting nothing, apparently doubling nothing, sustaining merely by the mechanisms of its own complex, irregular unfolding. Liberated in this sense from quotidian determinants, literary language acquires an unusual freedom and improvisatory force; but such improvisation is merely one of appearance. For the fact that literary language carries within itself the principles of its own veridicity produces a certain form of necessity: because such language is radically *irreducible* it is thereby fixed unalterably in itself, 'necessary' in so far as it is incapable of modification. (It is, indeed, *inferior* literature which, unable to produce the principles of its own veridicity, slips constantly towards an external order—tradition, morality, ideology— for verification.)

The necessity of the text, then, is not the index of a cohering authorial will; nor do we escape from that idealist problematic if we merely transpose it and posit, *à la* Goldmann, a 'collective unconscious' as producer. The necessity of the text—which is precisely what renders it *readable*, yields us a determinate object of analysis—inheres rather in the fact that the text *produces itself*—unfolds and activates its multiple lines of meaning without conformity to 'intention', pre-given normative model or external reality. The task of criticism is to discover in each text the laws of that self-production, or (what amounts to the same thing) the conditions of a work's possibility—'conditions' understood not as the point of departure, the primordial germ to which the process of production can be reduced back, but the real process of the work's self-constitution, the specific composition of the concrete diversity of its elements.

Macherey's insistence on the text's determinateness might seem at first glance in contradiction with his theory of criticism as transformative of its object. For if nothing in the text can be changed or added, how does this differ from the empiricist 'reception' of the work as spontaneous fact? The answer lies in properly discriminating the concepts of the work's *autonomy* and its *independence*. The work's autonomy consists in its establishing a *difference*, a separation, with the languages, ideologies, and histories which surround it—a measurable, determinate distance which may be the object of scientific knowledge. The work is constituted precisely by its relations with what it is not; if this were not so it would be wholly 'independent' of what surrounds it and thus unreadable and even invisible. The work is the production of a difference from what surrounds it; in being sundered from those surroundings, snatched into its own space, it ceaselessly alludes to them. No text can be 'independent': it subsists in its complex relations to other uses of language, and so to ideologies and social formations. But for Macherey these realities are inscribed within the letter of the text primarily by virtue of their *absence*. Every discourse presupposes the absence of that of which it speaks, installing itself in the empty space created by its distancing of the object. The 'truth' of a literary work, then, is not secreted within it like a nut in a fruit, awaiting extraction at the hands of 'interpretative' criticism. The work's significance lies in its relation to what it is not, and so, paradoxically, is at once interior and absent simultaneously.

It is for this reason that the work must be at once *treated*, transformed, for it to become a theoretical fact, and yet must also be left as it is, recognized in its determinateness. It is important to recognize first of all that the necessity of the text is founded on the conflictual multiplicity of its meanings, and that to explain the work is therefore to distinguish the principle of its diversity. The postulate of the work's *unity*, which has always more or less haunted bourgeois criticism, must be unequivocally denounced; it is not unity, but the distance which separates the work's several meanings, which is at issue. The mutual confrontation of those divergent meanings in the text signals a certain *incompleteness*: the work is not closed on itself, a 'totality' turning around a concealed centre, but radically decentred and irregular, unachieved and insufficient. Yet this incompleteness or 'hollowness' of the artefact is not one which criticism can correct by adding something to it; it is, rather, a *determinate* incompleteness which cannot be altered. The text is, as it were, complete in its incompleteness, unachieved by virtue of the very reality it is. *What is lacking to it—its absence—is precisely what constitutes it as an object.* It is necessary to determine what a text lacks—lacks without which it would not exist, would have nothing to say. To explain the work, then, is to demonstrate that it does not exist in itself as some ideal plentitude of meaning, but bears inscribed in its very letter the marks of certain determinate absences which are the very principle of its identity. 'Hollowed' by the elusive presence of other works against which it constructs itself, turning around the absence of certain words to which it incessantly returns, the literary work consists not in the elaboration of a single meaning, but in the conflict and incompatibility of several meanings. That conflict, moreover, is precisely what binds the work to reality: ideology is present in the text in the form of its eloquent silences, its significant gaps and fissures. The distance which separates the work from its ideological matrix embodies itself in a certain 'internal distance' which separates the work from itself.

How is this to be understood? In launching his literary project, Macherey would claim, a writer discovers that what he 'wanted' to say is blocked, contorted, and deformed by ideology; in trying to articulate one meaning, the work finds itself ideologically constrained to articulate another. Thus, Jules Verne's fiction 'wants' to represent bourgeois progress as a march forward to the future, yet finds itself (on account of certain contradictions inherent in that ideology[2]) enforced to represent this march in images bound to the past. The effect of this ideological torsion is a set of hiatuses within the work itself—a *découpage* which appears in Verne as a discrepancy between levels of 'representation' and 'figuration'. We may thus read a text, as it were, 'in reverse', constructing what it attempts to say, athwart what it actually finds itself saying.

Criticism, then, does not site itself in the same space as the text itself, allowing it to speak or completing what it leaves unsaid. On the contrary, it installs itself in the text's very incompleteness in order to *theorize* that lack of plentitude—to explain the ideological necessity of its 'not-said', its constitutive silences, that which it can show but not say. It is these silences which the critic must make speak; it is the 'unconsciousness' of the work which he interrogates, an unconsciousness which is nothing less than the play of history itself on the work's margins. In saying one thing, a text must at the same time say another, which is not necessarily the same; it is by its very nature unable to say simply one thing at a time. What the work 'says' as a whole, then, is not just this or that chain of meaning, but their conflict and difference; it articulates the hollow space which divides and binds together its multiple senses.

The relation between fiction and ideology is, for Macherey, one of considerable complexity. It is clear that the work does not 'reproduce' ideology, in a way which would make its own contradictions reflective of historical contradictions. On the contrary: the contradictions within the text are the product of the ideologically determined *absence* of such a reflection of real contradictions. It is the work's problematical *relationship* to ideology which produces its internal dissonances. Rather than 'reproducing' ideology, the text *produces* it, setting it in motion and endowing it with a form; and in doing so it reveals in its own internal dislocations the gaps

[2] Strictly speaking, there cannot for Macherey be 'internal ideological contradictions', since the function of ideology is to create an imaginary unity from real historical contradictions. There can only be contradiction between an ideology and what lies beyond its repressive limits—history itself. The text '*puts* the ideology into contradiction' by illuminating its gaps and limits, revealing ideology as a structure of absences. In doing so, the text puts itself into question too, manifesting a lack or dissonance within itself.

and limits which signify that ideology's contradictory relation to real history. In the text, that is to say, the ideology begins to speak of its absences and manifest its limits—not in the Lukácsian sense that the work's aesthetic potency allows it to overreach ideological mediations into a more direct encounter with historical truth (a position Macherey rejects as naively empiricist), but because, in transforming rather than merely reproducing ideology, the text necessarily illuminates the 'not-said' which is the significant structure of the 'said'.

The literary work, then, does have a significant relation to historical reality, although one of a highly mediated and refracted kind. For Macherey, literary language occupies a kind of intermediate space between science and ideology: it resembles scientific discourse in the rigour of its internal organizations and in bearing within itself the criteria of its own veridicity; but it also mimes quotidian discourse, which is the language of ideology. It is at once the analogue of a true theoretical knowledge and the caricature of ideology. Rather than imitating reality, it deforms it; it is capable of becoming an 'image' of reality only by virtue of the distance which separates it from what it imitates, since the image which conforms wholly to its object confounds itself with it and loses its imaging character. Baroque art, founded on the principle that the more one distances the more one imitates, is for Macherey a fundamental model of all literary production. Yet though literary discourse deforms and distances reality, it is not thereby the mere play of an illusion, an objectless message (as Barthes would have it) whose substance is reducible to the codes which formulate and communicate it. Fiction, by endowing the ideological illusion with a form, fixing it within determinate limits, 'interrupts', 'arrests', 'realizes', and completely transforms it, to the point where it ceases to be merely illusory. The literary work, in thus transforming the ideological illusion, implicitly yields a critique of its own ideological status, becoming the substitute for, if not the equivalent of, a theoretical knowledge. Fiction is not *truer* than illusion; but by establishing a transformative relation to ideology, its own deceptions begin to betray and uncover the more radical deceptions of ideology itself, and in so doing contribute to our deliverance from them.

Macherey's theory of literary production entails a concept of *structure* radically distinct from that of the structuralist ideology. The structuralist critical enterprise revolves on the decipherment of the text's enigma, the disengagement from it of a cryptic but coherent sense. The literary artefact is constructed as a message, and the critic's function is to isolate the transmitted information. The work, accordingly, has no autonomous value in itself: it is an intermediary, the simulacrum of a concealed structure. Structuralist analysis, which elaborates a 'copy' of the work itself, is thus the simulacrum of a simulacrum. It is, in that precise sense, Platonic: the writer's production is merely the appearance of a production, since its true object lies behind it. To criticize is thus to reduce the 'externality' of the text to the structure secreted in its 'interior'—to *extract* the truth of the object from its inner space. Such extraction, for Macherey as for Althusser, is merely another form of empiricist epistemology—an adequation and conformity of 'knowledge' to its privileged object. But the work has, in fact, neither exterior nor interior; it is not to be conceived in the metaphysical terms of depths and surfaces. If the work has an interior in any sense at all, it is one exhibited as an exterior: the work hides nothing, keeps no secret, is entirely 'readable' and offered to view. Structuralism, like 'normative' criticism, refuses the text's autonomous reality; it seeks for the laws immanent in a work, as one might seek for the laws of gravity within a falling body. But just as the laws of gravity are in fact *elsewhere*, situated on the quite distinct terrain of scientific knowledge, so scientific criticism gives the work a new dimension rather than discovers a deep meaning buried within it. It does not rest in its object, repeating its discourse in other terms; it is a matter not of an 'otherwise-said' but of a 'never-said'. An analogy can be drawn with Freud, who rather than searching for a hidden meaning in the depths of conscious discourse, situates this meaning elsewhere, in the structure he names the unconscious.[3] The 'structure' of the literary work, similarly, is not to be discovered *in* the work itself; it is a structure to which the work *belongs*, without copying or containing it. To speak of the work in terms of structure, then, can be to fall easy victim to the organicist fallacy of the work as harmonious totality; it is to forget that structure is the principle of *difference* rather than unity, and so must necessarily be absent from the relations it serves to explain. (Contradiction, for example, can be thought only as absence, not as positive presence.) It is in its very conflictual diversity that the work can be said to belong to an ideological structure, which disrupts its manifold meanings. The text's significance is to be found not 'in 'but 'beside' it, on its margins, where it relates to what it is not, in the conditions of its very possibility.

This exposition of Macherey's critical theory has been extremely partial and schematic: I have said nothing, for example, about his cardinally important analysis of Lenin's critique of Tolstoy, and little of his lengthy dissection of the work of Verne. The critical comments which follow must be equally truncated and selective.

In ascribing the power he does to literary form, Macherey runs the risk of a peculiarly Marxist variety of formalism. For though his contention

---

[3] There are other, fruitful comparisons to be drawn between Macherey and Freud. In *The Interpretation of Dreams*, Freud is clear that the task of the analyst of dreams is not simply to lay bare the meaning of a distorted text, but to explain the *meaning of the text-distortion itself*—a distortion which produces a radically mutilated discourse characterized by gaps, obscurities and ambiguities, by 'breaks in the text'.

that form distantiates the ideological is suggestive, why should this distantiation automatically be *subversive*? Why is 'form', in some new essentialism, ascribed a single, eternal effect? For such distantiation is surely also capable of powerfully *underwriting* the ideology of the text. And whether it subverts or underwrites depends not merely upon the particular transaction between form and ideology in question, but upon the concrete historical and ideological situation in which the text is situated and received. Macherey's early work, committed as it is to an 'intrinsicist' literary science which treats the text solely in terms of its production rather than also in terms of its consumption, completely suppresses the reality of the literary text as an historically mutable practice which 'lives' only in the process of its transaction with particular readers. It thus damagingly reproduces the 'scientism' of Althusser's work, presupposing some quite unproblematized, transcendental reader/critic.

Macherey's formalism is in part a result of his Althusserian notion of ideology. For if ideology is conceived of as an essentially *non-contradictory* region, as homogeneous 'illusion', then it would indeed take something like art to press it up against its own limits and force it into handing over its guily secrets. Ideology, however, has no such homogeneity: it is certainly *homogenizing* in tendency, but it nowhere, fortunately, has the success which Macherey assigns to it. Althusser's own work has grievously underplayed the degree to which ideology, as a terrain of *class-struggle*, is itself labile, internally contradictory, non-monolithic: his essay on ideology in *Lenin and Philosophy* images it, in effect, as an omnipotent superego which inexorably submits the individual subject to its needs, and links this undialectical view with an equally undialectical functionalism and economism, whereby ideology exists merely to reproduce the conditions whereby the subject is inserted into its economic place. Behind this theory lurks a particular politics, one shared by Macherey himself: the counter-revolutionary politics of the French Communist Party, whose political collaborationism finds itself reflected in a view of ideology divorced from class struggle. For Althusser and Macherey, ideology is effectively co-terminous with the 'lived'; but it is difficult to see what cutting-edge such an 'expansionist' definition of ideology can have. Since Macherey (although not Althusser) is prepared to term ideology 'illusion', fiction really alludes to another fiction (ideology), which in turn alludes to historical reality. Now it is certainly true that fiction is, in this sense, constituted by what one might term a 'double-deformation', whereby ideological materials which are already a 'misrecognition' of the real are raised to the second power, 'produced' in their turn by certain fictional devices. Fiction, by 'fixing' the ideological in this process, establishes what Althusser terms an 'internal self-distantiation' from the ideology in which it bathes, breaks it up and reassembles it into a peculiar visibility; so the 'double-deformation', we might say, partially cancels itself out, inverting itself back into an analogue of theoretical knowledge. But ideology does not have to have recourse to fiction to become the analogue of a knowledge, since it is more than just the bad dream of the infrastructure: it is not, in a word, just 'false consciousness', the very truth to which Althusser and Macherey wish to attest, but which Macherey seems at times to end up denying. (And if Macherey seems to this extent to fall back into the Hegelian–Marxist tradition he rejects, so do both Macherey and Althusser in their implicit desire to salvage a certain *privileged status* for art, to rescue it from the 'shame' of the 'merely ideological', and elevate it almost—but not quite—to the rank of theory.)

Since *Pour une théorie de la production littéraire*, Macherey's work has undergone radical new development. In two seminal articles, 'On Literature as an Ideological Form: Some Marxist Propositions', and 'The Problem of Reflection',[4] he appears to have broken decisively with his earlier intrinsicism and formalism—that is to say, with the residues of bourgeois aesthetics still lurking in his book. Abandoning the bourgeois-idealist category of 'literature' which still dominates *Pour une théorie*, he is now prepared to see what counts as an artefact as historically and conjuncturally determined; and he has shifted his attention away from the 'text-in-itself' to its material determinants, to the process whereby 'Literature' signifies those pieces of writing ephemerally and variously *constituted* as such by being inserted into the ideological apparatuses in such a way as to produce specific 'literary effects'—effects which, in so far as they have definite ideological functions, intervene into the class struggle. His model for this work has been the suggestive enquiries of Renée Balibar into the fostering, within the French pedagogical system, of a linguistic division (between *français ordinaire* and *français littéraire*) which plays its role in the enforcement, within the post-Revolutionary creation of a 'national language', of certain class divisions which that common language threatens.

Macherey's later work, then, has been considerably more materialist in outlook, and has already had a pervasive influence in England. Two problems in particular wait to be resolved. The first is the conflict between the 'scientism' of the early work and the 'conjuncturalism' of the later. If the former tends to reify the text to an immanent structure of meaning, the latter threatens to reduce the text to no more than the ensemble of its various moments of reception. It still remains to be shown how a 'literary' text (i.e. a text constituted as literary at a certain historical point for a certain reader) is at once amenable to scientific analysis, in the complex interaction of its 'ideological' and 'aesthetic' devices, and yet will generate from that interaction a whole field of multiple possible

---

[4] The first article, reprinted from the journal *Littérature* (No. 13), can be found in the *Oxford Literary Review* **3**, No. 1 (1978); the second has appeared in the American journal *Sub-stance* No. 15 (1976).

readings in particular situations which the 'science of the text' cannot itself pre-limit or predict.

The second problem concerns the vexed question of 'reflection'. Macherey's comments on Lenin's treatment of Tolstoy (the 'mirror of the Russian Revolution') brilliantly succeed in retrieving Lenin's critique from a crude reductionism: if Tolstoy's work is indeed a mirror, then it is, as Lenin recognizes, an angled, selective one thronged by fragmented images, as notable for what it does not, as for what it does, reflect. But such a drastically modified mirror might hardly be said to be a mirror at all; and indeed, by the time of his later essays, Macherey has effectively transposed the epistemological question of the 'text-reality' relationship to an ontological one: that of the *material reality* of art itself, which is an active force in the reproduction of social reality, rather than a mere reflex of it. This is a crucial reminder; but it does not solve the epistemological problem. Whether Macherey continues with his work in literary theory remains to be seen: when I had the opportunity of telling him how significant his book has been in England, he shrugged bemusedly, appeared to have difficulty in recalling having written it, and announced that he was a philosopher, not a literary critic. His latest book is a study of Spinoza and Hegel. But perhaps one should take that Gallic shrug with a pinch of salt.[5]

Wadham College, Oxford

[5] Part of this paper has been published previously in an article, 'Pierre Macherey and the Theory of Literary Production', *Minnesota Review* N.S. **5** (Fall 1975), 134–144. Grateful acknowledgement is made to the editors of the *Minnesota Review* for permission to re-use this material.

Theory and Practice in Marx and Marxism

RICHARD KILMINSTER

> The identification of theory and practice is a critical act, through which practice is demonstrated rational and necessary, and theory realistic and rational (Antonio Gramsci).[1]

I

In contemporary sociological and political theory the opposition of theory and practice refers to a number of aspects of the relationship between theories of various kinds and social life. It can refer, for example, to the relationships between the various sciences (particularly the social sciences) and their 'objects', between scientific knowledge and its necessary practical applications and broadly between social science and politics.[2] Many Marxist writings since Lenin attempt to unite those three levels in a theory of the total society with a practical intent. This theory is intended to inform practical political activity in order radically to change the complex of social institutions which make the theory itself possible, in this way abolishing the theory in practice. That theory and practice in this sense can inseparably inform each other in this way within the politics of the labour movement, is one meaning in Soviet Marxism of the phrase 'the unity of theory and practice'.[3] Following Marx's *Theses on Feuerbach*, Marxists have assumed that if a social theory is true, it will be transcended (abolished) in the practical activity undertaken informed by it. It is to try to conceptualize such putative moments of transition when theory becomes real that Anglo-Saxon writers in this field have adopted the German word

---

[1] *Selections from the Prison Notebooks of Antonio Gramsci*, edited and translated by Quintin Hoare and Geoffrey Nowell-Smith (London: Lawrence & Wishart, 1971), 365.

[2] See Brian Fay, *Social Theory and Political Practice* (London: Allen & Unwin, 1975), Ch. 1.

[3] See John Lachs, *Marxist Philosophy: A Bibliographical Guide* (Chapel Hill: North Carolina Press, 1967), 90–92, Alfred Meyer, *Marxism: The Unity of Theory and Practice* (Cambridge, Mass.: Harvard University Press, 1954), 104–107; and Gustav A. Wetter, *Dialectical Materialism: A Historical and Systematic Survey of Philosophy in the Soviet Union* (London: Routledge & Kegan Paul, 1958), 256–257.

Richard Kilminster

praxis, although it is clear that this concept cannot be a category of empirical, sociological enquiry. Conversely, if the theory is untrue, then the activity undertaken will demonstrate its inadequacies, necessitating the elaboration of further theory, which will suggest further action, and so on.[4] Hence, in this tradition, epistemological matters of the verifiability or falsifiability of social science hypotheses are, therefore, considered to be issues which cannot be settled solely in theory. They are in part practical questions.[5]

So it is clear that the issue of the relationship between theory and practice in the writings of Marx and later Marxists does not, strictly speaking, constitute a 'topic' for discussion, like Marx's analysis of feudalism or his critique of political economy or Gramsci's theory of hegemony or Marxist theories of the state. Rather, it articulates what has been the whole *raison d'être* of Marxist social theory and practice. Each development in Marxist theory has sought its own abolition. Because of that practical intent, exponents of Marxist theory have spent a good deal of time trying to demonstrate the implicit practical intent embodied in other social theories which do not explictly have the same practical orientation as their own, e.g. those informed by positivism or hermeneutics. This implicit practical application is related to the function such theories perform in society and then ploughed into their own general theory. Jürgen Habermas, for example, has described his own aim as to develop a theory of society with a practical intention and 'to delimit its status with respect to theories of different origins'.[6] For all these reasons it is more accurate to refer to Marx's theory, and many of the later Marxist versions, as a *practical–theoretical* framework. Habermas[7] summarizes well the practical orientation of the Marxist tradition which I have been characterizing:

> Historical materialism aims at achieving an explanation of social evolution which is so comprehensive that it embraces the interrelationships of the theory's own origins and application. The theory specifies the conditions under which reflection on the history of our species by mem-

---

[4] See Georg Lukács, *History and Class Consciousness: Studies in Marxist Dialectics* (1923), translated by Rodney Livingstone (London: Merlin Press, 1971), 197–199; and Karl Mannheim, *Ideology and Utopia: An Introduction to the Sociology of Knowledge* (1929) (London: Routledge & Kegan Paul, 1968), 112–113, for accounts of this aspect of Marxist thought. Mannheim also discusses (104ff.) the conceptions of theory and practice found in four other historical-political parties and tendencies in addition to the socialist–communist one.

[5] Karl Marx, *Economic and Philosophic Manuscripts of 1844*, translated by Martin Milligan (Moscow: Progress Publishers, 1967), 102 and 95.

[6] *Theory and Practice*, translated by John Viertel (London: Heinemann, 1974), 1.

[7] Ibid, 1–2.

bers of this species themselves has become objectively possible; and at the same time it names those to whom this theory is addressed, who then with its aid can gain enlightenment about their emancipatory role in the process of history. The theory occupies itself with reflection on the interrelationships of its origin and with anticipation of those of its application, and thus sees itself as the necessary catalytic moment within the social complex of life which it analyses; and this complex it analyses as integral interconnections of compulsions, from the viewpoint of the possible sublation—resolution and abolition—of all this.

My approach to discussing what Marx and certain European Marxists have said about those kinds of questions is a sociological one. But this stance should not discourage philosophical readers, because I think that Marx's work raises some fundamental questions about the human sciences, including that of the status of philosophy itself. By philosophy here, and in the paper generally, I am not referring to the official philosophy of Russian communism—dialectical materialism.[8] Rather, I mean traditional European philosophy in two aspects (which may of course overlap to some degree with the concerns of 'Diamat'): (a) as the repository for issues of justice, freedom, democracy, happiness, fulfilment, the good life, Ought-questions, etc.; and (b) as traditional epistemology. Later on I will discuss the relationship between these two aspects of philosophy in Marx.

Much of my argument draws on conclusions I have established in my book *Praxis and Method*.[9] There I argued, *inter alia*, that the practical–theoretical social science inaugurated by Marx constituted an early stage of the historical transcendence of philosophy. That is, first, its supersession as the competent discipline to analyse the complex societies in course of formation in Marx's time: the social sciences took on this task. Moreover, secondly, the category of *practice* in Marx provided for the transcendence of philosophy in the other two senses previously mentioned: as wisdom and as traditional epistemology. Putting the matter sociologically, Marx's theories can be seen as a symptom of a stage in a long historical process whereby philosophers have become increasingly defunctionalized. I realize that put baldly in that way, the thesis sounds provocative and declaratory, begging a number of important questions. What has become of the grand questions of philosophy in this transition? Isn't there a job for philosophy as logic? Doesn't philosophy function in certain circumstances as social critique? Isn't philosophy a method? In any case, didn't Pascal say that the minute we doubt philosophy is the minute we begin

---

[8] See Gustav A. Wetter, op. cit.

[9] *Praxis and Method: A Sociological Dialogue with Lukács, Gramsci and the Early Frankfurt School* (London, Boston and Henley: Routledge & Kegan Paul, 1979).

doing it? I have tried to advance a preliminary sociological characterization of this problem elsewhere[10] and I cannot deal directly with these questions in this paper. But the point is that the status and role of philosophy is placed on the agenda as a consequence of the practical character of Marx's theories and by the historical experiences of putting them into practice.

The opposition between theory and practice is used in everyday speech in a variety of ways, as when people say that in theory everyone should have a television licence, but that in practice not everyone has. The terms are also commonly used to refer to the body of principles of proper procedure in a profession, trade or craft, as opposed to their practical application. In the social sciences, as I have said, the dualism refers to a cluster of aspects of the relationship between sciences (particularly social sciences) and practical social life. In Marx's statement[11] that his conception of history 'does not explain practice from the idea but explains the formation of ideas from material practice', we find formulated abstractly what has become the central proposition of the sociology of knowledge. It is not my object to undertake a full-scale classification of these and other usages. This whole area is a prime target for the kind of conceptual clarification which has become the characteristic occupation of modern Anglo-Saxon philosophers in the historical transformation of philosophy I referred to above. (Although such an exercise would, in my view, need to be supplemented by a sociological analysis of the genesis of the various usages of the terms which could explain their interrelatedness, transferences of use from one sphere to another and their connection with wider societal developments.) But even a preliminary glance at the contemporary commonsense and technical meanings in English of the traditional opposition between theory and practice reveals two important features which will be relevant to the later discussion.

First, in virtually all uses of the dualism people usually have in mind practical, lived social life as opposed to abstract ideas, or perhaps action (practice) versus reflection or thinking (theory). This feature points to the opposition in its modern form being a product of the same stage of social development to which also corresponded the dualistic metaphysics of

---

[10] Ibid., especially Part Four. See also Paul Nizan, *The Watchdogs: Philosophers and the Established Order*, translated by Paul Fittingoff (New York and London: Monthly Review Press, 1972); J. M. Cohen, 'Philosophy in the Academy', *Radical Philosophy* (Summer 1972); A. R. Manser, 'The End of Philosophy: Marx and Wittgenstein', Inaugural Lecture, University of Southampton, 1973; and *Metaphilosophy* **8**, Nos. 2 and 3 (April/July 1977) (papers by Nathanson, Becker and Lazerowitz).

[11] Karl Marx and Frederick Engels, *The German Ideology* (1845) (London: Lawrence & Wishart, 1965), 50.

traditional European philosophy after Descartes.[12] That tradition of philosophy also operates with distinctions of a fundamentally similar kind to theory and practice: mind and matter, consciousness and being, thought and reality and ideality and materiality, around which polarities epistemological and ontological debate revolves. (The antithesis theory and practice is also a specifically philosophical polarity.) Its level of abstraction means that a number of theoretical problems, social activities and social phenomena I have mentioned, can be accommodated under the dualism. A further example of this flexibility is that the Marxist philosophers discussed in this paper lump together under the term 'theory' both sides of the sociological enterprise—theory and empirical observations; and 'practice' for them refers loosely to any social activity or circumstances. For the Greek philosophers, by contrast, *theoria* and *praxis* were not separate spheres of thought and action but different walks of life, called by Aristotle the contemplative and the political or practical.[13] I will not be concerned with the Greek writers since for my purposes the proximate origins of Marxist conceptions of the issues identified by the opposition lie in the modern European tradition of philosophy, particularly in the work of Kant and Hegel.

Secondly, and much more speculatively, modern usages sometimes, though not always, also carry a connotation of ideality, which may bespeak the same origin. On the level of method, we find this idealization in formulations of theory such as Max Weber's ideal-types or Boyle's law of gases, both of which refer to ideal states of affairs in society or nature which may not appear in empirical cases (practice). Another kind of idealization occurs when, for example, the opposition of theory to practice refers to principles or rules of proper procedure and their application, where there is often a strong implication present that practice *should* be congruent with theory. Here a state of play between theory and practice is implied which *ought* to exist.

That there is a significant relationship between practical social life and the theories of various kinds which people develop within it, was a legacy of the Enlightenment which was first given a systematic social-scientific formulation by Marx. He enshrined it in his theory of social being and consciousness or base and superstructure. It is epitomized by his frequent

---

[12] Theory, meaning a set of principles of an art or technical subject as distinct from its practice, were first juxtaposed in that sense in English in 1613. The opposition was used to refer to abstract knowledge opposed to practice in 1624. The use of the word 'theory' to refer to a mental scheme or conception of something to be done dates from 1597. The adjective 'practical' was opposed to theoretical, speculative or ideal from 1617 onwards. (*Shorter Oxford Dictionary*.)

[13] Nicholas Lobkowicz, *Theory and Practice: History of a Concept from Aristotle to Marx* (Indiana: Notre Dame University Press, 1967), 3–5.

inversions of the kind of advocating explaining the theory by the practice
and not the practice by the theory or not to look everywhere in history for
the category but to explain the category from real history.[14] It was an
insight developed in a dialogue with idealist philosophers and theologians
who seemed to be suggesting that consciousness was the motor of social
and natural reality. In his time Marx had to fight for the contrary view
against people who thought of practical affairs as in some ways secondary
or vulgar. The concept of the primacy of practical, social conditions in
society and its determinacy in explaining human thinking and action, was
for Marx what Paul Tillich called a *Kampfbegriff*, a polemical concept
born in argument, debate and controversy.[15] It had, obviously, important
political resonances. But Marx's declaration in the *German Ideology*[16]
that 'The premises from which we begin are not arbitrary ones ... but
real premises ... the real individuals, their activity and the material conditions under which they live' is, in social science today, a trusim. But this
characterization does not denigrate Marx. By a process of historical trans-
mission and sedimentation (not solely from Marx, although he is an important exemplar) this fundamental, secular starting point for a social
science is today built into social theory and historiography as an assumption, hardly even in need of being made explicit. Indeed, it may even be
said to have become part of the modern mentality.[17]

Hence, no secular school of social science would deny the general principle of the primacy of the structure of practical, human social relations as
the sole locus for the adequate explanation of the ways in which people
come to develop ideas about those relations, human relations in general
and about the natural world. Today we do not have to ask the question 'Is
human thought determined by the structure of social relations?', but rather
the key question is exactly *how* it is. And the trajectory of what Karl
Mannheim called a sociology of the mind[18] since Marx, has been that the
basic insight has been systematically differentiated and empirical enquiries
undertaken into *kinds* of correspondences between consciousness and
practical social life. The young Marx's remarks on knowledge and action,
on the other hand, were pervaded by a Utopian vision of a self-determining
mankind, creating in *praxis* a more or less total reconciliation of subjectivity

[14] *The German Ideology*, 50.

[15] *The Socialist Decision* (1933), translated by Franklin Sherman (New York:
Harper & Row, 1977), 114.

[16] *The German Ideology*, 31.

[17] See Gunter W. Remmling, *Road to Suspicion: A Study of Modern Mentality
and the Sociology of Knowledge* (Englewood Cliffs, New Jersey: Prentice-Hall,
1967).

[18] *Essays on the Sociology of Culture* (London: Routledge & Kegan Paul,
1956), Part One.

and objectivity and of philosophy and social life. Not surprisingly, he would never be drawn on which relations between 'thought' and 'reality' might remain the same whilst others may change as the result of forms of action. Nor on which were more readily subject to being altered by specified forms of practical activity on various levels.[19] Marx's formulation of the problem is undiscriminating, woolly and abstract. 'Explaining the theory by practice', as another way of referring to the sociology of knowledge, often entails demonstrating empirically that groups of people have been concealing, dissimulating, justifying or in various ways legitimating their activity (which is what one finds in investigating developments in Marxism). But the connection between 'consciousness' and social activity is not necessarily always of this kind. As Norbert Elias has shown, once one makes the necessary differentiations, the sociological approach to explaining the genesis of thought forms need not entail that one asserts relativistically the ideological character of all knowledge, in the sense of all knowledge being reducible to its justifying or rationalizing function in given cases.[20] So, tackling developments in Marxist theory sociologically exemplifies his legacy in modern social thought, which compels us to view him and his successors in this way.

Also, this method has an important advantage. Traditionally, as I have said, Marxists have assumed that if a social theory is true then it will be transcended (abolished) by the practice undertaken on its basis; and if it is not true, then the extent of its error will be revealed by the practice it initiates. I would not be the first to point out that this notion lends itself to powerful political groups legislating by fiat whether or not such a transcendent state of affairs has indeed ensued from a phase of action of one kind or another. Or, conversely, consistent with this conception, powerful groups can easily claim, as a way of legitimating their power, to have special access to a 'correct' theory of social dynamics *prior* to its supposed realization in various kinds of practical activity.[21] In other words, the doctrine of the 'unity of theory and practice' in this sense can have an ideological function. A sociological analysis, however, can potentially better enable us to understand whether either of those two kinds of legitimation is occurring in given cases, something which relying on the self-descriptions of the groups concerned would not. (Although, as I explain in the next section, space does not permit me to undertake this kind of inquiry in this paper.)

[19] Kilminster, *Praxis and Method*, Ch. 2.
[20] 'Sociology of Knowledge: New Perspectives', *Sociology* 5, Nos. 2 and 3 (1971).
[21] Georg Lukács's concept of the 'imputed' consciousness of the proletariat is a doctrine which notably lends itself to the kind of legitimation of power mentioned in the text. See Kilminster, op. cit., Part Two.

Richard Kilminster

II

In looking sociologically at the relations between changes in Marxist theory and modern social developments, there is a balance to be maintained between two aspects of the explanation. That is, between showing how (a) the character of the theory was tailored to particular actions and policies contemplated or being rationalized by the groups concerned; and (b) in each case a relatively autonomous framework—Marx's theory itself—was being employed. In other words, there is, in a given case, an interplay between the needs of the circumstances and the wider structure of assumptions in the theory which the people in those contexts had inherited. Norbert Elias has called these two inseparable levels of inquiry, respectively, knowledge-transcendent and knowledge-immanent developments.[22] Lack of space prevents me from undertaking the first part of the task. (This would involve tracing in detail Marxist theoretical responses to social and political developments such as the collapse of the Second International, the Bolshevization of Russia, the decline of working class revolutionary commitment, Stalinism and the events of 1968.[23]) Instead, I shall concentrate on the second level of the explanation.

In what follows, then, I shall examine the basic structure of Marx's practical–theoretical framework, i.e. the conceptual baggage, as it were, which the later writers and practitioners carried with them. I want to place it further back into its more far-reaching, remote, longer-term structural and historical presuppositions. My aim is to try to detect fundamental, but historically produced, patterns of thinking and assumptions present in Marx's social theory which shape in advance the ways in which society is grasped and, consequently, the way in which the theory is held to relate to practical social life. As a preliminary characterization, I find helpful the time-honoured formulation that Marx's social science was a synthesis of English political economy, French Utopian socialism and German philosophy.[24] Political economy provided the social-scientific concepts

---

[22] Norbert Elias, 'Theory of Science and History of Science', *Economy and Society* 1, No. 2 (May 1972), 132.

[23] See Tom Bottomore, *Marxist Sociology* (London: Macmillan, 1975), and George Lichtheim, *From Marx to Hegel and Other Essays*, (London: Orbach & Chambers, 1971). I would add that a systematic sociological comparison of the three modern historical configurations in which the relations between theory and practice became a burning issue for intellectuals—Germany in the 1840s, the Weimar Republic in the 1920s and Western Europe and the USA in the late 1960s—remains to be undertaken.

[24] V. I. Lenin, *The three sources and three component parts of Marxism* (1913), in Karl Marx and Frederick Engels, *Selected Works in One Volume* (London: Lawrence & Wishart, 1973).

from the most developed social science of the time and Utopian socialism the desirable vision of a classless society of human association and planful co-operation. A 'secularized' version of the Hegelian dialectic united the first two traditions in the notion of the historical necessity of socialism, scientifically shown to be built into history.

From the point of view of epistemology, I think the significance of Marx's use of the category of *practice* is as follows. At the historical stage at which he stood Marx inherited the philosophical vocabulary of traditional European epistemology, mediated to him via the legacy of Kant and Hegel. Following in the wake of Newtonian science, traditional epistemology had a particular cast in which, polarized into rationalists and empiricists, philosophers from Descartes onwards debated the foundations of knowledge in terms of the two sides of cognition: the individual thinking mind and what it experiences. Debates thus circulated around the issues of how the human mind comes to know what it does and what part it and the 'external', mechanical, world, known to humans through the senses, respectively play in the creation of ideas. Some of the characteristic dualisms of the tradition I have already mentioned. The epistemological ones include subject/object, thought/reality, reason/experience, the intellect versus the senses, the ideal and the real and consciousness and being. For Marx, the various positions taken in these debates are epitomized by the polar doctrines of idealism and materialism. Kant and Hegel had both insisted in different ways that consciousness was active in shaping its perception of the world. In the *Theses on Feuerbach* Marx mentions that idealists had stressed this side but says that idealism was, however, out of touch with real sensuous reality. Materialism, on the other hand, stressed that experience was the final arbiter in knowledge and materiality the fundamental stratum of reality. This meant that materialism gave force to the real sensuous world, although materialists tended to regard the mind as passive in the process of cognition.

Utilizing the category of practice, meaning mundane human social activity, Marx argues against materialism in an idealist fashion and against idealism in a materialist fashion, their unity constituted practically.[25] For

---

[25] This formulation is Alfred Schmidt's, from *The Concept of Nature in Marx*, translated by Ben Fowkes (London: New Left Books, 1971), 114. Although, like Marx's remarks on the transcendence of idealism and materialism via the category of practice, it does not separate the epistemological and ontological dimensions in the two doctrines. Consequently, in this respect the text is ambiguous at this point. In Marx, however, the ambiguity may be a product of his attempting to recast the debate in a way which moves away from the older philosophical materialism towards a theory of social mediations in which extra-human nature is independent of human beings but not a final ontological level. (See Schmidt, ibid., Ch. 1 and 113ff.)

Marx, there is no point in reducing cognition to either of its material or ideal poles because both sides are, and always have been, in an active relation in human practical activity. Objective reality is ineradicably subjectively constituted through practice since conscious, labouring mankind is part of Nature. Hence, Nature inevitably has a socially imprinted character and an autonomous role in human affairs at the same time. Human beings only encounter, and hence know, the world through their active contact with it. As Kolakowski has put it, for Marx 'Active contact with the resistance of nature creates knowing man and nature as his object at one and the same time'.[26] In the literature, this world-constituting active sense contact takes another meaning of the term *praxis*. Interestingly, though, Marx is unable to carry through this Hegelian drive away from ontological reductionism and his social theory remains burdened with the dualistic ontology of traditional metaphysics. The sociological theory of base and superstructure, or the determination of social consciousness by 'social being', falls back into the old static dualism, implicitly assuming that the reified economic base and the superstructure of ideology are two separate entities.[27]

As has been pointed out by many philosophers, Marx's practical theory of truth, even if he himself never made it explicit, meant that the classical definition of truth (agreement of concept with reality) was thrown into question. Marx said that if the correspondence of thought and reality, or knowledge and the world, was ongoingly maintained by human practical activity in ordinary life, then the relationship between them was, therefore, subject to being changed by practical activity. In other words, the question of truth as the correspondence between thought and reality could not be settled entirely in theory—it was partly a practical question. (Philosophers have discussed the apparent affinity between Marx's theory of truth and that of pragmatism,[28] but beyond asserting that I do not regard them as comparable, I cannot go further into this interesting question here.[29]) What is important, however, is that since Marx was talking about human practical activity here in a social sense, then the practical aspect of the

---

[26] 'Marxism and the Classical Definition of Truth' in *Marxism and Beyond* (London: Paladin, 1971), 75. See also Ernst Bloch, *On Karl Marx* (New York: Herder and Herder, 1971).

[27] See Kostas Axelos, *Alienation, Praxis and Techne in the Thought of Karl Marx* (Austin and London: University of Texas Press, 1976), 145ff.

[28] See Kolakowski, op. cit.; Stanley Moore, 'Marx and the Origin of Dialectical Materialism', *Inquiry* 14, No. 4 (Winter 1971), 420–429; and Norman D. Livergood in *Activity in Marx's Philosophy* (The Hague: Martinus Nijhoff, 1967).

[29] On the difference between Marx's theory of truth and that of pragmatism I agree with Ernst Bloch (op. cit., 92) that 'for Marx an idea is not true because it is useful, but useful because it is true'.

problem of knowledge as he saw it inevitably began to shade over into politics.

Hence, Marx's (often unsystematic and polemical) ruminations about epistemology in the traditional categories of idealism and materialism, were not just intended as contributions to that field. The whole point of his discussions of materialism and idealism was that various positions defined within that polarity carried with them (once one had switched to regarding socio-natural reality as actively constituted by praxis) *by their very nature*, practical, political implications. The idea that consciousness was cognitively active in real, practical, productive activity, suggested that people could actively move to change the world that their active, practical cognition constituted. This was something which a passive materialist theory could not theorize. Indeed, adherence to such a one-sided theory actually justified a kind of political practice by its epistemological exclusions. For example, the kind of materialist theory which stated that ideas were simply a reflection of the circumstances and environment surrounding people, implied politically that if one changed people's circumstances then they would correspondingly be changed as well. Such a view lent itself to elitist forms of Utopian socialism. Similarly, Marx implicitly links the inherent epistemological individualism of forms of materialism with the individualism of bourgeois liberalism: 'The highest point attained by that materialism which only observes the world . . . is the observation of particular individuals and of civil society'.[30] I will mention shortly how Marx integrates conservatism into this framework.

In the 1840s, when Marx was most concerned to develop a unified theory of society and history which would inform politics, Left Hegelians like Bruno Bauer were rabidly anti-liberal through *critique*. This Hegelian exercise entailed the critical comparison of some aspect of society with its ideal, or perfect potentiality. They would critically compare, for example, a given particular set of judicial institutions with the pure, universal category of Justice, of which the institutions were only an imperfect embodiment; or, say, a particular constitution with the universal idea of Democracy. Marx sees this procedure as ineffective verbal radicalism only, and enjoins 'practical–critical activity'.[31] This would be activity which did not just compare—on the theoretical plane of ethics—reality with what it ideally ought to be, but actually tried to *make* reality accord with what it ought to be, in practice. In this situation, the ought-ridden postulates of philosophy as wisdom would be transcended (abolished) in practice. This is, I think, the force of Marx's dictum 'You cannot transcend philosophy without realizing it and you cannot realize it without

[30] T. B. Bottomore and M. Rubel (eds.), *Karl Marx: Selected Writings in Sociology and Social Philosophy* (Harmondsworth: Penguin, 1967), 84 (*Theses on Feuerbach*).
[31] Ibid., 82.

transcending it'.[32] He is, in effect, talking about creating a society which no longer requires ethics.[33]

In a word, Marx tries to unite epistemology and ethics by yoking together the traditional epistemological doctrines of idealism and materialism with the great ideologies of the nineteenth century—liberalism, conservatism and socialism. The result is, he hoped, a more comprehensive synthesis epistemologically and ethically, the practical, political implications of which refer not to bourgeois society but to the whole of humanity: 'the standpoint of the new materialism is human society or social humanity'.[34] So for Marx mankind makes its own world, which it constitutes by its practical activity, which therefore means that it can potentially consciously change it in various ways. Under conditions of social class fettered historical alienation, however, this constituting process has become lost to consciousness, exacerbated by social life under advanced stages of the division, and alienation, of labour.[35] For sequences of mass action mentioned by Marx whereby the given circumstances of social life and their being consciously changed by people somehow coincide, recent writers have reserved the term *revolutionary praxis*.

The point is that for Marx questions of knowledge and questions of ethics are to be fed into a scientifically informed politics on behalf of the current underprivileged class. Its task is to hasten the historical process towards the idealized state of socialism, which is in any case built into its tendency. What others think merely ought to be (a socialist society) is actually embodied in what is as its *telos*, as Hegel taught. It reaches real, historical maturity whether people have ideals about it or not. The key quotation from Marx about this is:[36]

> Communism is for us not a state of affairs which is to be established, an ideal to which reality will have to adjust itself. We call communism the real movement which abolishes the present state of things.

Another way of putting these matters which will bring out the issues from a different angle, is to see Marx's project, following Rotenstreich,[37]

[32] Paraphrased from the Introduction to the 'Contribution to the Critique of Hegel's *Philosophy of Right* (1843–44), in *Karl Marx: Early Texts*, David McLellan (ed.) (Oxford: Basil Blackwell, 1971), 121–122.

[33] See the contribution to this volume by Steven Lukes.

[34] *Theses on Feuerbach.*

[35] On unresolved tensions and ambiguities in Marx's concept of labour and their consequences for attempts to put his theories into practice, see R. N. Berki 'On the Nature and Origins of Marx's Concept of Labour', *Political Theory* 7, No. 1 (February 1979), 35–56.

[36] *The German Ideology*, 48.

[37] Nathan Rotenstreich, *Theory and Practice: An Essay on Human Intentionalities* (The Hague: Martinus Nijhoff, 1977), 58–82.

as seeking in practical politics the unity of the philosophical realms, theoretical and practical reason. In attempting to reconcile the 'starry heavens above me and the moral law within me', Kant had separated nature and practical reason (ethics) or, more broadly, science and morality. Both theoretical and practical reason were spontaneous aspects of Reason, the former the domain of categories which limited knowledge and the latter the domain of ethical imperatives, a practical sphere separate and alongside the reality of nature. Hegel, however, claimed, against Kant, that the world is knowable because it is inherently rational. Reason has complete spontaneity on the intellectual plane as Kant had said, but this only made reality knowable because the object was the objective embodiment of Reason anyway. The embodiment of Reason in the world meant that it could be demonstrated that history was its gradual teleological unfolding in various spheres as determinations of the Idea. But it also meant that practical reason (ethics) could not be maintained as a separate sphere on the Kantian model, because, like Reason in general, it must also be embodied in the world as well. So, for Hegel, there was no need to assure the actualization of Reason in practical life by the creation of a separate Kantian ethical sphere: the level of speculation in his system assured their unity.

But for Marx, the Young Hegelians who embraced this position could only put to real people in real societies the 'moral postulate of exchanging their present consciousness for human, critical . . . consciousness'.[38] In other words, there was no passage from the achieved level of speculation to the practical realization of the unity of Reason in the world. The Young Hegelians were the 'staunchest conservatives'.[39] For Marx, however, history is the arena for the practical actualization of Reason. This translates into the proposition (expressed as the development of the forces of production outstripping their necessary relations of production) that in practice people must realize the inherent rational potentiality for social organization, development and progress spontaneously bequeathed to the bourgeois epoch. It is this potential which is fettered by archaic social class relations, necessitating revolutionary change. In my view, Marx's whole theory of history as a series of progressive socio-economic formations is predicated on the assumption that they have been mediated by their necessary *telos* of socialism as the end to the alienated 'pre-history' of mankind. Indeed, the Hegelian version is seen by Marx as a 'metaphysically travestied'[40] version of what is a real, scientifically describable, historical process. The forces and relations of production dialectic in Marx parallels Hegel's categorial unity of content and form, whereby it is the developing *content*

---

[38] *The German Ideology*, 30. See also 276, 282 and 290.
[39] Ibid., 30.
[40] Karl Marx and Frederick Engels, *The Holy Family* (1845) translated by R. Dixon (Moscow: Progress Publishers, 1956), 164.

(forces of production) which determines changes of *form* (relations of production) towards the self-development of the Idea (socialism). Once Marx has translated the Hegelian conception of history as the embodiment and realization of Reason into the terms of a socio-economic theory of development, then the theory articulating the process and a moral indictment of society were for him necessarily the same thing.

III

By way of an epilogue, I will briefly discuss some of the implications of the questions dealt with in this paper and highlight some problem areas. Changes in Marxist theory in Europe this century have been conditioned by many social developments, events, practical exigencies and policies, which the theories have in various ways reflected, legitimated or rationalized. At the same time, the theory which the various protagonists brought to bear on those situations contained more remote, longer-term presuppositions which go back a long way in the development of European societies. These fundamental, but historically produced, patterns of thinking shape in advance the ways in which society is conceptualized and, consequently, the ways in which the theory was held to relate to practical social life. When one is assessing the degree of success and consequences of attempts to put Marx's theories into practice, both these two levels—the circumstances and the basic structure of assumptions in the theory—must be taken into account.

The framework of practical–theoretical social science handed down by Marx was permeated with the traditional philosophy in a dialogue with which it had been forged, both epistemologically and ethically. Marx reconciles idealism and materialism on the plane of social practice but still refers to his synthesis by the metaphysical term 'materialism.' The dualistic social theory of base and superstructure reproduces the being and consciousness polarity of traditional metaphysics; and the notion of active subjective cognition indissolubly constituting its objects in practice is still a resolution of the subject–object problem within the duality itself. (Lukács' later vision of proletarian class consciousness overthrowing 'the objective form of its object' and constituting the identical subject–object of history, is a view of the possibilities of mass human action profoundly steeped in these presuppositions.) And, finally, Marx's attempt to unite the traditional philosophical dualism of idealism and materialism with socialism, conservatism and liberalism in order to link epistemology and ethics in politics, carried forward a particular epistemological–political synthesis. This established for later generations within the Marxist tradition the idea that various philosophical positions about the nature of ideas defined in terms of sense perception were somehow significantly related to political ideologies.

Marx had already tried to sublate debate within the categories of idealism and materialism by reference to social practice, but he was unable to consummate the break, remaining burdened with the philosophical heritage he was trying to overcome. Like Comte and St Simon, Marx was grappling with the important problems of how a theory of society was related to human social development, its subject matter, and what were the practical implications of types of social theory. He shared with them also the Enlightenment view that an adequate theory of society facilitates the practical steering of social processes for the benefit of mankind. Because of the stage at which he stood, however, he could only articulate the problem with the traditional epistemological vocabulary available to him, synthesized with the great nineteenth century ideologies. The epistemology had been a product of philosophers ruminating upon the implications of Newtonian science for human knowledge, as well as the kind of self-awareness associated with that stage of the civilizing process (Elias);[41] and the ideologies related to the stage of development of social class antagonisms Marx was living through. Today, however, we have to ask ourselves whether we can any longer relevantly pose the general problem of the relation between theories of various kinds and practical social life (traditionally identified as issues of theory and practice) in those terms. If not, then the problem has to be thought out in a different way.

Marx was only able to incorporate ethics into his practical–theoretical framework by paying the price of teleology. He translated the Hegelian conception of the historical realization of Reason embodied in the world into a historical, dialectical progression of socio-economic epochs preparing mankind for the ideal state of socialism. He thus wrote the Utopian ideal of socialist equality, freedom and human co-operative association, which others merely thought desirable, or for the lack of which they indicted bourgeois society in moral terms, into the real movement of history and claimed this process to be scientifically demonstrable. Later on, in the 1920s, it was the removal from Marx's theory of this supposition that social reality was inherently meaningful and rational in its tendency towards what society Ought to be, which gave rise to the problem for Marxists of how to re-incorporate this ethical level into a social science denuded of historical necessity.

In non-Marxist forms of social enquiry today it is common to find a pre-Hegelian logical separation of matters of fact from questions of value, of Is and Ought, science and morality and factual and normative questions, enshrined in the different disciplines of sociology and social philosophy. These separations are not only regarded as logically or methodologically

---

[41] Norbert Elias, *The Civilizing Process*, I (Oxford: Basil Blackwell, 1978). See also *Human Figurations*, Peter R. Gleichmann, Johan Goudsblom and Hermann Korte (ed) (Amsterdam: Sociologisch Tijdschrift, 1977).

sound, but also as providing a bulwark against the abuse of the supposed Marxian fusion of Is and Ought by bureaucratic socialist elites who have justified directive and totalitarian practices by claiming that their policies are based in a correct scientific analysis of historical development and are thus also morally right. It is significant that in Eastern Europe philosophy often serves the function of critique under conditions of generalized censorship and repression, with the considerable development of philosophies of value and philosophical anthropology, ultimately designed to develop criteria for indicting the social order.

To return more specifically to Marx, the image of man built into the theory was a correspondingly rationalistic one. Human beings should be self-determining, self-conscious and freed from the constraints of social alienation. It is an image of people as knowing, choosing and acting, but not as also affective, constrained and interdependent. Later followers of Marx have striven to realize that one-sided, idealized model of man in practice, or it is an image which implicitly guides their social-scientific enquiries. They generally, therefore, fail to take cognizance of the fact that observations of people living in real societies at various stages of development suggest that social life would be impossible without some social constraints, in the broadest sense.[42] Consequently, one finds a tendency in Marxist writings, stemming from the assumptions of the theory they inherit, to champion more or less total human freedom as a political goal The more realistic question as to *how far* this is possible is seldom asked. (I think Habermas has realized this, but I will mention him in a moment.)

Marx's theory, then, defines methodologically the relevant theoretical problems, shapes the way in which theories are seen as related to social life, moulds in advance the parameters of sociological enquiry and delimits in a characteristic way the questions which can be put to society. First, methodologically speaking, the inherently dualistic character of the theory has inevitably led to the problem of how to resolve the reciprocal effectivity of 'ideal' and 'material' factors in the historical process, 'material' having been linked by Marx with economic activity. This characteristic has thus *structured* later inquiries into adaptations and sophistications of the base and superstructure model.[43] But these elaborations still reproduce the

[42] See Norbert Elias, 'Sociology and Psychiatry' in S. H. Foulkes and G. Stewart Prince (eds), *Psychiatry in a Changing Society* (London: Tavistock, 1969), and 'Problems of Involvement and Detachment', *British Journal of Sociology* **7** (1956), 226–252.

[43] See Raymond Williams, 'Base and Superstructure in Marxist Cultural Theory', *New Left Review* No. 82 (Nov–Dec. 1973); Jeff Coulter, 'Marxism and the Engels Paradox' in *The Socialist Register* 1971, R. Miliband and J. Saville (eds) London: Merlin; and Zygmunt Bauman, 'Praxis: The Controversial Culture–Society Paradigm', in *The Rules of the Game: Cross-Disciplinary Essays on Models in Scholarly Thought*, Teodor Shanin (ed.), (London: Tavistock, 1972).

fundamentally metaphysical structure of the theory and thus remain trapped within its basic antinomy. Secondly, even though the practical questions asked by the later Marxist practitioners related closely to the circumstances they lived through, the way they interpreted their society was determined by the framework's basic assumptions. It induced its adherents into asking questions such as: What is preventing 'the revolution' from taking place, given that the level of social development seems apposite? What are the cultural mechanisms whereby working class consciousness is systematically dismantled? Is there a substitute proletariat to be seen? And against the proposition that political activity should be geared towards the goal of the revolutionary victory of the proletariat which will usher in socialism, all other activity towards, for example, minimizing social inequality or social constraints can only be described as reformism. Revolution versus reform is an antinomy which flows directly from a theory which assumes that practical activity can hasten the arrival of an idealized state of equality said to be embodied in the historical process.

The two examples of Adorno and Habermas will illustrate my general point. In both cases we see the fascinating interplay between the social developments they are responding to and the presuppositions of the theory they are bringing to bear on them. Adorno justified his doggedly philosophical stance after the late 30s because the historical opportunity of the emancipation of mankind by the revolutions of the proletariat (the realization of philosophy) had been 'missed'.[44] As a result, he was condemned to maintain a 'negative' critique of society which shows the existing order as perennially capable of becoming something other than it is. This philosophizing keeps alive the possibility of emancipation. This strategy still assumed, however, that 'the revolution' *should* have occurred and that *if it had done so* it would have liberated mankind. It therefore took seriously, as a real possibility, social consequences predicted by the mythological strand in Marx's thought, i.e. the practical fusion of Is and Ought in a future world of human association for which history had been preparing humanity. Once one has made that assumption, then its non-arrival leads to the conviction that the idealized sequence is more real than the empirical reality and something to which reality must ultimately adjust itself. But if it is held that the moment to realize human emancipation has been lost, then we have in this position a kind of theological picture that in the present conditions man is living, if not in a fallen state, then certainly in purgatory. The result is a tragic pessimism and nihilism.

In the work of Habermas we can see how he operates within the inertia of the Marxist tradition and takes up from Adorno the redefinition of the

---

[44] Theodor W. Adorno, *Negative Dialectics*, translated by E. B. Ashton (London: Routledge & Kegan Paul, 1973), 3.

problems of theory and practice after Stalinism, fascism and the thesis of the disenchantment of the world elaborated by philosophers in modern times.[45] I will take up only one aspect of his later work in order to illustrate the point I am making about the presuppositions of the Marxist framework; that is, the notion of the ideal speech situation.[46] Built into all individual speech acts, he says, is the assumption that one can be understood by potential interlocutors who are equal partners in discourse. This is a transcendental presupposition for all communication. This idealized state of affairs is, however, no mere abstract Utopia, for it is partly present now, in society, in every individual speech act. It is, therefore, not an arbitrary postulate of a total community of equality, for it is already, as it were, partly realized. The postulate thus provides a critical yardstick for objectively evaluating given societies as only providing conditions of 'distorted communication' compared with those of the ideal speech situation, which those instances of distorted communication also *are*. In this respect, at least, Habermas's work constitutes the reappearance of Left Hegelian critique in a modern guise. The ideal-speech situation corresponds to Hegel's *telos* of self-knowing Reason embodied as universality in all particularity, which was reworked by Marx as the Utopian tendency of history. Habermas has grounded more systematically Adorno's later Hegelian stress on the 'Utopian moment of the object' and his crusade against 'identity thinking' as the means of negatively criticizing what is in terms of what it could ideally be.[47]

The point is that the Marxist tradition itself, as adapted to twentieth century conditions, provides the framework which has posed the problems and the parameters of their solutions. Critical theory and critical sociology reproduce the Marxist socialist theory but without the original agent, the proletariat, and without the original catalyst, the party. The result is that the critical theory remaining after those excisions must necessarily have to replace the old *telos* of history with an idealized state of affairs which *cannot* be realized.

There are four reasons for this. (a) The Utopia cannot any longer be justified as the outcome of historical necessity. The critical theorists are

[45] See F. H. Heinemann, *Existentialism and the Modern Predicament* (London: Adam and Charles Black, 1953), and George Steiner, *Heidegger* (London: Fontana/Collins, 1978), Chs. II and III.

[46] Jürgen Habermas, 'Toward a Theory of Communicative Competence' in Hans Peter Dreitzel (ed.) *Recent Sociology No. 2* (New York: Macmillan 1970) and *Communication and the Evolution of Society* (London: Heinemann, 1979), Ch. 1.

[47] See Gillian Rose, 'How is Critical Theory Possible? Theodor W. Adorno and Concept Formation in Sociology', *Political Studies* **24**, No. 1 (1976).

'modernists' who, following Weber and the existentialists, know that since the Middle Ages European societies have become increasingly depleted of inherent religious meaning. After the death of God, the Marxist concept of historical necessity only reproduces Christian theology in a secular form, with socialism taking the place of heaven. In any case, the moment to realize this outcome was missed. Moreover, historical necessity was associated with orthodox, bureaucratic, positivistic Marxism, which was at least a necessary condition for Stalinism.[48] (b) Suggesting that there was a *real* possibility of the realization of any idealized state would lend itself to abuse by bureaucratic socialist elites in practice because it would give them the theoretical means by which to claim that a given society *was* its embodiment. This would thus preclude further social critique since the standard had been proclaimed as realized. The ideal speech situation, however, although present in all individual speech acts, is never totally realizable. Habermas has implicitly developed the later Marx's acknowledgment of the perennial 'realm of necessity' in human affairs, which the early Frankfurt School enshrined as the notion of the necessity of some form of alienation in society;[49] and there is a distant echo in this aspect of his work of the existentialists' insistence that both authenticity *and* inauthenticity are distinctive, necessary and irreducible modes of existence.[50] Consequently, his theory entails that conditions maintaining some distorted communication must, dialectically, *always* be present for the ideal-speech situation to have any existence and critical purchase. Indeed, it is this state which sustains for humanity's good positivism as instrumental reason. (c) More remotely, the inertia of the socialist tradition perpetuates an early nineteenth century rationalistic image of human fraternity which implicitly guides the inquiry. (d) Lastly, at a deeper conceptual level, the work is permeated with the philosophical categories of European rationalism, particularly the philosophies of Kant and Hegel, which have left behind in social science and European culture in general, a profoundly idealizing mode of thought.

The result of all these factors is that the socialist Utopia here had to become a postulate, a possibility, grounded in some way that was more amenable to empirical reference than the Hegelian dialectics of Adorno and in a way which provided a non-arbitrary, objective criterion of social critique which had more power than mere moralizing. The answer lay

[48] See Zygmunt Bauman, *Socialism: The Active Utopia* (London: Allen & Unwin, 1975).

[49] Kilminster, op. cit., Ch. 14.

[50] See George Steiner, op. cit.,; and Deena Weinstein and Michael A. Weinstein, 'An Existential Approach to Society: Active Transcendence', *Human Studies* 1, No. 1 (1978).

in the ideal speech situation, knowable in theory but by definition un-realizable in practice.[51]

University of Leeds

[51] I am grateful to Aidan Foster-Carter, Ahmed Gurnah and Alan Scott for many stimulating discussions of this paper and to Zygmunt Bauman and Bill Rees for detailed comments on an earlier draft.

Marxism, Morality and Justice

STEVEN LUKES

A paradox, according to the OED, is 'a statement seemingly self-contra-dictory or absurd, though possibly well-founded or essentially true'. In this article I shall try to show that the classical orthodox Marxist view of morality is a paradox. I shall seek to resolve the paradox by trying to show that it is only seemingly self-contradictory or absurd. But I shall not claim the standard Marxist view of morality to be well-founded or essentially true. On the contrary, I shall suggest that, though coherent, it is ill-founded and illusory.

To this end, I shall first illustrate the highly distinctive position that Marxism has always taken towards morality in general and justice in particular. I shall then try to analyse and explain the recurring pattern which emerges from this inquiry, namely, a paradoxical, seemingly contra-dictory attitude to morality. From this analysis it will, I hope, emerge in what sense Marxism has a moral point of view and in what sense it does not.

I

There is a certain pattern of argument relating to morality which con-stantly reappears throughout the history of Marxism: one set of positions, central to Marxism, when set beside another set of positions, no less central, appears to generate a striking contradiction. On the one hand, it is claimed that morality is a form of ideology, that any given morality always arises out of a particular stage of the development of productive forces and relations and is always relative to a particular mode of production and particular class interests, that there are no eternal truths of morality, that the very form of morality, and general ideas such as freedom and justice, that are 'common to all states of society' cannot 'completely vanish except with the total disappearance of class antagonisms',[1] that Marxism is opposed to all moralizing and that the Marxist critique of both capitalism and political economy is not moral but scientific. On the other hand, as has often been pointed out, Marxist writings are full of moral judgments, both implicit and explicit. From his earliest writings, where Marx expresses his hatred of servility through the discussions of alienation in the *Paris Manuscripts* and the *German Ideology* to the excoriating attacks on factory

---

[1] Marx and Engels, *The Communist Manifesto. Collected Works*, VI (London: Lawrence & Wishart, 1975), 504.

conditions and inequalities in *Capital*, it is plain that Marx was fired by outrage and indignation and the burning desire for a better world that it is hard not to see as moral. The same applies to Engels, author of *The Condition of the Working Class in England*, a work full of moral condemnation of the social conditions created by advancing industrial capitalism, which remained basic to his thought.[2] And the same surely applies to their followers down to the present day. And it is clear that, at least in capitalist societies, most people become Marxists for mainly moral reasons.

In illustrating this paradoxical pattern, let us begin with Marx. In the *German Ideology* he and Engels wrote of 'Morality, religion, metaphysics, all the rest of ideology and their corresponding forms of consciousness' that they 'no longer retain the semblance of independence. They have no history, no development but men, altering their material production and their material intercourse alter—along with these—their real existence and their thinking and the products of their thinking.'[3] The communists, they wrote,

> do not preach *morality* at all, as Stirner does so extensively. They do not put to people the moral demand: love one another, do not be egoists, etc.; on the contrary, they are very well aware that egoism, just as much as selflessness, is in definite circumstances a necessary form of the self-assertion of individuals.[4]

One central part of their objection to the moral vocabulary of the 'true socialists' attacked in the *German Ideology*, foreshadowing later attacks by Kautsky, Luxemburg and Lenin on 'ethical socialists', was clear:

> In reality, the actual property owners stand on the one side and the propertyless communist proletarians on the other. This opposition becomes keener day by day and is rapidly driving to a crisis. If, then, the theoretical representatives of the proletariat wish their literary activity to have any effect, they must first and foremost insist that all phrases are dropped which tend to dim the realization of the sharpness of this opposition, all phrases which tend to conceal this opposition and may

[2] And which Marx endorsed, as when he wrote: 'The moral degradation caused by the capitalistic exploitation of women and children has been so exhaustively depicted by F. Engels ... and other writers, that I need only mention the subject in this place. But the intellectual desolation artificially produced by converting immature human beings into mere machines for the fabrication of surplus value ... finally compelled even the English Parliament to make elementary education a compulsory condition ... ' Marx, *Capital*, I (Moscow: Foreign Languages Publishing House, 1959), 399–400.

[3] Marx and Engels, *The German Ideology, Collected Works*, V; 36–37 (amended translation—S.L.).

[4] Ibid., 247.

even give the bourgeoisie a chance to approach the communists for safety's sake on the strength of their philanthropic enthusiasms ... it is ... necessary to resist all phrases which obscure and dilute still further the realization that communism is totally opposed to the existing world order.[5]

As for communism, it was 'not for us a *state of affairs* which is to be established, an ideal to which reality [will] have to adjust itself. We call communism the *real* movement which abolishes the present state of things. The conditions of this movement result from the now existing premises.'[6] Moral thinking, in effect, stemmed from a cognitive inadequacy that was itself historically determined and only surmountable at a certain stage of historical development:

It was only possible to discover the connection between the kinds of enjoyment open to individuals at any particular time and the class relations in which they live, and the conditions of production and intercourse which give rise to these relations, the narrowness of the hitherto existing forms of enjoyment, which were outside the actual content of the life of people and in contradiction to it, the connection between every philosophy of enjoyment and the enjoyment actually present and the hypocrisy of such a philosophy which treated all individuals without distinction—it was, of course, only possible to discover all this when it became possible to criticize the conditions of production and intercourse in the hitherto-existing world, that is, when the contradiction between the bourgeoisie and the proletariat had given rise to communist and socialist views. That shattered the basis of all morality, whether the morality of asceticism or of enjoyment.[7]

Marx maintained these positions throughout his life. It is true that in 1864 he helped draft the General Rules of the International Working Men's Association, whose members were enjoined to acknowledge 'truth, justice, and morality, as the basis of their conduct towards each other and towards all men, without regard to colour, creed, or nationality', and the principle of '*no rights without duties, no duties without rights*', while the struggle for the emancipation of the working classes is described as a struggle 'for equal rights and duties, and the abolition of all class rule'.[8] Moreover, in his Inaugural Address, Marx urged workers to 'vindicate

---

[5] Ibid., 469.
[6] Ibid., 49.
[7] Ibid., 418–419.
[8] *General Rules of the International Working Men's Association: Preamble* (1864), Marx and Engels, *Selected Works*, I, (Moscow: Foreign Languages Publishing House, 1962), 386–389.

the simple laws of morals and justice, which ought to govern the relations of private individuals, as the rules paramount of the intercourse of nations'.[9] On the other hand, he explained these unfortunate phrases in a letter to Engels of 4 November 1864: 'I was obliged', he wrote, 'to insert two phrases about "duty" and "right" into the preamble, ditto, "truth, morality and justice", but these are placed in such a way that they can do no harm'.[10]

In *Capital*, Marx scorns Proudhon's appeal to an ideal of justice. What opinion, he asks,

> should we have of a chemist, who, instead of studying the actual laws of the molecular changes in the composition and decomposition of matter, and on that foundation solving definite problems, claimed to regulate the composition and decomposition of matter by means of 'eternal ideas', of 'naturalité' and 'affinité'? Do we really know any more about 'usury' when we say it contradicts 'justice éternelle', 'équité éternelle', 'mutualité éternelle', and other 'vérités éternelles' than the fathers of the church did when they said it was incompatible with 'grace éternelle', 'foi éternelle' and 'le volonté éternelle de Dieu'?[11]

And in the *Critique of the Gotha Programme* he once more makes clear his rejection of moral vocabulary:

> I have dealt more at length with . . . 'equal right' and 'fair distribution' . . . in order to show what a crime it is to attempt, on the one hand, to force on our Party again, as dogmas, ideas which in a certain period had some meaning but have now become obsolete verbal rubbish, while again perverting, on the other, the realistic outlook, which it cost so much effort to instil into the Party but which has now taken root in it, by means of ideological nonsense about right (*Recht*) and other trash so common among the democrats and French Socialists.[12]

Morality had at best a purely derivative role to play in the analysis of capitalist relations and the explanation of social change. In his *Ethnological Note-books*, Marx annotates a passage in which Henry Sumner Maine writes of 'the vast mass of forces, which we may call for shortness *moral*'

---

[9] *Inaugural Address of the Working Men's International Association*, Marx and Engels, *Selected Works*, I, 385.

[10] Mark and Engels, *Selected Correspondence* (Moscow: Foreign Languages Publishing House, n.d.), 182.

[11] Marx, *Capital*, I, 84–85.

[12] Marx, *Critique of the Gotha Programme*, *Selected Works*, II, 15.

which 'perpetually shapes, limits or forbids the actual direction of the forces of society by its Sovereign'. Marx comments that

> this 'moral' shows how little Maine understands of the matter; as far as these influences (*economical* before everything else) possess [a] 'moral' modus of existence, this is always derived, secondary modus and never the prius.[13]

Finally, a passage in *The Civil War in France* sums up Marx's continuing denial of the relevance of utopias and ideals to working class action. The working class, he wrote,

> have no ready-made utopias to introduce *par décret du peuple*. They know that in order to work out their own emancipation, and along with it that higher form to which present society is irresistibly tending by its own economical agencies, they will have to pass through long struggles, through a series of historic processes, transforming circumstances and men. They have no ideals to realize, but to set free elements of the new society with which old collapsing bourgeois society itself is pregnant.[14]

On the other hand, as this last quotation shows, this new society was clearly seen as a 'higher form' of society, characterized, in the Tenth Thesis on Feuerbach, as '*human* society, or associated humanity'.[15] As is well known, Marx in turn divided that higher form into two phases, a lower and a higher, which Lenin christened socialism and communism respectively. The former abolishes exploitation but not yet exchange; the latter—full communism—represents Marx's ultimate ideal. It has recently been plausibly argued[16] that its superiority over socialism, or the lower phase, rests for Marx on moral and philosophical principles, derived from Feuerbach in the *Economic and Philosophical Manuscripts* and from Hegel in the *Critique of the Gotha Programme* and *Capital*. Of course, Marx's descriptions of post-capitalist society are extremely thin and scattered throughout his writings. It appears from an 1851 outline of what was to become *Capital* that he intended to present his views about communism in a systematic manner in a final volume. As it was, he never wrote what

---

[13] *The Ethnological Notebooks of Karl Marx* (Studies of Morgan, Phear, Maine, Lubbock) translated and edited with an introduction by Lawrence Krader (Assen: Van Gorcum & Co., 1972), 329.

[14] Marx, *The Civil War in France, Selected Works*, I, 523.

[15] Marx, *Theses on Feuerbach, Collected Works*, V, 8.

[16] By Stanley Moore in his *Marx on the Choice between Socialism and Communism* (Cambridge and London: Harvard University Press, 1980).

Engels in a letter to him described as 'the famous "positive", what you "really" want'.[17]

What is clear is that the ideal society to which Marx expectantly looked forward would be one in which, under conditions of abundance, human beings can achieve self-realization in a new, transparent form of social unity, in which nature, both physical and social, comes under their control. What is wealth, he asks, 'other than the universality of individual needs, capacities, pleasures, productive forces, etc., created through universal exchange? The full development of human mastery over the forces of nature, those of so-called nature as well as of humanity's own nature?'[18] In *Capital* he describes production in such a society as consisting in

> socialized man, the associated producers, rationally regulating their interchange with Nature, bringing it under their common control, instead of being ruled by it as by the blind forces of Nature; and achieving this with the least expenditure of energy and under conditions most favourable to, and worthy of, human nature.[19]

Beyond this sphere of production, which 'still remains a realm of necessity', there begins that development of human energy which is an end in itself, the true realm of freedom, which, however, can blossom forth only with this realm of necessity as its basis.[20] Such a society is variously described by Marx in terms of true freedom, as the overcoming of alienation and the realization of the human essence or human nature, and in utilitarian terms of welfare and happiness. Above all, however, he seems always to have linked three central ideas together: (1) the self-realization of individuals, the full development of their essentially human powers, of the 'rich individuality which is as all-sided in its production as in its consumption, and whose labour also therefore appears no longer as labour';[21] (2) the establishing of new, harmonious and rational social relations which involves the abolition of 'the contradiction between the interest of the separate individual or the individual family and the common interest of all individuals who have intercourse with one another', which in turn involves abolishing the division of labour and private property;[22] and (3) a prior

[17] Marx and Engels, *Briefwechsel* (Berlin, 1949), 348, cited by B. Ollman in a helpful essay on 'Marx's Vision of Communism' in B. Ollman, *Social and Sexual Revolution* (Boston: South End Press, 1979).

[18] Marx, *Grundrisse: Foundations of the Critique of Political Economy* (Rough Draft), translated by Martin Nicolaus (Harmondsworth: Penguin Books in conjunction with *New Left Review*, 1973), 488.

[19] Marx, *Capital*, III, (Moscow: Foreign Languages Publishing House, 1962), 799–800.

[20] Ibid.

[21] Marx, *Grundrisse*, 325.

[22] Marx and Engels, *The German Ideology, Collected Works*, V, 46–47.

history of 'total alienation' in which the productive forces are developed by means of a 'sacrifice of the human end-in-itself to an entirely external end',[23] in which 'man's own deed becomes an alien power opposed to him which enslaves him instead of being controlled by him'.[24] The linkage of these three ideas is well brought out in the following passage from the *Grundrisse*:

> Universally developed individuals, whose social relations, as their own communal (*gemeinschaftlich*) relations, are hence also subordinated to their own communal control, are no product of nature, but of history. The degree and the universality of the development of wealth where *this* individuality becomes possible supposes production on the basis of exchange values as a prior condition, whose universality produces not only the alienation of the individual from himself and from others, but also the universality and the comprehensiveness of his relations and capacities.[25]

Marx's projected future coincided with this ideal of a higher form of 'human society' to which he saw humanity as imminently progressing. He made the claim in a letter to Ruge, that 'we do not anticipate the world dogmatically, but rather wish to find the new world through the criticism of the old'.[26] But that claim, and his belief that the new order was latent in the womb of the old, does not make his ideal and his criticism any the less evaluative and, in one sense, moral. And indeed his life's work is full of critical judgments that only make sense against the background of the ideal of social unity and individual self-realization to which we have just alluded. Hence for example all the passages about the stunting effects of the division of labour under capitalism on the labourer, enabling him to achieve 'only a one-sided, crippled development',[27] or the way the capitalist mode of production in producing surplus value confronts 'the labourer as powers of capital rendered independent, and standing in direct opposition therefore to the labourer's own development'.[28] Hence the many passages decrying gross inequality: the bourgeois are 'indifferent to the sufferings of the proletarians who help them acquire wealth',[29] the proletariat 'has to bear all the burdens of society without enjoying its

---

[23] Marx, *Grundrisse*, 487–488.
[24] Marx and Engels, *The German Ideology, Collected Works*, V, 47.
[25] Marx, *Grundrisse*, 162.
[26] *Writings of the Young Marx on Philosophy and Society*, translated and edited by L. D. Easton and K. H. Guddat (New York, 1967), 212.
[27] Marx and Engels, *The German Ideology, Collected Works*, V, 262.
[28] Marx, *Capital*, III, 858–859.
[29] Marx, *The Poverty of Philosophy, Collected Works*, VI, 176.

Steven Lukes

advantages',[30] and capitalism involves 'coercion and monopolization of social development (including material and intellectual advantages) by one portion of society at the expense of the other'.[31] And hence the sceptical treatment of bourgeois claims that free competition is the ultimate development of human freedom, on the grounds that

> it is nothing more than free development on a limited basis—the basis of the rule of capital. This kind of individual freedom is therefore at the same time the most complete suspension of all individual freedom, and the most complete subjugation of individuality under social conditions which assume the form of objective powers, even of overpowering objects—of things independent of the relations among individuals themselves.[32]

How, indeed, can one fail to see the moral force of all these passages, and of those in which Marx speaks of machinery 'transforming the workman, from his very childhood, into a part of a detail-machine', a 'lifeless mechanism independent of the workman, who becomes its mere living appendage' so that 'factory work exhausts the nervous system to the uttermost [and] does away with the many sided play of the muscles, and confiscates every atom of freedom, both in bodily and intellectual activity?[33] Under the capitalist mode of production according to Marx, 'the labourer exists to satisfy the needs of self-expansion of existing values, instead of, on the contrary, material wealth existing to satisfy the needs of development on the part of the labourer'.[34] Consider finally the following passage from *Capital* about the production of relative surplus value within the capitalist system:

> all methods for raising the social productiveness of labour are brought about at the cost of the individual labourer; all means for the development of production transform themselves into means of domination over, and exploitation of, the producers; they mutilate the labourer into the fragment of a man, degrade him to the level of an appendage of a machine, destroy every remnant of charm in his work and turn it into a hated toil, they estrange from him the intellectual potentialities of the labour process in the same proportion as science is incorporated in it as an independent power, they distort the conditions under which he works, subject him during the labour process to a despotism the more hateful for its meanness; they transform his life-time into working-time,

[30] Marx and Engels, *The German Ideology*, Marx and Engels, *Collected Works*, VI, 52.
[31] Marx, *Capital*, III, 819.
[32] Marx, *Grundrisse*, 652.
[33] Marx, *Capital*, I, 422.
[34] Ibid., I, 621.

and drag his wife and child beneath the wheels of the Juggernaut of capital . . . Accumulation of wealth at one pole is . . . at the same time accumulation of misery, agony of toil, slavery, ignorance, brutality, mental degradation, at the opposite pole, i.e. on the side of the class that produces its own product in the form of capital.[35]

As for Engels, he wrote this in *Anti-Dühring*:

We therefore reject every attempt to impose on us any moral dogma whatsoever as an eternal, ultimate and for ever immutable ethical law on the pretext that the moral world, too, has its permanent principles which stand above history and the differences between nations. We maintain on the contrary that all moral theories have been hitherto the product, in the last analysis, of the economic conditions of society obtaining at the time. And as society has hitherto moved in class antagonisms, morality has always been class morality; it has either justified the domination and the interests of the ruling class, or, ever since the oppressed class became powerful enough, it has represented its indignation against this domination and the future interests of the oppressed.[36]

Of equality, he wrote that 'the idea of equality, both in its bourgeois and its proletarian form, is . . . itself a historical product, the creation of which required definite historical conditions that in turn themselves presuppose a long previous history. It is therefore anything but an eternal truth.' Of justice, he remarked that

According to the laws of bourgeois economics, the greatest part of the product does *not* belong to the workers who have produced it. If we now say: that is unjust, that ought not to be so, then that has nothing immediately to do with economics. We are merely saying that this economic fact is in contradiction to our sense of morality. Marx, therefore, never based his communist demands upon this, but upon the inevitable collapse of the capitalist mode of production which is daily taking place before our eyes to an ever greater degree . . . [37]

Justice, Engels wrote, attacking Proudhon, is 'but the ideologized, glorified expression of the existing economic relations, at times from their conservative, and at other times from their revolutionary side':

While in everyday life, in view of the simplicity of the relations discussed, expressions like right, wrong, justice and sense of right are accepted

---

[35] Ibid., I, 645.

[36] F. Engels, *Anti-Dühring* (Moscow: Foreign Languages Publishing House, 1959), 131.

[37] Preface by Engels to the first German Edition of Marx, *The Poverty of Philosophy* (Moscow: Progress Publishers, 1978), 13.

without misunderstanding even with reference to social matters, they create, as we have seen, the same hopeless confusion in any scientific investigation of economic relations as would be created, for instance, in modern chemistry if the terminology of the phlogiston theory were to be retained.[38]

Moreover, just before his death, Engels wrote a letter decrying attempts to specify details about communism: to do so, he wrote, was impossible 'without falling into utopianism or empty phrasemaking'.[39]

And yet, on the other hand, Engels also wrote in *Anti-Dühring* of 'the proletarian morality of the future', as containing 'the maximum elements promising permanence'; and he also argued the claim that

> there has on the whole been progress in morality, as in all other branches of human knowledge, no one will doubt. But we have not yet passed beyond class morality. A really human morality which stands above class antagonisms and above any recollection of them becomes possible only at a stage of society which has not only overcome class antagonisms but has even forgotten them in practical life.[40]

In earlier speeches and writings, Engels had certainly been prepared to sketch the outlines of such a society,[41] and, as we have seen, his writings are as replete as those of Marx with sharp and biting morally-based critiques of class societies.

The only sustained treatment of these questions in the Marxist canon is Karl Kautsky's *Ethics and the Materialist Conception of History*. It is important to note that Kautsky was writing in the context of the influence of Kantianism on Marxists, both German and Austrian. To Kantian-influenced Marxists and sympathizers with Marxism, the distinction between facts and values was central. Even if the Marxist philosophy of history were true, and socialism was therefore inevitable, it would not follow that socialism must therefore be accepted as good, desirable, and worth striving for. Some further value judgments were required, based on grounds other than historical materialism. As Staudinger put it, a rotten apple can only be the way it is, but it is rotten for all that.[42] Many thought that the Kantian ethic could provide the requisite grounds, showing that the socialist order is one where society has no other end than to treat the human person as an end in himself; moreover, the principles of socialist

[38] Engels, *The Housing Question*, Marx and Engels, *Selected Works*, I, 624–625.
[39] Marx and Engels, *Werke*, XXXIX (Berlin, 1968), 195.
[40] Engels, *Anti-Dühring*, 130, 132.
[41] See, e.g., the Speeches in Elberfeld (1845) and the *Principles of Communism* (1847).
[42] Cited in L. Kolakowski, *Main Currents of Marxism*, II, (Oxford: Clarendon Press, 1978), 251.

ethics were universal, applying to all persons, as moral subjects and objects, appealing to universal human values and not only to working class interests. Kantian ethics was seen as a natural completion of Marxism: it furnished the formal definition of the conditions which any moral precept must fulfil, while Marxism set out which concrete actions would lead to the aims it shared with Kantianism, namely universal brotherhood and solidarity, together with recognition of the irreducible value of every human individual. As Kolakowski has put it, the Kantian Marxists' 'main drift was always the same: the scientific interpretation of society and history tells us what is or what will be; no historical or economic analysis can tell us what ought to be, yet we must have a measure by which to judge present conditions and determine our aims'.[43] Thus Hermann Cohen argued that the socialist idea of human brotherhood, in which all men were equal and free, was a logical deduction from Kantian doctrine;[44] Karl Vorländer argued similarly,[45] as did the Austrian Marxists Adler[46] and Bauer,[47] though Conrad Schmidt offered a more utilitarian basis for ethical socialism.[48]

Against all this, Kautsky echoed Marx's and Engels's criticisms of Proudhon and Lassalle, speaking with scorn of 'Ethical Socialism' as 'endeavours . . . in our ranks to modify the class antagonisms, and to meet at least a section of the Bourgeoisie half way', the 'historical and social tendency' of the Kantian ethic being 'that of toning down, of reconciling the antagonisms, not of overcoming them through struggle'.[49] For Kautsky, moral tenets 'arise from social needs', 'all morality is relative', what is 'specifically human in morality, the moral codes, is subject to continual change': 'the moral rules alter with the society, yet not uninterruptedly and not in the same fashion and degree as the social needs', indeed 'it is

---

[43] Ibid., Kolakowski further rightly observes that in their debates with the orthodox the Kantians 'did not realize that the absence of this distinction is fundamental to Marxism and that in consequence the whole argument on both sides was being conducted in non-Marxist terms (historical determinism versus moralism)' (ibid., 254). It was left to Lukács to make this clear.

[44] See H. Cohen, *Ethik des reinen Willens* (Berlin, 1904).

[45] See K. Vorländer, *Kant und der Sozialismus* (Berlin, 1900) and *Kant und Marx. Ein Beitrag zur Philosophie des Sozialismus*, (Tübingen, 1911).

[46] See Max Adler, *Kausalität and Teleologie im Streit um die Wissenschaft* in *Marx-Studien*, I (Vienna, 1904), and *Kant und der Marxismus* (Berlin, 1925).

[47] See O. Bauer, 'Marxismus und Ethik', *Die Neue Zeit*, **XXIV**, No. 2 (1905–6), 485–499.

[48] On these writers generally, see R. de la Vega and H.-J. Sandkühler (eds), *Marxismus und Ethik* (Frankfurt, 1970), and Kolakowski, op. cit., II, Ch. 12.

[49] K. Kautsky, *Die Ethik und die materialistische Geschichtsauffassung* (1906), translated as *Ethics and the Materialist Conception of History*, by J. B. Askew, 4th edn revised (Chicago: Charles H. Kerr & Co., n.d.), 69.

with the principles of morality as with the rest of the complicated sociological superstructure which raises itself on the method of production. It
can break away from its foundation and lead an independent life for a
time.'[50] It was, he writes, 'the materialist conception of history which has
first completely deposed the moral ideal as the directing factor of the
social evolution, and has taught us to deduce our social sins solely from
the knowledge of the material foundations'.[51] Even with Marx, Kautsky
says, 'occasionally in his scientific research there breaks through the
influence of a moral ideal. But he always endeavours and rightly to banish
it where he can. Because the moral ideal becomes a source of error in
science, when it takes on itself to point out to it its aims. Science has only
to do with the recognition of the necessary. It can certainly arrive at
prescribing an *ought* but this can arise only as a result of insight into what is
necessary. It must decline to discover an *ought* which is not recognizable
as a necessity founded in the world of phenomena.'[52]

On the other hand, Kautsky wrote that with the expansion of capitalism,
there had formed a basis for 'a general human morality'. This was formed
by

> the development of the productive forces of man, by the extension of
> the social division of labour, the perfection of the means of intercourse.
> This new morality is, however, even today far from being a morality of
> all men even in the economically progressive countries. It is in essence
> even today the morality of the class conscious proletariat, that part of
> the proletariat which in its feeling and thinking has emancipated itself
> from the rest of the people and has formed its own morality in opposition
> to the bourgeoisie.[53]

It is, he adds, 'capital which creates the material foundation for a general
human morality, but it only creates the foundation by treading this morality
continually under its feet'.[54] On this basis, the proletariat will 'create a
form of society, in which the equality of man before the moral law will
become—instead of a mere pious wish—reality'.[55] Kautsky insisted that
'though the conscious aim of the class struggle in Scientific Socialism has
been transformed from a moral into an economic aim it loses none of its
greatness': where, he asks, 'is such a moral ideal which opens such splendid
vistas?'[56] As Kolakowski has observed, Kautsky

agreed with the neo-Kantians that Marxism proved the historical

[50] Ibid., 178, 192, 184.
[51] Ibid., 201.
[52] Ibid., 202–203 (amended translation—S.L.).
[53] Ibid., 159–160.
[54] Ibid., 160.
[55] Ibid., 160–161.

necessity of socialism, and this in his view was all that required to be shown. The working class was bound to develop a consciousness that would regard socialism as an ideal, but this attitude of mind was itself no more than the consequence of a social process. The question why a person should regard as desirable what he believes to be inevitable is ignored by Kautsky, who gives no reason for not answering it.[57]

Other classical Marxists took an exactly similar line. Thus Plekhanov, in replying to the objections of Stammler along these lines, saw no need to supply moral grounds for joining a movement certain to succeed.[58] He seems simply to have supposed that since human purposes are determined by productive forces and social conditions, the provision of such grounds is rendered unnecessary. He altogether failed to understand Stammler's neo-Kantian objections, regarding himself, as Kolakowski writes,

> as a necessary link in the process of socialist change, implying that it could not take place without him: this may have been true in his case, but it conflicts with his own principles as to the historical role of the individual, and it still does not explain why he, or anyone else, should have taken upon themselves to be the necessary link.[59]

Lenin likewise fiercely combated what he called the subjective and moralistic viewpoint of populist writers which he contrasted with Marxism as a scientific determinist doctrine which does not ask questions about what ought to be but considers all processes including the phenomena of consciousness as natural events determined by the relations of production. Lenin indeed describes the proletariat as 'the intellectual and moral motive force and the physical executor' of 'the inevitable advent of socialism' but states that for Marx that inevitability is deduced 'wholly and exclusively from the economic law of development of contemporary society'.[60] Marx, he wrote,

> treats the social movement as a process of natural history, governed by laws not only independent of human will, consciousness and intentions, but, on the contrary, determining the will, consciousness and intentions of men . . . if the conscious element plays so subordinate a part in the history of civilization, it is self-evident that a critique whose subject is civilization can least of all take as its basis any form of, or any result of, consciousness.

[56] Ibid., 204, 206.
[57] Kolakowski, op. cit., II, 39.
[58] G. Plekhanov, *Fundamental Problems of Marxism*, English translation (London, 1929).
[59] Kolakowski, op. cit., II, 343.
[60] V. I. Lenin, *Karl Marx, Collected Works*, XXI, 71.

Everybody knows, he wrote, that 'scientific socialism never painted any prospects for the future as such: it confined itself to analysing the present bourgeois regime, to studying the trends of development of the capitalist social organization, and that is all.'[61] There was, he remarked in *State and Revolution*,

> no trace of an attempt on Marx's part to make up a utopia, to indulge in idle guess-work about what cannot be known. Marx treated the question of communism in the same way as a naturalist would treat the question of the development of, say, a new biological variety, once he knew that it had originated in such and such a way and was changing in such and such a definite direction.[62]

He agreed with Sombart that there was in Marxism 'not a grain of ethics from beginning to end' since 'theoretically, it subordinates the "ethical standpoint" to the "principle of causality"; in the practice it reduces to the class struggle'.[63] And there are many passages in Lenin's writings where he takes an aggressively instrumentalist view of morals, arguing that moral rules about labour discipline could, for example, 'properly be ignored by the proletariat under bourgeois rule' though their practical application by the Soviet state was a 'condition for the final victory of Socialism'.[64] And in 1920 he told the Komsomol Congress

> We say that our morality is entirely subordinated to the interests of the proletariat's class struggle ... Morality is what serves to destroy the old exploiting society and to unite all the working people around the proletariat, which is building up a new, a communist society ... To a communist all morality lies in this united discipline and conscious mass struggle against the exploiters. We do not believe in an eternal morality, and we expose the falseness of all the fables about morality.[65]

Yet, on the other hand, Lenin's writings are full of passionate moral denunciations of the ills of capitalism, as when he wrote in 1917 of 'these survivals of accursed capitalist society, these dregs of humanity, these hopelessly decayed and atrophied limbs, this contagion, this plague, this ulcer that socialism has inherited from capitalism'.[66] In *State and*

[61] V. I. Lenin, 'What the "Friends of the People" are and How they Fight the Social Democrats', *Collected Works*, I, (London: Lawrence & Wishart, 1960), 166, 184.

[62] V. I. Lenin, *State and Revolution*, *Collected Works*, XXV, 458.

[63] V. I. Lenin, 'The Economic Content of Narodism and the Criticism of it in Mr Struve's Book', *Collected Works*, I, 421.

[64] V. I. Lenin, *Selected Works*, II, (Moscow, 1950), Part I, 453–454.

[65] V. I. Lenin, *Collected Works*, XXXI, 291–294.

[66] V. I. Lenin, 'How to Organize Competition', *Collected Works*, XXVI, 410.

Revolution, Lenin clearly suggests that Marx's higher phase of communism will consist in a more *just* distribution of consumer goods and writes of the lower phase as 'by no means our ideal, or our ultimate goal. It is only a necessary *step* for thoroughly cleansing society of all the infamies and abominations of capitalist exploitation *and for further* progress.'[67] In the process of that development, 'the working man can reveal his talents, unbend his back a little, rise to his full height, and feel that he is a human being';[68] while (in more utilitarian vein) socialism alone

> will make possible the wide expansion of social production and distribution along scientific lines and their actual subordination to the aim of easing the lives of working people and of improving their welfare as much as possible.[69]

The proletariat, he wrote in 1919, are 'not only overthrowing the exploiters and suppressing their resistance, but are building a new and higher social bond, a social discipline, the discipline of class-conscious and united working people';[70] and in 1920 he wrote of communist labour as 'labour performed because it has become a habit to work for the common good, and because of a conscious realization (that has become a habit) of the necessity of working for the common good—labour as the requirement of a healthy organism'. It will, he proclaimed,

> take many years, decades, to create a new labour discipline, new forms of social ties between people, and new forms and methods of drawing people into labour. It is a most gratifying and noble work.[71]

Materialism for Lenin 'includes partisanship, so to speak, and enjoins the direct and open adoption of the standpoint of a definite social group in any assessment of events.'[72] Was that standpoint not self-evidently moral?

Trotsky's celebrated debate with John Dewey, initiated by his pamphlet *Their Morals and Ours,* reveals the same pattern of argument and the same resulting paradox. Trotsky enjoins his readers to agree that 'morality is a product of social development; that there is nothing immutable about it; that it serves social interests; that these interests are contradictory; that morality more than any other form of ideology has a class character'.

[67] *State and Revolution, Collected Works,* XXV, 466, 474.
[68] V. I. Lenin, 'How to Organize Competition', *Collected Works,* XXVI, 407.
[69] V. I. Lenin, 'Speech at the First Congress of Economic Councils', 26 May 1918. *Collected Works,* XXVII, 411.
[70] V. I. Lenin, *A Great Beginning* in *Collected Works,* XXIX, 423.
[71] V. I. Lenin, 'From the Destruction of the Old Social System to the Creation of the New' in *Collected Works,* XXX, 518.
[72] 'The Economic Content of Narodism . . . ', *Collected Works,* I, 401.

Though a few 'elementary moral precepts exist, worked out in the development of mankind as a whole and indispensable for the existence of every
collective body', their influence is 'extremely limited and unstable' and
it declines 'the sharper the character assumed by the class struggle'.[73]
Indeed, the 'highest form of the class struggle is civil war which explodes
into mid-air all moral ties between the hostile classes'.[74] 'Moral evaluations',
for Trotsky, 'together with those political, flow from the inner needs of
struggle.'[75]

On the other hand, he also writes, discussing the relation between
means and ends, that

> A means can be justified only by its end. But the end in its turn needs
> to be justified. From the Marxist point of view, which expresses the
> historical interests of the proletariat, the end is justified if it leads to
> increasing the power of man over nature and to the abolition of the
> power of man over man . . . That is permissible . . . which *really* leads
> to the liberation of mankind. Since this end can be achieved only through
> revolution, the liberating morality of the proletariat of necessity is
> endowed with a revolutionary character. It irreconcilably counteracts
> not only religious dogma but all kinds of idealistic fetishes, these philo-
> sophic gendarmes of the ruling class.

But then he adds a sentence on which Dewey focuses his critical attention:
'It deduces a rule for conduct from the laws of the development of society,
thus primarily from the class struggle, this law of all laws'.[76]

I could go on multiplying examples from the history of Marxism: for
instance, the recent critique by Althusserian structuralist Marxists of so-
called 'humanist' Marxists has in part taken the same form of denying
any role for moral judgment and evaluation, even going so far as to deny
the idea that human beings are acting 'subjects', capable of exercising
moral choice, while at the same time being plainly committed to the idea
that there are compelling grounds for engaging in class struggle within
the present capitalist order with the aim of bringing about a superior
socialist order. The fact that these grounds are not rendered explicit does
not render them any the less indispensable.

It may, however, be worth concluding this illustrative survey of the
Marxist tradition's paradoxical view of morality by referring to the recent
lively debate between E. P. Thompson and Perry Anderson, which touches
among many other matters on this central issue. In the 1976 Postscript to

[73] L. Trotsky, J. Dewey and G. Novack, *Their Morals and Ours: Marxist
versus Liberal Views on Moralists*, 4th edn (New York: Pathfinder Press, 1979). 15.
[74] Ibid., 15–16.
[75] Ibid., 38.
[76] Ibid., 36–37.

his magisterial *William Morris: Romantic to Revolutionary*, Thompson argues that Morris's 'use of moral criteria and his assertions of "ideal" ends and of prior values' indicates 'a direction towards which historical development may move, suggests choices between alternative directions, asserts a preference between these choices, and seeks to educate others in his preferences'. He notes Engels' dismissal of Morris as a 'sentimental socialist' (and Morris's unrepentant 'I *am* a sentimentalist . . . and I am proud of the title') and comments on the crack that 'lies between Morris's avowed and conscious positions and a moral determinism (from these relations of production, these values and this common morality) which has occupied much Marxist thought'. Indeed for Thompson, the case of Morris raises

> the whole problem of the subordination of the imaginative utopian faculties within the later Marxist tradition: its lack of a moral self-consciousness, or even a vocabulary of desire, its inability to project any images of the future, or even its tendency to fall back in lieu of these upon the Utilitarian's earthy paradise—the maximization of economic growth.[77]

In his polemical anti-Althusserian essay, 'The Poverty of Theory', he carries the argument further, urging the need to address 'experience' and 'culture', above all that half of it that may be described as 'affective and moral consciousness'—the ways in which people 'handle their feelings within their culture, as norms, familial and kinship obligations and reciprocities, as values or (through more elaborated forms) within art or religious beliefs'. He argues, not that morality is an autonomous region of human choice and will, arising independently of the historical process, but that values and interests are inseparable, that 'every class struggle is at the same time a struggle over values; and that the project of Socialism is guaranteed by NOTHING—certainly not by "Science" or by Marxism–Leninism—but can find its own guarantees only by *reason* and through an open choice of values'. It is here, according to Thompson, that 'the silence of Marx, and of most Marx*isms* is so loud as to be deafening'. Noting, as we have done, that 'Marx, in his wrath and compassion, was a moralist in every stroke of his pen', Thompson argues that Marx's and Engels's battle against the triumphant moralism of Victorian capitalism led them to this neglect and silence. Moreover,

> This silence was transmitted to the subsequent Marxist tradition in the form of a repression. This repression, in its turn, made it more easy

---

[77] E. P. Thompson, *William Morris: Romantic to Revolutionary* (London: Merlin Press, 1977), 803, 792.

for the major tradition to turn its back upon Morris (and many other voices) and to capitulate to an economism which, in fact, simply took over a bourgeois utilitarian notion of 'need'; and, as a necessary complement to this, to foster a paltry philistinism towards the arts. It was only necessary for Marxist Science to enter into the kingdom of Socialism, and all else would be added thereunto. And Marxism–Leninism–Stalinism did. And we know with what results.[78]

Anderson in reply agrees with Thompson that 'Marx and Engels left no Ethics, and that the resultant gap was never made good in the Marxism which ensued after their deaths—to the danger of historical materialism as a theory and of the socialist movement as a practice', though he accuses Thompson of underrating the '*difficulty* of developing a materialist ethics, at once integrally historical and radically non-utilitarian'. Anderson sees Thompson's text as scored in a key

> fundamentally at variance with the mainstream of historical materialism. Neither Marx or Engels—as Thompson notes—were in any way reluctant to express social–moral judgments. They did not, however, ever systematize these into a separate discourse. In a certain sense, Thompson is right to tax their legacy with this relative silence—whose most serious result in their own life-time was, he justly points out, Engels's impatience and insensibility towards the pecular genius of Morris. But what he fails to see is that the reason why the founders of historical materialism were so chary of ethical discussions of socialism— a reason which has not lost its relevance to his own present championship of them—is their tendency to become *substitutes* for explanatory accounts of history. Aggressively claiming to reinstate 'moralism' as an integral part of any contemporary culture of the Left, Thompson has forgotten the distinction which the term itself is designed to indicate in ordinary usage. Moral consciousness is certainly indispensable to the the very idea of socialism: Engels himself emphasized that 'a really human morality' would be one of the hallmarks of communism, the finest product of its conquest of the age-old social divisions and antagonisms rooted in scarcity. Mora*lism*, on the other hand, denotes the vain intrusion of moral judgments in lieu of causal understanding—typically, in everyday life and in political evaluations alike, leading to an 'inflation' of ethical terms themselves into a false rhetoric, which lacks the exacting sense of material care and measure that is inseparable from true moral awareness. This process is all too evident and familiar in contemporary politics outside the socialist movement, and against it. Solzhenitsyn

[78] E. P. Thompson, *The Poverty of Theory and Other Essays* (London: Merlin Press, 1978), 363, 364.

since his exile is a signal example. Its end-result is to devalue the writ of moral judgment altogether.[79]

II

How, then is this recurring, paradoxical pattern of argument to be understood? How is one to reconcile the persistent attacks on morality and moralizing as such (as against particular forms of morality and moralizing) with the no less persistent wrath and compassion and belief in humanity's progress towards a higher form of social life? Of course, Marxism may on this point simply be self-contradictory, but I shall assume that it is worth striving to resolve the apparent contradiction, even if it be at the cost of showing Marxism's view of morality to be implausible.

One, superficial, approach would be to focus on the question of tactics. As we have seen, one common theme has been that the use of moral concepts gives comfort to the class enemy and dilutes class antagonisms, in Kautsky's words, meeting 'a section of the bourgeoisie half way'. This argument has always been especially used against 'utopias' and detailed projections of the future, seen as deviations from the hard business of struggle. But at best this is an argument about what it is appropriate to say and write in certain circumstances, not about what is right to believe; it does not resolve the paradox, on the assumption that the attacks on morality are to be taken as genuine statements of belief. To assess the consequences of those statements is not to assess the statements themselves.

Another approach would be to focus on the question of relativism. Moral judgments are typically objective, universal and non-relative in form, appealing to what Engels called 'permanent principles which stand above history and the differences between nations'. Perhaps the Marxist view of morality can be understood as a self-consistent attack on non-relativist ethics, itself advancing moral judgments and ideals that are, however, themselves understood as no less relative (and socially determined) than those of other classes and previous periods. But not only is this interpretation incompatible with what Marxists have said on the matter (they *deny* that their criticisms and projections are moral as opposed to scientific, that is, objective and certainly not relative). It is also far from clear how the wrath and compassion and projections of a better world could be made compatible with a serious relativism, especially when combined with a functionalist determinism (i.e. relating moral codes to class interests or to the stabilization of relations of production). Could I *both* believe that capitalist accumulation means 'the accumulation of

[79] Perry Anderson, *Arguments within English Marxism* (London: NLB and Verso Editions, 1980), 97–98, 86.

misery, agony of toil, slavery, ignorance, brutality (and) mental degradation'
for workers and *also* believe (1) that it is so only relative to my historically
located point of view and (2) that I believe it because to do so fulfils a
social need? (Of course, I might believe it to be, non-relatively, true and
also believe that my believing it is socially determined or fulfils a social
need, but that would not be a relativist position')

A third approach would be to focus on the alleged 'abstractness' of
morality. There is, I think, much to be said for the view that Marx, at
least, took over Hegel's critique of abstract Kantian *Moralität*, as against
Sittlichkeit (roughly, the 'concrete morality of a rational social order
where rational institutions and laws provide the content of conscientious
conviction').[80] In this sense, moral judgments are one-sided and irrelevant
and inadequate to the reality they purport to judge. This part of Marx's
world-view, inherited from Hegel, retained, I believe, its influence on the
subsequent Marxist tradition, though detached from its Hegelian origins.
As I shall suggest below, it forms part of the canonical Marxist view of
morality.

Perhaps the most promising approach is to focus on those aspects of
morality which Marx and subsequent Marxists have singled out as ideological and as relative to class interests and particular modes of production.
The most obvious sphere of moral appraisal that meets this criterion is that
of *justice*. As we have seen, Marx and Engels particularly attacked Proudhon and Lassalle for their condemnations of capitalism as unjust.
What, then, was their view of justice?

This is a matter of some controversy,[81] but I think it plausible to hold
that Marx's official view of justice (and Engels followed him in this)
is most clearly expressed in two passages, the first from *Capital*, the
second from the *Critique of the Gotha Programme*. In the first, Marx writes
that the

---

[80] *Hegel's Philosophy of Right*, translated with notes by T. M. Knox (Oxford:
Clarendon Press, 1942), 319. For illuminating discussions of Hegel's distinction,
see C. Taylor, *Hegel* (Cambridge: Cambridge University Press, 1975), Ch. XIV,
and C. Taylor, *Hegel and Modern Society* (Cambridge: Cambridge University
Press, 1979), Ch. 2, and also Michael B. Foster, *The Political Philosophies of
Plato and Hegel* (Oxford, 1935).

[81] See Allen W. Wood, 'The Marxist Critique of Justice', *Philosophy and
Public Affairs* (Spring 1972), Zlyad I. Husami, 'Marx on Distributive Justice',
ibid. (Fall 1978), George G. Brenkert, 'Freedom and Private Property in Marx',
ibid (Winter 1979), and Allen W. Wood, 'Marx on Right and Justice: A Reply
to Husami', ibid. (Spring 1979): all reprinted in M. Cohen, T. Nagel and T.
Scanlon (eds), *Marx, Justice and History* (Princeton: Princeton University Press,
1980). (Page references refer to this volume.) See also Allen Buchanan, 'Exploitation, Alienation and Injustice', *Canadian Journal of Philosophy* 9 (March 1979),
121–139.

justice of the transactions between agents of production rests on the fact that these arise as natural consequences out of the production relationships. The juristic forms in which these transactions appear as wilful acts of the parties concerned, as expressions of their common will and as contracts that may be enforced by law against some individual party, cannot, being mere forms, determine this content. They merely express it. This content is just whenever it corresponds, is appropriate, to the mode of production. Slavery on the basis of capitalist production is unjust; likewise fraud in the quality of commodities.[82]

And in the second passage, Marx asks 'What is a just distribution?' and answers

Do not the bourgeois assert that the present-day distribution is 'just'? And is it not, in fact, the only 'just' distribution on the basis of the present-day mode of production? Are economic relations regulated by legal conceptions or do not, on the contrary, legal relations arise from economic ones? Have not also the socialist sectarians the most varied notions about 'just' distribution?[83]

In short, for Marx and Engels, transactions are just if they correspond or are appropriate to, or are functional to, the prevailing mode of production: judgments about justice are not made by reference to abstract or formal principles independent of the existing mode of production, indicating some ideal to which social reality could be adjusted; rather, they are 'rational assessments of the justice of specific acts and institutions, based on their concrete functions within a specific mode of production'.[84] Thus, for example, since the exploitation of wage labour by capital is essential to the capitalist mode of production, there is nothing unjust about the transactions through which capital exploits labour: the worker is paid the full value of his labour power (unless, of course, he is defrauded) and the capitalist, in subsequently appropriating surplus value is not required

---

[82] *Capital*, III, Ch. 21, 333–334.

[83] *Critique of the Gotha Programme*, I:3, in Marx and Engels, *Selected Works*, II, 21 (amended translation.—S.L.). On the other hand, there are obviously passages where Marx and Engels plainly contradict this, their 'official' view, as for example when Marx after referring to the prospective 'development of the social individual which appears as the great foundation-stone of production and of wealth', goes on to write: '*The theft of alien labour time, on which the present wealth is based,* appears a miserable foundation in face of this new one, created by large-scale industry itself' (*Grundrisse*, 705). I can only note this contradiction between 'official' and 'unofficial' views. Marx and Engels plainly believed that capitalism was unjust, but they did not believe that they believed this (I am grateful to Jerry Cohen for this way of putting the matter).

[84] Wood, 'The Marxian Critique of Justice', 16.

to pay the worker an equivalent for it, since under capitalism the worker has no right to the full value created by his labour. He did have such a right under the petty-bourgeois system of 'individual private property', but the very productive success of capitalism required its abolition.

In the *Critique of the Gotha Programme*, Marx criticized 'Vulgar socialism (and from it in turn a section of the democracy)' for considering and treating 'distribution as independent of the mode of production and hence the presentation of socialism as turning principally on distribution'; his view, on the contrary, was that 'at any given time the distribution of the means of consumption is only a consequence of the distribution of the conditions of production themselves'.[85] I think it is clear that he saw the concepts and principles governing such distribution as no less such a consequence: they prevail because they are functional. 'Justice' is a juridical concept (*Rechtsbegriff*) whose role is to govern juridical relations (*Rechtsverhältnisse*) which, as Marx remarked, 'like forms of state, are to be grasped neither through themselves nor through the so-called universal development of the human spirit, but rather are rooted in the material conditions of life, whose totality Hegel . . . comprehended under the term "civil society"'.[86] This is why Engels remarked that 'social justice or injustice is decided by the science which deals with the material facts of production and exchange, the science of political economy'.[87] The principles of *Recht* do not provide a set of independent rational standards by which to measure social relations, but must themselves always in turn be explained as arising from and controlling those relations.

How, then, did Marx and Engels conceive of *Recht*—that is, roughly, the sphere of rules specifying claims by people against others that are justifiable on legal or moral grounds? I think that the clue to answering this question can be found in the passage in the *Critique of the Gotha Programme* in which Marx discusses distribution in the lower phase of communism. In this phase, he writes, where each producer receives back from society means of consumption costing the same as the labour he has expended (minus various deductions),

> *this equal right* is still always encumbered with a bourgeois limitation. The right of the producers is *proportional* to the labour they supply; the equality consists in measurement by a common standard, labour.
>
> But one man is superior to another physically or mentally, and so supplies more labour in the same time or can work for a longer time;

[85] Marx, *Critique of the Gotha Programme, Selected Works*, II, 25 (amended translation—S.L.).

[86] Marx, *Preface to A Contribution to the Critique of Political Economy, Selected Works*, I, 362 (amended translation—S.L.).

[87] Marx and Engels, *Kleine Ökonomische Schriften* (Berlin, 1955), 412, cited in Wood, op. cit., 15.

and labour, to serve as a measure, must be defined by its duration or intensity, otherwise it ceases to be a standard of measurement. This *equal* right is an unequal right for unequal labour. It recognizes no class differences, because everyone is only a worker like the rest; but it tacitly recognizes unequal individual endowments, and thus productive capacities, as natural privileges. *It is, therefore, a right of inequality, in its content, like every right. Right (Recht) by its very nature can consist only in the application of a common standard; but unequal individuals (and they would not be different individuals if they were not unequal) are measurable by a common standard only in so far as they are brought under a common point of view, are considered in one particular aspect only, for instance, as in the present case, are regarded only as workers, everything else being disregarded.* Further, one worker is married, another not; one has more children than another, and so on and so forth. Thus, with an equal contribution of labour, and hence an equal share in the social consumption fund one will in fact receive more than another, one will be richer than another, and so on. To avoid all these defects, right instead of being equal would have to be unequal.[88]

But what exactly are the defects? The first is simply that workers with higher productive capacities benefit by higher incomes. But this defect could simply be rectified by paying them all the same. Another is that some workers have dependants—members of their families—who do not work. But in an earlier paragraph of the *Critique* Marx has already allowed for taxes to provide funds for those unable to work; and there seems to be no reason in principle why socialism could not provide non-working members of families with adequate incomes.

Aside from these particular and remediable defects, it is, however, the third defect, indicated by the passage in italics, which takes us to the heart of the matter. For here the objection is not that a particular principle of distribution is unfair, but rather that *any* system of rules specifying justifiable claims (*Recht*) treats people unequally, since *by its very nature* it applies a common standard to them, considering them in one particular aspect only. But, as Moore has pointed out, this amounts to a general argument that any social system is inequitable to the extent that it operates through general rules. According to this argument, 'no system of general rules, however complicated, can consider all the aspects in which indivi-

---

[88] Marx, *Critique of the Gotha Programme, Selected Works*, II, 23–24 (amended translation and added italics—S.L.). Marx's critical attitude to *Recht* was consistent throughout his life. In *The German Ideology*, Marx and Engels wrote: 'As far as *Recht* is concerned, we with many others have stressed the opposition of communism to *Recht*, both political and private, as also in its most general form as the rights of man' (*Collected Works*, V, 209). They refer to their early writings in the *Deutsch-Französische Jahrbücher* to support this assertion.

duals differ from one another. To apply such rules entails applying the same standard to different cases.'[89] Marx would clearly not be satisfied by increasing the number of aspects in which people are considered, since his view appears to be that every respect in which individuals differ from one another could in principle be relevant; accordingly, *no* common standard could ever fit the bill. In short, he seems here to be taking all too seriously his doctrine of the 'universality of individual need, capacities . . .', etc., and 'rich individuality that is as all-sided in its production as in its consumption'. He seems to have supposed that any rule of law or morals, which by its very nature singles out certain differences between people as grounds for differential treatment, is for that very reason 'abstract' and 'one-sided'. In the higher phase of communism, which the *Critique* goes on to describe,

> after the productive forces have . . . increased with the all-round develop-ment of the individual, and all the springs of co-operative wealth flow more abundantly—only then can the narrow horizon of bourgeois right be crossed in its entirety . . . [90]

I take this to mean, not merely that there will no longer be *bourgeois* right, but that there will be no more *Recht*, no more legal and moral rules.[91] The principle that such a society would inscribe on its banners—'From each according to his ability, to each according to his needs'—would not be such a rule, since (1) those abilities and needs would be infinite, that is

[89] Moore, op. cit., 48.

[90] Critique . . . in *Selected Works*, II, 24.

[91] This interpretation of Marx's view of *Recht*, encompassing law and morality, is similar to that of the early Soviet jurist Pashukanis. He writes that 'morality, law and the state are forms of bourgeois society', that they are forms 'incapable of absorbing [a socialist] content and must wither away in an inverse ratio with the extent to which this content becomes reality'. He writes of 'the social person of the future, who submerges his ego in the collective and finds the greatest satisfaction and the meaning of life in this act' as signifying 'the ultimate trans-formation of humanity in the light of the ideas of communism'. Morality is 'a form of social relations in which everything has not yet been reduced to man himself. If the living bond linking the individual to the class is really so strong that the limits of the ego are, as it were, effaced, and the advantage of the class actually becomes identical with personal advantage, then there will no longer be any point in speaking of the fulfilment of a moral duty, for there will be no such phenomenon as morality' (E. B. Pashukanis, *Law and Marxism: a General Theory*, translated by B. Einhoven (London: Ink Links, 1978), 160, 159). Pashukanis also exhibits the paradoxical pattern we have identified, arguing that there will, however, be a morality in the society of the future, understanding 'morality' in 'the wider sense' as 'the development of higher forms of humanity, as the transformation of man into a species-being (to use Marx's expression)' (Ibid., 160–161).

unlimitable in advance and unspecifiable by any rule; (2) the former would be harnessed to 'the common interest of all individuals who have inter-course with one another' through what Marx called *gemeinschaftlich* relations (and Lenin 'a new and higher social bond'); and (3) the latter would all be satisfiable, without conflicting claims, because of those relations and because of material abundance.

Now we begin to see the sense in which Marxism rejects morality as ideological in class societies and postulates its withering away under full communism. In so far as morality is seen as a part of *Recht*, and analogous and complementary to law,[92] it is relative to class interests, functional to modes of production and destined to disappear. Of course, there are wider senses of 'morality' in which Marxism has, or rather *is* in part, a morality—such as 'a doctrine touching the fundamental human good and the way to realize it, where "fundamental" good is taken to mean a good which is inescapably and universally the good of man',[93] or more widely still, an all-inclusive theory of human conduct such that someone's morality would be 'whatever body of principles he allowed to guide or determine his choices of action'.[94] The fundamental human good for Marxism, as we have seen, incorporates self-realization in community, freedom as the over-coming of alienation, mastery over nature and the maximization of welfare; as Trotsky saw, the principles guiding choices of action are entirely dictated by this (complex) end.

What, then, is it that distinguishes this narrow sense of morality, which Marxism officially rejects as a standard of judgment and basis of criticism, and whose withering away it foretells? To answer this, we may usefully turn in what may appear to be a surprising direction: to the philosopher Hume, who wrote '*that 'tis only from the selfishness and confined generosity of man, along with the scanty provision nature has made for his wants, that justice derives its origin*'.[95] Citing this view of Hume's, alongside Prota-

---

[92] H. L. A. Hart isolates four features distinguishing morality (in this sense) from law: importance, immunity fron deliberate change, the voluntary character, of moral offences, and the distinctive form of moral pressure. See H. L. A. Hart, *The Concept of Law* (Oxford: Clarendon Press, 1961).

[93] Charles Taylor, 'Marxism and Empiricism' in B. Williams and A. Monte-fiore (eds), *British Analytical Philosophy* (London: Routledge & Kegan Paul, 1966), 244–245.

[94] J. Mackie, *Ethics: Inventing Right and Wrong* (Harmondsworth: Penguin, 1977), 106.

[95] D. Hume, *A Treatise of Human Nature*, Book III, Part II, Section II, L. A. Selby-Bigge (ed.) (Oxford: Clarendon Press, 1888), 495. Compare Rawls's account of the 'circumstances of justice' which 'obtain whenever mutually disinterested persons put forward conflicting claims to the division of social advantages under conditions of moderate scarcity': J. Rawls, *A Theory of Justice* (Oxford: Clarendon Press, 1972), 128.

goras, Hobbes and Warnock, John Mackie has sought to identify what he calls a 'narrow sense of morality' as 'a system of a particular sort of constraints on conduct—ones whose central task is to protect the interests of persons other than the agent and which present themselves to an agent as checks on his natural inclinations or spontaneous tendencies to act'.[96] Mackie argues, following Hume, that morality, in this narrow sense, thus defined, is needed to solve a basic problem inherent in the human predicament: that 'limited resources and limited sympathies together generate both competition leading to conflict and an absence of what would be mutually beneficial co-operation'.[97] Accepting the centrality of self-love and confined generosity in human motivation and behaviour, he suggests that competition and conflict between individuals and between groups is inevitable and that 'rival social and political ideals offer different ways in which co-operation, competition and conflict may be institutionalized and regulated, but every real alternative includes some combination of all three of them'.[98]

This Humean argument shows clearly enough in what ways Marxism offers neither a morality nor a social and political ideal. Those making moral judgments, invoking moral principles or advancing moral ideals (in the narrow sense) are, on this argument, responding to these invariant features of the human predicament. But it is a peculiar and distinctive feature of Marxism that it precisely denies that limited sympathies and resources are invariant features inherent in the human condition. On the contrary, it maintains that they are historically determined, specific to class societies and inherently removable. Neither limited resources, nor limited sympathies, nor in general conflicts of interest and antagonistic social relations are fundamental to the human predicament. To assume that they are is itself an ideological error—ideological in serving to perpetuate the existing class-bound social order. Marxism supposes that a unified society of abundance is not merely capable of being brought about but on the historical agenda, and indeed that the working class is in principle motivated to bring about and capable of doing so. At worst, morality

---

[96] Mackie, *Ethics*, 106. Compare Alan Gewirth's definition of 'a certain core meaning' of 'morality' as 'a set of categorically obligatory requirements for action that are addressed at least in part to every actual or prospective agent and that are concerned with furthering the interests, especially the most important interests, of persons or recipients other than or in addition to the agent or speaker' (Alan Gewirth, *Reason and Morality* (Chicago and London: University of Chicago Press, 1978), 1).

[97] Ibid., 111.

[98] Ibid., 170–171.

which serves existing modes of prodcution, delays that outcome; at best, morality which fuels indignation and protest, can bring it nearer.[99]

Thus Marxism's distinctive attitude to morality is explained and the paradox within it removed. Prevailing moralities (in the narrower sense, as part of *Recht*) provide part of the ideological cement of class societies and all moralities in this sense purport to accommodate interests to the mutual advantage of all. By contrast, Marxism holds that, broadly, all major conflicts of interests are to be traced back to class divisions and that to reconcile them is to promote class compromise and delay the revolutionary change that will make possible a form of social life that has no need of morality, because the conditions of morality, or what John Rawls calls the 'circumstances of justice' will no longer obtain. Marx wrote of religion that 'The abolition of religion as the illusory happiness of the people is a demand for their true happiness. The call to abandon illusions about their condition is the call to abandon a condition which requires illusions.'[100] It seems that Marx held a parallel view about morality as part of *Recht*. Morality (as the fundamental human good) requires abandoning a condition which requires morality (as part of *Recht*). The good consists in eliminating the conditions of morality and the circumstances of justice.

I hope to have shown that Marxism's traditional view of morality is not self-contradictory. But is it plausible? To attempt to answer this would require at least another paper, but it may be worth concluding this one by pointing to a number of reasons for thinking that it is not. First, Marxism has always neglected all other bases than class for social antagonism, whether they be social or psychological, or else it has tried to root them in class divisions.[101] This has always rendered Marxism at best insensitive to both the depth and the complexity of social conflict, both at the level of everyday life and of social movements, above all where questions of culture and of identity are at stake. Second, there is no reason to suppose that any feasible form of post-class social unity could eliminate the most deep-rooted conflicts of interests in a society. Indeed, third, many such conflicts are inherent in any complex form of social life, and many of these derive neither from selfishness nor from scarcity but from the nature of the ends that are pursued, not all of which can be

---

[99] See Allen Buchanan, 'Revolutionary Motivation and Rationality' in Cohen, Nagel and Scanlon (eds), *Marx, Justice and History* (Princeton: Princeton University Press, 1980).

[100] K. Marx, *A Contribution to the Critique of Hegel's Philosophy of Right: Introduction* in *Marx: Early Writings*, translated by T. B. Bottomore (London: C. A. Watts, 1963), 44.

[101] See Frank Parkin, *Marxism and Class Theory: A Bourgeois Critique* (London: Tavistock, 1979).

realized simultaneously.[102] Fourth, the Marxist tradition has never satisfactorily explained, practically rather than philosophically, just how *gemeinschaftlich* social unity is to be reconciled with a rich and many-sided individuality for all, nor does it (with some few exceptions)[103] offer any theoretical grounds, as the liberal tradition does, for resisting pressures towards the former in the name of the latter. And, fifth, it is at best an illusion to suppose that the pursuit of the social goal and fundamental human good to which it is committed can suffice as a basis for action-guiding principles in the present.

Marxism has, indeed, always lacked any basis for establishing a system of constraints upon what it is permissible to do in the process of struggling for its ends. The only limits it recognizes—at Trotsky made clear—are set by the complex, vague and only dimly adumbrated ends themselves (whatever really leads to them is permissible), and about them infinite debate is possible. The fact of this lack was graphically commented upon by Lev Kopelev (whom Solzhenitsyn portrayed as Rubin in *The First Circle*) in his memoirs, *No Jail for Thought*. Describing the horrors of the 1930s in the USSR, Kopelev writes that with

> the rest of my generation I firmly believed that the ends justified the means. Our great goal was the universal triumph of communism, and for the sake of that goal everything was permissible—to lie, to steal, to destroy hundreds of thousands and even millions of people, all those who were hindering our work or could hinder it, everyone who stood in the way. And to hesitate or doubt about all this was to give in to 'intellectual squeamishness' and 'stupid liberalism', the attributes of people who 'could not see the forest for the trees'.

He describes how the communists of that time became

> unprincipled liars and unrelenting executioners, all the while seeing themselves as virtuous and honourable militants—convinced that if they are forced into villainy, it is for the sake of future good, and that if they have to lie, it is in the name of eternal truths.

It was, he writes, only later that he came to see things differently:

> I had already begun to wonder, and had decided that what we lacked was a set of absolute moral norms. Relativist morality—whatever helps us is good, whatever helps the enemy is bad, the creed we proselytized

[102] See F. Hirsch, *The Social Limits to Growth* (London: Routledge & Kegan Paul, 1977).

[103] Notably, Rosa Luxemburg: see, for a thought-provoking discussion of this question, Norman Geras, *The Legacy of Rosa Luxemburg* (London: New Left Books, 1976), 133–194.

under the name of the 'materialist dialectic'—would debase us in the end, and would debase the cause of socialism, raising a species of immoral craftsmen of death. Today they apply themselves to killing enemies, real or imaginary; tomorrow they will turn just as willingly against their own.[104]

And this, of course, raises the question of questions in relation to Marxism and morality: just what links are there between Marxism's view of morality in theory and its moral record in practice?

Balliol College, Oxford

---

[104] Lev Kopelev, *No Jail for Thought* (Harmondsworth: Penguin, 1979), 31–34.

Habermas on Truth and Justice

PHILIP PETTIT

1. Introduction

The problem which motivates this paper bears on the relationship between Marxism and morality. It is not the well-established question of whether the Marxist's commitments undermine an attachment to ethical standards, but the more neglected query as to whether they allow the espousal of political ideals. The study and assessment of political ideals is pursued nowadays under the title of theory of justice, the aim of such theory being to provide a criterion for distinguishing just patterns of social organization from unjust ones. The main rivals in the field represent justice respectively as legitimacy, welfare and fairness.[1] Marxism does not put forward a distinctive conception of justice itself and the question is whether the Marxist is free to choose as he thinks fit among the candidates on offer.

There is a sting in the question. The various conceptions of justice elaborated in the literature of political philosophy are all of them paradigms of that sort of thinking castigated by Marxists as bourgeois or ideological, undialectical or unhistorical. This indeed is no accident, for the method whereby the argument between the conceptions is advanced seems particularly vulnerable to such criticism: it is invariably characterized as depending at crucial points on an appeal to intuition about matters of justice, and intuition of this kind is surely susceptible to the influences of social formation with which Marx among others has made us familiar.[2]

In face of this depressing state of affairs the Marxist might think of disallowing altogether the investigation of the nature of justice. And yet that is scarcely an attractive option. For if the demands of justice are not something that we can sensibly think of construing in an objective manner, then what is it that vindicates the Marxist criticism of existing social structures? It will not do for the Marxist to invoke the march of history, for the fact that present structures are doomed, if indeed they are so, does nothing to show that their demise should be applauded or hastened.

---

[1] See my *Judging Justice: An Introduction to Contemporary Political Philosophy* (London: Routledge & Kegan Paul, 1980).

[2] See *Judging Justice*, Chapter 4.

Philip Pettit

The Marxist, it appears, is in a dilemma.[3] If he countenances the enterprise of political philosophy, the investigation of the nature of justice, he must weaken the received theory of social formation. If he does not countenance it, he must give up all claim to the rational criticism of social arrangements and play the role of blind collaborator to the historical process. My own view is that his best recourse is to adopt the first horn and reconsider the nature of ideology, but in this assay I would like to examine the approach to the problem which Jürgen Habermas has sponsored in his recent writing.

Habermas is the principal representative today of that tradition of Marxist thinking known as critical theory. This tradition goes back to the Frankfurt Institute of Social Research which was founded in 1923: its main exponents in earlier years were Theodore Adorno and Max Horkheimer but it also encompassed such thinkers as Walter Benjamin, Erich Fromm and Herbert Marcuse.[4] Habermas has wrought a powerful transformation of Marxist thinking in his work of the last twenty years, although one which maintains many of the emphases of his heritage in critical theory. He rates on any estimate as one of the most important Marxist theorists writing today.

The key to Habermas's reworking of Marxism is his importation from the hermeneutic tradition of a distinction between the interventionist disposition that we adopt towards systems which we seek to control and the interactive one that we take up *vis-à-vis* persons with whom we wish to communicate. What he has done, in a nutshell, is to elaborate the significance for Marxist theory and praxis of accepting that this distinction is a valid one. At the level of praxis he has emphasized that if one thinks of revolution on the model of the party steering the proletariat, or if one sees social organization as ideally tending towards finer bureaucratic

---

[3] The problem is nicely described in a passage from Alasdair MacIntyre, *Against the Self-Images of the Age* (London: Duckworth, 1971), 92–93. 'Marx originally indicted capitalist values as well as capitalist methods. His belief that any appeal to the exploiters on a moral basis was bound to embody the illusion of common standards of justice governing human behaviour made him suspicious of all moralizing. But when Eduard Bernstein attempted to find a Kantian basis for socialism, the defenders of Marxist orthodoxy Karl Kautsky and Rosa Luxembourg were forced to reopen the question of the nature of the moral authority of the Marxist appeal to the working class. This question, as the experience of Luxembourg and of Lukács, of Trotsky and of Guevara shows, was never satisfactorily answered'.

[4] See Paul Connerton (ed.), *Critical Sociology* (Harmondsworth: Allen Lane, 1976), and Martin Jay, *The Dialectical Imagination* (London: Heinemann, 1973).

rationalization, one condones a treatment of human beings which sees them only as systems to be technically controlled. At the level of theory he has stressed that only an interest in securing such technical control licenses the deterministic ambitions of historical materialism, and that a more liberal sense of the cognitive interests which theory ought to serve, in particular social theory, makes possible a richer interpretation and development of the historical materialist tradition.[5]

But what Habermas has to say on these general matters I must leave aside. I want to consider in this paper only the response which he has underwritten to the dilemma posed above. He has recently put forward a consensus theory of justice which is meant to slip between the horns of that dilemma, indicating a valid basis for social criticism and yet escaping the charge of ideological distortion. The feature of the consensus theory which turns the necessary trick is what I shall call its agnosticism. The theory gives us a criterion of justice, identifying the just social scheme as that which would attract rational consensus, but it denies that the criterion can be applied with certainty in an imperfect world, holding that we cannot now know what would command rational agreement. The criterion is one which the Marxist critic may claim, with due diffidence, to be applying; he is gambling on what people would opt for in a rational consensus. However, it is not a criterion which can raise ideological worries, for by leaving us in an agnostic position about what scheme would satisfy the condition it defers appropriately to the constraints of social formation.

My discussion of Habermas's theory will divide naturally into two parts. Habermas rejects the view that evaluative matters, and in particular matters having to do with justice, are any less objective and decidable than empirical ones.[6] He does not go so far as to say that evaluative statements are true or false in the same way as empirical, but he does think that the method whereby empirical truth is established provides a model for the

---

[5] For a comprehensive introduction to Habermas's thought see Thomas McCarthy, *The Critical Theory of Jürgen Habermas* (London: Hutchinson, 1978). Richard Bernstein has a useful shorter account in *The Restructuring of Social and Political Theory* (London: Methuen, 1976). Books of Habermas which have appeared in English are: *Towards a Rational Society* (London: Heinemann, 1971), *Knowledge and Human Interests* (London: Heinemann, 1972), *Theory and Practice* (London: Heinemann, 1974) and *Legitimation Crisis* (London: Heinemann, 1976). For a bibliography see McCarthy.

[6] 'Wahrheitstheorien' in *Wirklichkeit und Reflexion: Walter Schulz zum 60 Geburtstag* (Pfullingen: Neske, 1973), 226–227. We speak of justice where Habermas uses the word 'Richtigkeit'.

corresponding evaluative procedure.[7] Thus in the first part of this discussion I shall consider his approach to empirical truth and in the second I shall look at his parallel treatment of the evaluative counterpart to truth, something that might be called evaluative adequacy: the phrase however is not one that we shall need, for where the adequacy of political evaluations is under discussion we may equally well speak of justice, this being what such adequacy betokens. As we shall see, Habermas defends what he calls a consensus theory of truth and it is this which gives him his model for a consensus theory of justice.[8]

2. The Consensus Theory of Truth

Truth, according to Habermas, is something which a speaker implicitly claims for any assertion that he makes.[9] In being bold enough to speak, the speaker invites us to believe that what he says is intelligible, that he is sincere in saying it, that he is not speaking out of turn, at least not in any serious sense of that phrase, and that he is speaking the truth: these are the four validity claims, as Habermas calls them, of any assertion.[10] Although it is said to be the job of a universal pragmatics of speech to isolate these claims, the case for the truth claim is readily made. Any assertion 'p' is equivalent to the assertion ' "p" is true' and, this being

[7] 'Wahrheitstheorien', 219. It is doubtful whether Habermas has any good reason for not speaking of evaluative truth. For a discussion of the case for ascribing truth-value to evaluate assertions see David Wiggins 'Truth, Invention and the Meaning of Life', *Proceedings of the British Academy* **26** (1976), and my own 'Evaluative "Realism" and Interpretation' in S. Holtzmann and C. Leich (eds), *Wittgenstein: To Follow a Rule* (London: Routledge & Kegan Paul, 1981).

[8] The main source on Habermas's theory of truth, and indeed also on his theory of justice, is the still untranslated paper 'Wahrheitstheorien'; this will henceforth be referred to as 'W' and any quotations from it will be in my own translation. McCarthy provides a faithful commentary on Habermas's views on truth and justice in the book mentioned under reference 5. For a critical commentary on his theory of truth see Mary Hesse, 'Habermas's Consensus Theory of Truth', *Proceedings of the Philosophy of Science Association* 1978, **2** (1979). Reprinted in Mary Hesse, *Revolutions and Reconstructions in the Philosophy of Science* (Hassocks: Harvester, 1980).

[9] Habermas also holds that there is a truth claim implicit in non-assertoric speech acts, as there is held to be a claim of each of the other sorts mentioned later. See 'Was heisst Universalpragmatik?' in K. O. Apel (ed.), *Sprachpragmatik und Philosophie* (Frankfurt: Suhrkamp, 1976). What he has in mind seems to be a claim to the truth of the existential presuppositions of such acts.

[10] On the four claims see 'Was heisst Universalpragmatik?'. The claim to intelligibility is not so much a claim as an assumption. The other claims might be suitably rendered as claims to knowledge, honesty and authority.

general knowledge, a speaker who says that 'p' must expect to be taken to believe, and in that sense must implicitly claim, 'p' is true.[11]

It is a feature of communication that a speaker must be prepared to back up the claims which he implicitly makes if he is challenged by his hearers. The attempt to redeem the truth claim of an assertion gives rise to what Habermas calls theoretical discourse. In such discourse arguments are advanced for and against the truth of the proposition in question. The structure of the arguments is described by Habermas on a model derived from Stephen Toulmin.[12] The contentious proposition, say 'Harry is a British subject', will be traced by the speaker to a piece of *evidence* or data, such as 'Harry was born in Bermuda'. If the force of this evidence is questioned an attempt will be made to provide a *warrant* for the connection: this will take the form of a rule such as 'A man born in Bermuda will generally be a British subject'. Finally under yet further pressure an effort will be made to supply this warrant with a *backing*: say an account of certain legal provisions which explain why the rule in question holds.

But if truth is the topic of debate in theoretical discourse, what does it consist in? Habermas reasons that any answer to this question must maintain the connection between truth and argument: it must make truth out to be something operational, something that can be decided among partners in discourse. 'We call those statements true for which we are able to argue.'[13] On the basis of this consideration he rejects the assimilation of truth either to the subjective experience of certainty or to correspondence with objective fact. The first move would break the connection between truth and argument because certainty is a private experience and, while it may generally attend the acceptance of certain simple observation reports, it is not systematically responsive to the argument which guides propositional assent.[14] The assimilation to correspondence would also break the link between truth and argument, Habermas says, because, if they are taken seriously, the facts in correspondence with which truth allegedly consists must be admitted to be transcendent and inaccessible entities: they are not identifiable after all with the events and objects which form the data of our experience.[15]

At this point it would appear that there are two options open to Haber-

---

[11] See W 213–215: notice Habermas's supposition that every assertion is true or false.

[12] W 241ff. See Stephen Toulmin, *The Uses of Argument* (Cambridge: Cambridge University Press, 1964).

[13] W 219.

[14] W 223–226. Cf. 'A Postscript to *Knowledge and Human Interests*' in *Philosophy of the Social Sciences* 3 (1973), 170.

[15] W 215–219.

mas. He might maintain the operational character of truth through identifying the property methodologically, by reference to the procedure of verification, or sociologically, by reference to the circumstance licensing assent. The methodological approach is part of the heritage of logical positivism and it would identify truth with that property which belongs to propositions and theories that satisfy certain confirmation tests. This identification may be understood analytically or not, depending on whether truth is defined as the ability to pass the tests or is taken as the property, whatever it is, which explains that ability: depending on whether it is said to be necessarily or contingently connected with test-passing. Habermas has no truck with it however, in either sense.[16] He is not explicit about his reasons for rejecting the account but one may conjecture that he would object to it on the grounds that there is no plausible set of confirmation tests which would pick out just those theories that we take to be true. What he has to say on the underdetermination of theory-choice by observation and induction suggests that he would go along with the presently fashionable view that there is no canonical procedure of verification, or even of falsification, by reference to which truth might be identified.[17]

The sociological approach to the identification of truth is that which Habermas prefers. This says that truth is that property which belongs to propositions and theories that are capable of commanding consensus. 'I may ascribe a predicate to an object if and only if every other individual who could enter into discussion with me would ascribe the same predicate to the same object. In order to distinguish true from false statements, I refer to the judgement of others—in fact to the judgment of all others with whom I could ever undertake a discussion (among whom I include counter-factually all the partners in discussion that I could find if my life history were co-extensive with the history of mankind). The condition for the truth of statements is the potential agreement of all others. Every other person would have to be able to convince himself that I ascribed the predicate "p" correctly to the object x and would have to be able then to agree with me. Truth means the promise of achieving a rational consensus.'[18]

As with the methodological criterion of truth, the sociological allows of being construed in an analytical or non-analytical manner. We may pose a question parallel to that raised in Plato's *Euthyphro*, where it is asked whether the gods will something because it is good, or whether it is

---

[16] W 239.

[17] W 247. See Thomas Kuhn, *The Structure of Scientific Revolutions*, 2nd edn (Chicago: Chicago University Press, 1970), and Paul Feyerabend, *Against Method* (London: New Left Books, 1975).

[18] W 219.

good because they will it. The question is whether a proposition secures rational consensus because it is true, or whether it is true because it secures rational consensus. The identification of truth is analytical in the second event, truth consisting in the ability to command consensus, it is non-analytical in the first, truth being that which explains the attainment of the consensus.

One reason for thinking that Habermas must intend his sociological theory of truth to be understood non-analytically is that the he is a fallibilist and thinks that we can never be certain that we have attained the truth; if rational consensus is attained and truth is analytically tied to the achievement of such consensus then it would appear that fallibilistic doubts are out of place. This consideration is not compelling however because Habermas says that we cannot ever be certain that a consensus is properly rational, in which case we could never be certain that truth had been reached even if it was defined by the ability to command rational consensus.[19]

But there is a second consideration which also prompts the non-analytical reading of Habermas's criterion. This is that Habermas obviously thinks of propositions that attract rational consensus as having a property which accounts for that distinction: if nothing else, this is the property of offering reasons which move people to give the proposition their assent. 'The truth of a proposition stated in discourses means that everybody can be persuaded by reasons to recognize the truth claim of the statement as being justified.'[20] This truth is best taken as consisting for Habermas in the inherent reasonableness of the statement: as he says himself, borrowing an English phrase, in its 'warranted assertibility'.[21] The property is not defined by the ability of the proposition to command consensus but serves rather to explain that ability.

As so far explicated Habermas's theory of truth is not anything very unusual. Like many contemporary approaches it is nurtured on C. S. Peirce's identification of truth with permanent credibility: 'The opinion which is fated to be agreed to by all who investigate is what we mean by the truth'.[22] Its origin is the rejection of two illusions commonly assaulted

---

19 See W 258 and *Kultur und Kritik* (Frankfurt: Suhrkamp, 1973), 381.
20 'A Postscript to Knowledge and Human Interests', 170.
21 W 240.
22 C. S. Peirce, 'How to Make Our Ideas Clear' in P. P. Wiener (ed.), *C. S. Peirce: Selected Writings* (New York: Dover, 1958), 133. For an interesting comment on the value of Peirce's definition see Nelson Goodman, *Ways of Worldmaking* (Sussex: Harvester Press, 1978), 123–124. Richard Bernstein discusses Habermas's interpretation of Peirce in his introduction to the German edition of his book on *Praxis and Action: Praxis und Handeln*, (Frankfurt: Suhrkamp, 1975).

in contemporary philosophy: the metaphysical illusion that a proposition or theory might be rationally quite satisfying and yet fail to be true[23]; and the methodological illusion, that it is possible to spell out in the form of procedural tests those things that make a proposition or theory rationally satisfying.[24] Reject both of these illusions and it is more or less inevitable that one will identify truth sociologically as the property which belongs to those claims that are found rationally satisfying. Habermas rings a change on this familiar theme; he does not force any great novelty upon us.

Things alter however as Habermas advances the specification of his consensus theory of truth. The further specification comes in two stages and at the second of these some very distinctive claims are put forward. The first stage consists in an account of the sort of discursive argument which a proposition should be able to survive if it is to count as warranting assertion. What Habermas says, and it is surely uncontentious, is that the argument should be radical in the sense of allowing questioning at every level: not just questioning of the evidence invoked to support the proposition, but of the warrant buttressing the evidence, and of the backing which reinforces the warrant; ultimately it must even tolerate interrogation of the very conceptual scheme within which the original claim was put forward. 'An argumentatively achieved consensus is a sufficient criterion for the resolution of a discursive validity claim if and only if freedom of movement between the argumentative levels is guaranteed by the formal properties of the discourse.'[25]

So far, again, so good. But now Habermas makes a move which is at once obscure and contentious. He puts forward the thesis, as he describes it himself, that the formal properties of discourse which guarantee the required freedom of movement, the necessary interrogative space, are those realized when the discourse is conducted in an ideal speech situation.[26] For such a situation to be brought about a number of things must happen: these are summed up in the general symmetry requirement, as he calls it, that participants enjoy a fair distribution of chances to speak; more specifically they mean that each participant can open or continue any line of discussion, that each can put forward any assertion or call any into question, that the participants are equally free in their relations with one

---

[23] For criticism of this illusion see Hilary Putnam, 'Realism and Reason' in *Meaning and the Moral Sciences* (London: Routledge & Kegan Paul, 1978).

[24] See the works of Kuhn and Feyerabend mentioned under reference 17.

[25] W 255. Compare the model of theory selection presented in Mary Hesse, 'Models of Theory Change' in P. Suppes *et al.*, *Logic, Methodology & Philosophy of Science* (Amsterdam, 1973).

[26] W 255.

another to express their most intimate feelings, and that they are equally free to make demands on each other and offer each other help.[27]

The move to the ideal speech situation is contentious because it is by no means obvious that to bring about such a situation would be to ensure interrogative space in the ensuing discourse; if the participants are lazy thinkers no amount of democratization will guarantee that their interrogation is radical. What I wish to explore however is not the contentious nature of this final step in Habermas's presentation, but rather its obscurity. Even if the ideal speech situation is what would be required to maintain interrogative space in discourse between a number of people, it is unclear why Habermas needs to go into such matters. Is it not enough to know that truth is that property which would cause a proposition to be accepted by anyone, even when the proposition is subjected to radical interrogation? Why does one have to be told how to ensure that the interrogation is radical in the case where a number of people open discussion with one another, rather than each thinking the matter out on his own?

The question is useful because it admits of an enlightening answer. The notion of consensus may be understood in either of two senses, the one a distributive sense, as I shall say, the other a collective one. A proposition admits of distributive consensus if and only if each person assents to it, whether or not after discussion with others and whether or not in awareness of what others think. A proposition admits of collective consensus on the other hand if the people involved discuss it as a group and come to a unanimous decision about it. Up to the last stage in his presentation it seemed that Habermas identified truth as the property of propositions which were rationally capable of distributive consensus: the property of propositions to which anyone would rationally have to give assent, i.e. have to give assent after radical interrogation. At the last stage however he reveals that he conceives of the consensus for which any true proposition must have the potential as a collective consensus. Thus he gives himself the problem of stating conditions that guard against a failure of collective reason, a foreclosure of radical questioning: this, since it is notorious that in collectivities people quickly succumb to pressures of conformity and co-ordination.

There is no obvious reason why Habermas should have to concern himself with the problem of how to maintain interrogative space, the free movement between levels of argument, in the search for collective consensus. His sociological account identifies truth as the property which belongs to those propositions to which anyone would rationally have to agree. 'The condition for the truth of statements is the potential agreement of all others.'[28] This perfectly reasonable account supposes only distribu-

[27] W 255–256. Cf 'Was heisst Universalpragmatik?'.
[28] W 219. See reference 18.

tive consensus. It is quite gratuitous to add the requirement that the agreement must be achieved in collective discussion and it is therefore quite unnecessary for an upholder of the theory to investigate how best to guard against collective irrationality. Only the first step in Habermas's specification of his theory of truth is to the point; to be rational a person's assent must indeed be able to stand the test of radical argument. There is no reason to say that the assent must be forthcoming as part of a collective consensus achieved in an ideal speech situation; it may coincide with the judgment that would appear on such an occasion, but that is neither here nor there. The discourse in which Habermas says that questions of truth are raised is normally an interpersonal affair and it may be this which leads him to put a collective construction on the consensus required by his theory. But, as Habermas himself admits, discourse may also be internalized, it may only involve a single thinking subject.[29]

In conclusion, a question: does anything turn on the construal of consensus in a collective rather than a distributive manner? Well, to be sure of the truth of a proposition I must be convinced, presumably from the weight of reasons in its favour, that the proposition would rationally command everyone's agreement; such consensus, rather than subjective certainty or correspondence with objective facts, is the hallmark of truth. Now if the consensus is understood distributively this might be taken to put truth more readily within my grasp than it would be if the consensus required were collective. Having become convinced by radical argument in my own case that a proposition deserves assent I may take it, by analogy, that anyone would respond to the considerations offered in similar manner; thus, if consensus is understood distributively, I may assume that the proposition is true. This line of thought might be held not to work so easily if consensus is construed collectively, for the collective requirement might be taken to introduce a dimension of inscrutability. Who, it might be asked, is to say what judgment on the proposition people would come to collectively? Group dynamics are sufficiently obscure to make the question telling. It appears then that the collective construal of consensus has the effect, at most, of making truth less accessible than the distributive construal would do, although it is doubtful if even this effect is achieved: the extra trouble which Habermas takes on himself may be lacking, not just in argumentative support, but also in strategic purpose.

3. The Consensus Theory of Justice

With this account of Habermas's consensus theory of truth we may turn to consider the theory of justice that he models on it. Our goal, it will be

[29] See *Theory and Practice*, 28.

recalled, is to see whether his theory of justice succeeds in slipping between the horns of the dilemma that we constructed in the introduction. Does it manage at once to provide a valid basis for social criticism and to evade the charge of ideological distortion? More sharply, does the criterion of justice which it supplies fulfil the task of telling us what justice is, while leaving us in an agnostic position as to what justice demands? It will be noticed that the consensus theory of truth performs something like this feat, for it tells us what truth is but it does not enable us unproblematically to distinguish true theories from false. The difficulty of applying the criterion to identify true theories is that the theories in question are empirical ones and identification must await the presentation of all relevant evidence. It does not primarily have to do with the problem of foreseeing which theories will attract consensus, even collective consensus: this point will come up again later.

For Habermas, although he is not explicit about the matter, there are two independent parallels between the case of truth and that of justice. The first, and we have already drawn attention to it, is that to debate justice is to discuss the adequacy of political evaluations—judgments of justice—and such adequacy is the evaluative counterpart to the truth of empirical statements. Thus just as truth is examined in theoretical discourse, so we may expect a discursive consideration of justice. The other parallel suggests a similar conclusion. We mentioned that for Habermas someone making an assertion presses, not just a truth claim, but a claim to be intelligible, a claim to be sincere, and a claim not to be speaking out of turn: as he says, a claim to *Richtigkeit*, i.e. appropriateness, rightness or justice. This latter claim, he says, resembles the truth claim in demanding discursive redemption and so, on a second count, justice is put in parallel to truth.[30]

In fairness to Habermas a word more must be offered on this second way of drawing the parallel between justice and truth, for the parallel may seem to engage questions of justice only very marginally. The main point to be made is that justice is implicitly claimed not only by someone making an assertion, but also by someone giving an order, putting a request, offering advice, and so on.[31] The redemption of such justice claims may be expected to lead quite far afield. A claim is vindicated when it can be backed up by a norm, a norm which proves itself to be justifiable, whether or not it is institutionalized in the society.[32] The investigation of the validity of such norms will cover the entire spectrum of social life for every norm is engaged in some speech act: 'at least one justified recommendation (or as the case may be, one just command) must correspond

[30] W 220ff. See reference 10.
[31] W 227–228.
[32] W 228–229.

to any norm which ought to have validity under given circumstances'.[33]

Where theoretical discourse is the forum for the consideration of truth, Habermas describes the forum for looking into justice as practical discourse. In practical discourse he thinks that we find the same abstract structure of argument as we found in theoretical. The discourse is inaugurated when the justice of some speech act is called into question: or, as we may also say, when the adequacy of the corresponding evaluation is challenged. The ensuing argument will look to *prima facie* evidence, overarching warrant and ultimate backing. In the practical case the evidence will take the form of a legitimating ground, the warrant that of a general norm or principle and the backing the form of an excursus on the beneficial features of the norm. Thus the justice of my telling you to repay money that you borrowed might be vindicated by my recalling that you promised to repay it (ground), by my invoking the norm that promises ought to be kept (warrant) and ultimately by my expounding on the benefits secured by the realization of such a norm (backing).[34]

But granted that there are all these similarities, what makes for the distinction between practical and theoretical discourse? According to Habermas the crucial difference is that whereas in theoretical discourse the bridge between backing and warrant is usually inductive, the backing consisting in observation reports that support the general laws invoked as warrant, the bridge in the practical case is provided by the principle of universalization. His idea is that a practical warrant consists in a norm, a practical backing in an account of the interests served by the norm, and that the interests support the norm in so far as they are impartially served by it: that is, in so far as the norm would be chosen by someone who took those interests universally into account, and did not look only to his own welfare. 'Induction serves as a bridge principle for justifying the logically discontinuous passage from a finite number of singular statements (data) to a universal statement (hypothesis). Universalization serves as a bridge principle for justifying the passage to a norm from descriptive comments (on the consequences and side-effects of the application of norms for the fulfilment of commonly accepted needs).'[35]

In passing it may be remarked that the distinction drawn by Habermas between practical and theoretical discourse, although he conceives of it as a difference of form,[36] depends on the acceptance of substantial assumptions. It is by no means uncontentious to claim that the justification of a norm can be pursued only by reference to interests that it fairly serves, needs that it impartially fulfils. Someone committed to a natural rights

---

[33] W 229.
[34] W 242–244.
[35] W 245.
[36] W 226–227 and 239.

approach might say that the satisfaction of interests and needs has nothing to do with the assessment of a norm, that the norm is to be judged by whether or not it meets certain general constraints.[37] Habermas offers no argument for the line that he takes. He notes in passing that 'norms regulate legitimate chances of need satisfaction'[38], but that this is so does not establish that the norms should be judged by the satisfaction they produce.

Putting these matters aside, we are now in a position to understand Habermas's claim that the justice of norms is assessed in practical discourse, as the truth of propositions, specifically empirical propositions, is examined in theoretical. The effect of the claim is to force on us a consensus theory of justice in parallel to the consensus theory of truth. For all the considerations which motivate the latter theory are taken by Habermas also to apply in the justice case. 'If justice can qualify as a discursively resoluble validity claim, side by side with truth, then it follows that just norms must allow of being grounded in the same way as true propositions.'[39] The upshot is that we are to think of justice as something that permits only indirect characterization: it is the property which belongs to norms that would rationally command anyone's assent. This characterization is to be understood, once again, in a non-analytical fashion so that the justice of the norms explains their ability to attract assent, rather than being defined by it: the norms are not just because they secure a rational consensus; on the contrary, they secure a rational consensus because they are just.

This characterization of justice is one with which it is difficult to quarrel, although it is far from clear that none other is available. In the truth case Habermas offered arguments against the direct analysis of truth by reference to certainty or correspondence, and he also gave us reason for opposing an indirect analysis in methodological terms. Thus an indirect sociological account seemed to be the only one in the offing. In the justice case similar considerations are ignored and we are unceremoniously invited to assume that the most enlightening account of justice approaches it along a sociological route parallel to that which access was gained to truth. The assumption is not irresistible but I propose to go along with it for the time being.

As in the case of truth, Habermas specifies his initial statment of his consensus theory of justice in two further stages. At a first stage, and once again the comment is unobjectionable, he says that the argument which a just norm is expected to be able to survive, the argument which is meant to elicit universal assent, must be of a radical kind that allows

[37] See my *Judging Justice*, mentioned under reference 1, Chapters 8–10.
[38] W 251.
[39] W 226.

questioning at every level. It must permit questioning of evidence, warrant and backing and even allow the encompassing moral framework to be submitted to examination. The remark quoted earlier is intended to apply to the consideration of justice as much as it is to that of truth. 'An argumentatively achieved consensus is a sufficient criterion for the resolution of a discursive validity claim if and only if freedom of movement between the argumentative levels is guaranteed by the formal properties of the discourse.'[40]

It is the second stage of specification, in this case as in the other, which causes problems. Once again Habermas assumes that the consensus by reference to which justice is identified must be a collective consensus, although there is no obvious reason why a distributive consensus will not do. That assumption made, he then concerns himself with the question of how to guarantee that in collective discussion the required freedom of movement between different levels of argument, the necessary interrogative space, will be preserved. His answer is: by realization of those conditions that define the ideal speech situation. But there is no reason given why he should have to go into this matter and it is not even certain that any difference is made by the assumption that the consensus required to identify justice is a collective one. As we saw with truth, it might be taken that the assumption makes justice less scrutable, the outcome of a collective consensus being taken to be more difficult to foresee than that of a distributive one; but this point is not readily decidable, since we cannot be certain that group dynamics would make the collective judgment different from the distributive one.

So much then by way of characterization of Habermas's consensus theory of justice. The question which we now have to ask is whether it fulfils the task of telling us what justice is, while leaving us in an agnostic position as to what justice demands. So far as the arguments presented up to this point go the answer must be that it does not. The theory would allow me to deduce that others would respond in a similar way if radical argument in my own case showed me that a particular norm deserved recognition; thus, taking consensus in the distributive sense, it would permit me to regard the norm as just. As we have seen there is no reason to construe the consensus demanded in a collective sense but even if there were it is not certain that the same line of thought would fail. And even if it did fail, group dynamics being such as to render the point of collective agreement unpredictable, it would seem to fail for reasons which suggest that we ought to have stuck with distributive consensus in the first place. For if group dynamics interfere to make people agree to something collectively that each on his own would have been moved by radical argument

[40] W 255.

to reject, that would seem to indicate that they are a force of distortion rather than enlightenment.

It appears then that to accept Habermas's theory of justice is not to have agnosticism thrust upon one. Peirce would not have wanted his theory of truth to stop scientists from putting forward hypotheses: he did not entertain the prospect of their sitting back and waiting to see what opinions were fated to be agreed upon; indeed the same holds, presumably, for Habermas. By parity of argument there is no reason why the consensus view of justice should inhibit anyone from speculating and arguing about questions of political right, laying down that this norm is compelling, the other objectionable, and so on. But that being so, one may wonder whether the dilemma that we originally posed has been successfully evaded. For it now seems that Habermas is committed to the validity of our investigating matters of justice when the Marxist theory of ideology to which he subscribes would castigate the enterprise as irremediably distorted: this, at least, on the assumption that the investigation licensed by the consensus theory of justice will follow the familiar lines of established political philosophy, an assumption which Habermas does nothing to belie.

At the beginning of this section I mentioned that the consensus theory of truth does secure a sort of agnostic result, for while it tells us what truth is, it does not give us a standard by reference to which we can begin to work out which theories are true and which false. The reason is that in order to begin to judge theories for their truth-value we need to have all the relevant empirical data available and this condition is patently unfulfilled so long as scientific research goes on. No parallel consideration applies however in the case of justice, since the arguments by which we are moved to make our judgments, and by which we think that anyone should be moved, are not vulnerable in the same way to the effect of novel empirical discovery. Thus someone who accepts the consensus theory can have no reason not to go right ahead with the enterprise of making up his mind between such rival criteria of justice as those which define it respectively as legitimacy, welfare and fairness.

Our case against Habermas might seem ready to be closed. The consensus theory of justice, whatever we think about it in other respects, does not meet the constraint of leaving us in an agnostic position on questions of justice; it licenses a variety of speculation which Marxists have traditionally dismissed as ideological. But the case cannot be closed quite yet for Habermas has other arguments to offer in favour of the conclusion that the consensus view of justice forces agnosticism upon us. These arguments are independent of the parallel with the consensus theory of truth and I shall deal with them in the remainder of this section. There are three arguments in all and they respectively invoke considerations of agreement, accessibility and autonomy: none, I shall urge, is irresistible.

Philip Pettit

The argument from agreement is by no means explicit in Habermas's work but it is suggested by the following remark. 'It is obvious that practical questions, which are posed with a view to the choice of norms, can only be decided through a consensus between all of those concerned and all of those potentially affected.'[41] This comment is made by way of drawing a contrast between the resolution of questions of justice and the settlement of questions of truth. It suggests that because the selection of a norm as just means the choice of a rule of behaviour which will affect others as well as oneself, one must wait on the consensus of others before the selection is made; otherwise one is scarcely treating them as equals. The situation is meant to contrast sharply with that of selecting a proposition or theory as true, where the choice made will only affect one's own beliefs and behaviour. If the reasoning is valid, what it indicates is that the attempt to work out on one's own the shape that the just society ought to have is both presumptuous and pointless: presumptuous, because it means that one assumes the role of a dictator who is ready to order other people's lives for them; and pointless, because it is unlikely to yield the social constitution which people would jointly decide upon.

This argument for the required agnosticism will not work, for the reason that it depends on a confusion of two procedures: on the one hand, the more or less cognitive exercise in which answers are sought to questions such as 'Is this or that sort of arrangement just or not?'; and on the other, the organizational enterprise in which responses are elicited to issues of the form 'Shall we follow this or that constitutional pattern?' There are those who deny the distinction between the two procedures: anyone who thinks that evaluation is undetermined, being ultimately a matter of decision for example, is free to reject it. But Habermas does not belong to this 'decisionist' party, as we have already seen. 'I suspect that the justification of the validity claims contained in the recommendation of norms of action and norms of assessment can be just as discursively tested as the justification of the validity claims implied in assertions.'[42] Thus he must admit that it is one thing for an individual to resolve the cognitive question of what sort of norms are just and another for him to take part in the normative organization of a society.[43]

Once this distinction is admitted however the force of the argument from agreement is dissipated. It is not presumptuous to try to work out one's views on cognitive questions of justice, simply because they affect one's opinions on how society ought to be organized and determine the broad lines that one would follow in organizational deliberations. If it were presumptuous to do this then so would it be to attempt to clarify one's

[41] W 250–251.
[42] W 226.
[43] Such a distinction is more or less explicit in *Theory and Practice*, 32ff.

mind on economic matters, since one's economic views must have a similar influence on one's organizational disposition. And neither is it pointless to try to elaborate one's beliefs about matters of justice in advance of multilateral deliberations on the organization of society. On detailed questions of arrangement the outcome of such deliberations must be impossible to predict but on broad issues of justice, assuming that reason prevails, the line taken must coincide with that which one's personal reflection selects as rational.

The second ancillary argument for the agnostic construal of Habermas's consensus theory of justice may be called the argument from accessibility. This is suggested in the following remark, although it is not explicitly developed. 'Norms regulate legitimate chances of need satisfaction and the interpreted needs are a matter of inner nature to which each person has a privileged access, in so far as he has a non-deceitful relationship with himself.'[44] This remark is made in the same context as that which presents the argument from agreement and it also is meant to mark a contrast between the consensus theory of justice and the consensus theory of truth. The idea behind it is that since justice can only be determined by reference to something on which each person is authority in his own case, there is no sense in trying to work out one's picture of the just society in advance of multilateral deliberation and consensus, whether of a distributive or collective kind. Once again support is proffered for the agnostic construal of Habermas's theory of justice.

In this remark Habermas makes a substantial assumption about the sort of reasoning appropriate for settling issues of judgment, an assumption on which we commented earlier. The assumption is contentious and neither is it intrinsically connected with the consensus theory of justice: one might have a different view of the sort of reasoning suitable for political matters and still hold by the essential core of the consensus theory. But even if we let the assumption pass, we must be unpersuaded by this second argument. We might baulk at the strongly anti-behaviourist assumption that each person has a privileged awareness of his own needs, so long as he is not self-deceived, but this is not the objection that I have in mind. The reason we must be unpersuaded by the argument is that the point which it makes could be applauded by certain non-agnostic political philosophers: for example, by a particular kind of utilitarian.

The utilitarian believes that the just social scheme is that which produces the greatest happiness among the people living under it. One species of utilitarian, whose procedure I have characterized in detail elsewhere,[45] argues that people are happiest when the satisfaction of their wants or needs is maximized, and that we must use an interview technique based

[44] W 251.
[45] See my *Judging Justice*, mentioned under reference 1, Chapter 13.

on the economic theory of utility and decision to establish which of the alternative schemes available is likely to secure this result. A political philosopher of this hue could have no objection to the point which is made in the argument fron accessibility. The argument would not inhibit him from going ahead with his interviews and his calculations, always trying to guard against the self-deception of his subjects, in the attempt to determine the outline of the just society. Thus the argument fails to reinforce the agnostic construal of the consensus theory of justice. It would do so only if it was impossible to get at a person's politically relevant needs other than by letting him cast a vote for his preferred scheme and only if, in addition, there was no possibility of eliciting a suitable vote in a poll. The first condition is, as a matter of empirical fact, unfulfilled and the second would be realized only if it were the case, which it patently is not, that collective discussion is required for the eliciting of suitable votes and, what is more, collective discussion under some unobtainable circumstances such as those of the ideal speech situation. (Notice that were the first condition fulfilled and the second not, then the argument would fail to be compatible with a utilitarian procedure but it would continue to be consistent with a well-known alternative in political philosophy: the majoritarian criterion, according to which the just scheme is that which secures the greatest number of votes.)

The third ancillary argument for the agnostic construal of the consensus theory of justice urges upon us the virtue of leaving judgments of justice to the wisdom of parties seeking collective agreement under the conditions of the ideal speech situation; it suggests that only such parties are in a position to make reliable judgments, and this for a reason that should caution us against trying to work out what they would decide. Specifically, it is claimed that collective consensus under ideal conditions of communication ensures, whether or not uniquely, that the interests satisfied by the scheme chosen are those of autonomous agents, in particular that they are real interests and interests held in common. 'If under these conditions a consensus about the recommendation to accept a norm arises argumentatively, that is, on the basis of hypothetically proposed, alternative justifications, then this consensus expresses a "rational will". Since all those affected have, in principle, at least the chance to participate in the practical deliberation, the "rationality" of the discursively formed will consists in the fact that the reciprocal behavioural expectations raised to normative status afford validity to a *common* interest ascertained *without deception*.'[46]

Let us take first the point that the ideal conditions of communication guarantee that people's real interests, that is, their interests as interpreted without distortion or deception, are satisfied by the scheme chosen.

[46] *Legitimation Crisis*, henceforth LC, 108. The italics are in the original.

Habermas foresees that under those conditions people are forced by the glare of unconstrained communication to bring their needs clearly to light. 'Even the interpretations of needs in which each individual must be able to recognize what he wants become the object of discursive will-formation.'[47] He contrasts this situation favourably with that which is countenanced on any approach that takes people's interests as given and then tries to satisfy them impartially, pursuing universalizability. 'The principle of justification of norms is no longer the monologically applicable *principle* of universalizability but the communally followed *procedure* of discursive redemption of normative validity claims.'[48] Needs are interpreted and established under the subtle influence of interaction,[49] and the approach favoured by Habermas does not take this formative process as finished but presses it rather towards perfection. 'It carries on the process of the insertion of drive potentials into a communicative structure of action—that is, the socialization process—"with will and consciousness".'[50]

The second point made in the argument from autonomy is that the ideal conditions of communication filter out, not only people's real interests, but also interests which are genuinely common or 'generalizable'. Habermas is not entirely clear about what he means by such interests. They are described as 'needs that can be communicatively shared'[51] and are contrasted with 'particular desires and private satisfactions or sufferings'.[52] Presumably they include universal self-regarding desires which each can fulfil compatibly with respecting similar desires in others. An example might be the desire which each of us has for freedom from arbitrary arrest, a desire which contrasts in its non-competitive nature with something like the desire for social position. They must certainly also include society—regarding desires which each person naturally has or comes to develop. An example of this sort of aspiration would be the desire for a peaceful or cohesive community. Both these kinds of desires are capable of being communicatively shared in the sense that each person can avow and pursue them consistently with welcoming their avowal and pursuit by others. The second point in the argument from autonomy is that under the conditions of the ideal speech situation such needs are filtered out from particular, divisive concerns, so that the scheme chosen is given a

---

[47] LC 108.
[48] *Zur Rekonstruktion des Historischen Materialismus* (Frankfurt: Suhrkamp, 1976), 85. Cf. *Theory and Practice*, 150–151.
[49] *Theory and Practice*, 151.
[50] LC 89.
[51] LC 108.
[52] 'A Postscript to *Knowledge and Human Interests*', 171.

satisfactory base. 'The interest is common because the constraint-free consensus permits only what all can want.'[53]

What are we to make of this final argument? Well, the second point is hardly a telling one, since there is no reason to think that we cannot work out which interests are common and which particular in advance of seeing what happens under ideal conditions of communication. Habermas himself insists that the distinction between these two sorts of interests is argumentatively based and not a matter of arbitrary decision.[54] In that case there seems to be no obstacle to our going through people's concerns and rationally establishing where the line ought to be drawn.

The first point in the argument is less easy to deal with since we may well agree that one of the faults with an approach such as that of impartial utilitarianism is that it takes people's interpretations of their needs as given. This might push us into attempting to identify the just scheme by reference to other factors such as natural rights, a possibility that Habermas does not consider, but if we think that justice ought to be judged on the basis of the satisfaction of human needs or wants we may be understandably downcast by the lack in question. In that case we must be at least responsive to the claim that debate in the ideal speech situation would bring to the surface people's real wants, undeceived and undistorted.

And yet, ought we even then to be persuaded to espouse agnosticism and put down justice as something on which we cannot trust our own judgments, although we know the circumstances under which judgments would be trustworthy? The cost of going that way is enormous, in that it entails a self-denying ordinance in the area of political philosophy. And moreover, there are two considerations that counsel against it. The first is that while our intrepretations of our needs, and the desires which they sponsor, are certainly subject to the influence of social formation, there is no ground for believing that they are indefinitely malleable. Thus we might reasonably hope that a social scheme which satisfied people's existing wants would not diverge radically from that which would satisfy their enlightened ones; and if we are unconvinced of this then we might plausibly have a go at working out what people would come to want under enlightenment and then prescribe that the just scheme is that which satisfies those hypothetical desires. The second consideration that counsels against the agnostic conclusion is that it is doubtful in any case whether the ideal conditions of communication would automatically guarantee clairvoyance on the part of those seeking political consensus. Habermas does not offer us any detailed argument on the point, and we may well remain unconvinced, taking the only guarantee of self-knowledge to be radical

---

[53] LC 108.
[54] LC 108.

reflection, and thinking it possible that people in ideal communication might yet escape this experience.[55]

But there is a doubt raised by the argument from autonomy which, in conclusion, I would like to confess. It sometimes seems in Habermas's comments that he is mooting a model of human needs other than that which is generally taken for granted, and if this model is sound, then his argument has more weight than we have allowed. The generally accepted model, which might be described as a biological one, assumes that human needs remain recognizable across cultural variations in their expression. The model mooted by Habermas is better characterized as an artistic one, for it suggests that at least some of the needs which a just society should fulfil appear under the right conditions, as if out of nowhere: that like the need that one finds satisfied in a novel form of art, they are undetectable in advance of their appropriate objects. If we think that many significant human needs are of this kind, then we may expect people under ideal conditions of communication to develop interests of which we can have no inkling, interests that are without precedents or parallels. In that case we must be less short with Habermas's final argument for the agnostic construal of his conception of justice. It will be certain that under the existing order of things we are not in a position to work out what regime will satisfy our real interests, for it will be guaranteed that we are without the resources to recognize at least some of the interests in question.

The artistic model of human needs may attract some derision as a piece of romantic mysticism, but it is deserving of serious consideration. We cannot give it such attention here and we must be content just to note that our case against Habermas's agnosticism depends on the assumption of the more commonly accepted biological model. If we speak confidently of having established our point of view, we do so with this weakness put aside. A fuller defence of our claims must raise the question of the nature of human needs, and the rationality of respecting needs in ourselves and others which we are presently incapable of identifying. My own hope is that such a defence is available, for I fear that putting justice out of cognitive reach may ultimately mean inhibiting social criticism, and indulging the seductive idea that someday everything will be changed, changed utterly.

4. Conclusion

It appears then that neither the parallel with the consensus theory of truth, nor the three ancillary arguments that we have considered, secure

---

[55] Notice that Habermas mentions self-reflection and artistic experience as sources of enlightenment about one's real needs in *Zur Rekonstruktion des Historischen Materialismus*, 344–345.

for Habermas the agnostic construal of his consensus theory of justice; this, assuming the biological model of needs. Even when justice is identified in the indirect sociological fashion that he proposes it is presented as something which we may legitimately hope to investigate; none of the considerations brought forward by Habermas can deny us the right to that ambition. But if the investigation of the nature of justice is licensed, and nothing is said to suggest that it will be radically different from the sort of inquiry traditional in political philosophy, then a seal of approval is given to a mode of theorizing which has always attracted the Marxist criticism of being ideologically contained. Habermas has not slipped between the horns of the dilemma which we posed in the introduction. His consensus theory of justice, conceived for the purpose of grounding social criticism, involves him willy-nilly in countenancing the enterprise of political philosophy, and it means therefore that he must modify the Marxist theory of ideology which would deny the validity of that pursuit.

If my argument is sound then we must welcome Habermas into the company of contemporary political philosophers such as John Rawls, Robert Nozick and Ronald Dworkin. These thinkers unashamedly pursue the articulation of the demands of justice and, while Habermas may wish to express reservations on the plausibility of the project, his commitments force him to take his part in it. But there should we place him in the constellation of positions taken up by contemporary political philosophers? Interesting to note, his consensus theory does not of itself force him into any particular position. Just as one might accept Peirce's account of truth, or indeed Habermas's own, and adopt any of an indefinite number of rival scientific theories, so the acceptance of a consensus account of justice leaves one free to spell out the requirements of justice in any of the many competing ways. However, Habermas does have substantive opinions on the nature of justice and these appear in his remarks to the effect that the just system is that which impartially and maximally satisfies people's real needs. What one would like to see in his future work is a defence of this criterion against competitors and a detailed elaboration of its consequences: the sort of elaboration which, I have argued, he has no good reason not to try to provide.[56]

University of Bradford

[56] I am grateful for comments received when this paper was read at university seminars in Cork and Leeds. I received helpful remarks from Zygmunt Baumann, Thomas MacCarthy, Albrecht Wellmer and David West.

Marxian Metaphysics and Individual Freedom

G. W. SMITH

The principles of historical materialism involve Marx in making two crucial claims about freedom. The first is that the revolutionary proletariat is, in an important sense, more free than its class antagonist the bourgeoisie. The second is that the beneficiaries of a successful proletarian revolution—the members of a solidly established communist society—enjoy a greater freedom than even proletarians engaged in revolutionary *praxis*. It is perhaps natural to take Marx to be operating here with what might be called a logically continuous notion of freedom, established communists enjoying to perfection (or as near as maybe) what revolutionary proletarians merely imperfectly experience and what the bourgeoisie entirely misses. But whatever one's views might be about what Marx in fact says about freedom this cannot be what he ought to say for his theory of freedom to work. The kind of line Marx (and Marxists) need to take finds a significant precedent in his economics where we find a theory implying two quite distinct logical dimensions in that the principles and concepts designed to apply to the transactions of capitalism (commodity, capital, wage-labour, surplus-value, and so on) necessarily lack descriptive purchase on communist economic reality. The existence of these two dimensions, and particularly Marx's comparative silence as to the nature of the second, reflect his conviction that the transition between the two systems must be marked by a profound conceptual as well as material break.[1] Consequently it is not unreasonable, perhaps, to look for an analogous discontinuity in his metaphysics and to expect to find two distinct varieties of freedom, the one reflecting the nature of class society, the other of human community. If in what follows some exegetical light is thrown upon difficult texts all well and good, but the primary aim will be analytical—

---

[1] It might be objected that certain crucial concepts straddle the economic divide, 'exploitation' being perhaps the most important. After all, Marx undoubtedly condemns capitalism for being exploitative and commends communsim on the grounds that it is non-exploitative. But the contrast here must be between contradictories rather than contraries, if only because the category of exploitation is defined in terms of a measure *a priori* inapplicable in communism, namely exchange-value. (The capitalist coercively extracts in the form of profit the difference between the exchange-value of the labour-power he purchases and the exchange-value of the commodities produced by the worker.)

to identify the concepts Marx logically requires for the transition from claim (i) about proletarian freedom to claim (ii) about communist freedom. It is from this analytical point of view that the conceptual discontinuities of the economics are particularly suggestive. In what follows I shall argue two things: firstly, that both logic and clarity demand that Marx's twofold claim about freedom must be met by the application of two distinct concepts of freedom; and secondly, that the notion applicable to the communist state of affairs is of such a kind as to bring the possibility of individual freedom in communism radically into doubt.

I

Let us begin by considering the notion of freedom that Marx requires to capture the sense in which the proletariat, engaged in revolutionary *praxis*, is more free than its class opponents. In the celebrated third thesis on Feuerbach Marx accuses the 'old materialists' of emphasizing the fact that circumstances determine men to the point where they forget that circumstances are also changed by men. However, Marx insists, 'the co-incidence of changing circumstances and of human activity or self-changing can be conceived and rationally understood only as revolutionary practice'.[2] The oracular utterances of the *Theses* admittedly present a quagmire for interpreters but at least here the general meaning seems clear enough: men are (as the materialists claim) shaped by their social circumstances but proletarians (the revolutionary class) are, unlike members of other classes, capable of changing the conditions that determine them; hence proletarians are capable of changing themselves. In this sense (however much they may be alienated or exploited) they are free, or at least more free than those classes that cannot change themselves by changing their circumstances. To carry his point all Marx needs to do here (and all he seems to be doing) is to rebut the inference to human unfreedom (understood as lack of self-determination) purportedly drawn by the old materialists from their deterministic premises. He is not called upon to reject the premises themselves. A reference to J. S. Mill's handling of the same problem might be helpful here. In an editorial aside Engels associates Marx's target in the third thesis—the old materialists—with the doctrines of the English socialist Robert Owen; Mill, too, in his chapter on freedom and determinism in the *System of Logic*, feels he must answer Owen's social passivism.[3] Like Owen, Mill accepts the principle of universal causal determinism, but he claims to be able to evolve a conception

---

[2] K. Marx and F. Engels, *The German Ideology*, (C. J. Arthur) (ed.) (New York: International Publishers, 1970), 121.

[3] J. S. Mill, *A System of Logic* (Toronto: Toronto University Press, 1974), Book 6, Chapter 2.

of freedom according to which men can still be described as active agents in a world which proceeds according to exceptionless causal laws. To put it slightly differently, Mill invokes a positivist conception of freedom designed to accommodate human self-determination in a deterministic world. As Mill's response to Owen is detailed, explicit, and careful, it is perhaps worth taking as a preliminary guide to the kind of line Marx must presumably pursue if the sketch of thesis 3 is to be filled out.

Let us then briefly consider Mill's argument. As he represents Owen's social passivism, men cannot be held responsible for what they are, nor for what they do. They cannot be held responsible because their actions are merely the expression of their desires and their desires flow from their characters which are merely effects of social circumstances. Mill puts it by saying that, in Owen's view, men's actions and their desires merely express a character that has been made for them and not by them. If Owen were right men would be society- rather than self-determined and, as such, unfree. But Mill is convinced that Owen is wrong. Human actions are indeed the invariable effects of prior causes, yet it by no means follows from this that a man's character must be determined by causes beyond his own control, for he can still change his character *if he has the desire to do so*. If the desire to alter one's own character occurs it will of course be as the effect of prior causes, but this clearly does not mean that it cannot occur, nor that one would be unable to satisfy it if it did. Those in fact able to satisfy the desire for self-change when it occurs are, says Mill, self-determined and hence free. Of course, not everyone is free in this sense. Mill concedes that some people might be unable to alter their characters when they want and try to do so; they are indeed passive victims of causes and conditions beyond their control. But, equally, they are the pathological exceptions to the 'normal' case. The normal individual possesses the power to alter his character if he wishes. Consequently, Owen's depressing picture of men as invariably creatures of circumstances, the hapless inheritors of socially determined personalities, misguidedly treats everyone as though they were prisoners of inveterate habits or of psychological compulsions which they can never master, however much they might want and try to do so. Mill's response to Owenism pivots on what at least appears to be an elementary point. Owen assumes that the causal relation must be one-way—that it must hold in one direction only, from society to character and thence to desires (and actions). But the normal case, says Mill, is for it to hold in both directions—from society to character to desires (the Owenite direction) and from desires to character to society. The key to human freedom clearly lies in the reciprocal nature of the causal chain. Once we see this, self-determination is revealed as a possibility without need to abandon determinism for any kind of contra-causal freedom.

According to Mill, then, human freedom is possible because, though character admittedly determines desire, desire also determines (or in normal cases can determine) character. According to Marx in the third thesis, the old materialists are right in their contention that circumstances determine men, but they forget that men also determine (or can determine) circumstances. As with Mill the key to the problem is apparently to be found in the recognition of causal reciprocity between men and circumstances. Moreover, Marx's notion of revolutionary *praxis* introduces a distinction parallel to that drawn by Mill between normal and abnormal cases. For only the proletariat is in a position (like Mill's normal man) to escape the one-way determination of circumstances and to change circumstances, and hence themselves, in their turn. Only the revolutionary proletariat finds itself in a position to achieve freedom by engaging reciprocally with social circumstances. Apart from presenting an attractive line for those who prefer their Marxism uncomplicatedly empiricist rather than obscurely dialectical, modelling Marx on Mill offers two further and perhaps more substantial advantages. To begin with, it furnishes a coherent and intelligible explanation of Marx's particularly hard saying about 'philosophy' having to give way to 'practice'. For the manner in which the philosophical problem is solved—by pointing out that though circumstances change men, men *who so desire* can change circumstances and hence change themselves—focuses immediate attention upon the essentially practical issue of precisely when and how men moved by the appropriate revolutionary desires (and charged with the appropriate capacities) may be expected to appear on the social scene; a question answerable only in historical and economic, i.e. practical, terms. The second advantage is less immediately obvious, indeed it might appear at first sight to be no advantage at all as it arises out of the objection, often made by critics of philosophical Compatibilism, that Mill's solution to the Owenite challenge is broken-backed. Mill maintains that you are free if you are able to change your character if you wish. But how does the wish to change arise? Either it must arise in a character already engaged in self-reform, in which case the question has to be asked again one step back, or it arises in a so far unreformed character, in which case it cannot be self-caused but must occur as the contingencies of one's social circumstances determine. Mill indeed admits as much: as for the desire for self-reform, he says, 'it comes to use from external causes, or not at all'.[4] On this basis Owen seems clearly to have the best of the argument—an individual's character is ultimately outside his own control and is determined by his circumstances.[5] Isn't Marx struck down by the same objection? We are asked to believe that a revolutionary proletariat, a proletariat engaged in revolutionary change and self-change, is free;

[4] Ibid., 840.
[5] For a less hasty treatment see my 'The Logic of J. S. Mill on Freedom', *Political Studies* **28** (1980), 238–252.

but they, like Mill's self-reformers, are free only in the sense that they can employ their capacities to respond to desires over the occurrence of which they have no control; and as such they are not really free at all. After all, Marx supposes the proletariat to be capable of freedom impossible for 'abnormal' classes such as the bourgeoisie precisely because the contingencies of history are such that they will *impel* the needs, and hence the desires, which (along with historically created social and economic powers) will enable them to engage reciprocally with their circumstances rather than remaining, as other classes do, mere passive creatures of prevailing conditions. Revolutionary practice may be 'active' in that it may eventuate in social changes which in their turn will change men, but it is (and given the *logic* of the positivist concept of freedom it must necessarily be) a kind of activity which remains a function of historical contingencies. Like Mill's men the proletariat are ultimately, and necessarily, society- rather than self-determined.

Marx can, however, escape the charge which apparently destroys Mill. Whereas Mill deploys the notion of reciprocal causality to demonstrate the possibility of an unqualified human freedom Marx need make no such strong claim. Indeed to do so would be inconsistent with his programme. For if the revolutionary proletariat were already completely free there would be no point in striving for communism. As an embattled class, locked in opposition with the bourgeoisie, proletarians are still in the position of being compelled to respond to circumstances which they themselves have not created. Complete freedom awaits the successful proletarian revolution, for only with the firm establishment of communism can social circumstances be brought under full human control. The logic of the positivist conception of freedom which, as we have seen, seems ultimately to collapse into the one-way determination of men by circumstances, is in fact peculiarly well suited to what must be one of Marx's main preoccupations, viz. distinguishing the *relative* freedom of the proletariat, whose situation impels them to change circumstances (and hence change themselves), from the unfreedom of other (abnormal) classes, whose situations impel them to passivity and impotence. The logical structure of the Millian notion of freedom very neatly captures the situation of the proletariat, pinpointing the respect in which they are more free than their class opponents and the respect in which they nevertheless remain unfree. They are not entirely free in that their revolutionary needs and desires arise mechanically so to speak out of the contradictions and conflicts generated by an anarchic economic system, but they are freer than the bourgeoisie and other, historically marginal, classes (who are equally subject to the same uncontrolled economic forces) in that they are in the process of developing the powers necessary for the creation of a rational social order and of conceiving the needs and wants which will impel them to apply their powers.

The sense of relative freedom captured by the positivist notion involves limitations along two dimensions. In the first place the collective action of the proletariat is compromised by contingency in the manner outlined above—they merely react (as a class) to the wants and needs engendered by historical and economic contingencies. But in addition the individual proletarian achieves this imperfect freedom only as an 'involuntary' member of a class—he is not free to select or to choose his social relations. Marx clearly expects freedom to increase in both respects with the establishment of communism. The contingencies compromising the self-determination of the proletarian class give way before the rational organization and control of the totality of social life. And the individual is released from the constraints of involuntary class membership and is enabled to express his true individuality by choosing his own social relationships. It is in these two central senses that those living in an established communist society are more free even than militant proletarians. Admittedly the notion of 'controlling' the conditions of social life suggests a quantitative continuum, control over something may be greater or less and one achieves greater freedom by way of greater control, but clearly the positivistic notion of freedom is ill designed for the job which has to be done. It simply cannot be stretched to cover the conditions which, in Marx's view, characterize communist freedom. For however far men might go in perfecting control over their social circumstances the greatest freedom of which they can be capable in positivistic terms involves the crucial compromise with contingency embodied in the logical structure of the concept—at any point freedom presupposes a response to heteronomously given (socially induced) desires. To put it in Marxian terms, men free in the positivistic sense are free only within the constraints set by history (proletarian revolutionaries), whereas true communist freedom demands that men be free within conditions set by themselves. It is precisely this fundamental logical disparity which suggests that the categorial discontinuities of the economics should find a reflection in the metaphysics of freedom.

II

The shift from proletarian revolution to established communism, from 'pre-history' to 'human history', suggests of course an analogous shift from positivist to dialectical freedom. The freedom appropriate to communist man has to be a materialized version of the kind of freedom Kant and Hegel attributed to the spiritual 'self'. The idea of perfected freedom necessarily involving men in controlling the totality of their circumstances implies that men can create the conditions of their own freedom. The Idealists never take this to imply that freedom requires activity in an entirely unconditioned vacuum. On the contrary, conditions continue to determine self-activity and the self may even be described as being reciprocally engaged with these conditions. The crucial difference lies in the denial that these conditions are in any way external to the self. Instead the conditions admitted to govern the activity of the self facilitate rather than impede freedom because freedom means freedom of the self and the determining conditions are constitutive of the self, i.e. constitute the possibility of self-activity. Whereas causal reciprocity involves an external and contingent relationship between ontologically distinct items, a dialectical relationship holds between elements internally connected and mutually constitutive. Pretty clearly, if Marx is to be able to vindicate the claim that established communists are more free than revolutionary proletarians he must show how they can be related to their social circumstances in a dialectical rather than in a merely reciprocal manner. Perfected freedom ascribed to the collectivity of men furnishes no real difficulty. Marx claims to show how the abolition of private property and division of labour will enable men democratically to turn productive forces to the satisfaction of their needs and to replace the operation of natural laws by conscious planning. Under these circumstances it is not entirely implausible to hold that at least those who have lived for several generations under communism and who therefore may be assumed to inhabit a system purged of all evidence of unplanned or natural contingency will come to regard the social conditions they inherit as an extension of their own activities, needs, and purposes. At least I shall assume that the achievement of a dialectical self-identity of the social collective and the conditions under which it acts are unproblematical because I want to concentrate attention upon the second basic sense in which communist freedom is supposed to be an advance on revolutionary *praxis*, viz. individual freedom.

Individual liberty in communism is an issue for Marx because far from repudiating it, far from 'submerging' the individual in society, he insists that only in communism can the individual flourish and develop into a genuinely autonomous agent capable of giving full expression to his individual distinctiveness. Indeed, this is a claim that constitutes a vitally important element in his assertion of the moral superiority of communism over capitalism. This much is uncontroversial. What is problematic, however, is the precise nature of individual freedom in communism. The tendency of commentators is to deal with this question on a rather superficial level. On the one hand some critics maintain that there is no difficulty in the idea of individual freedom being secured in a system bereft of the apparatus of law and rights usually associated with individual liberty, whereas others argue that it is literally inconceivable without formal provisions of this kind. Both sides, however, neglect a logically prior issue, namely whether Marx can be said to have a coherent notion of what an individual person is in communism, and hence of what individual freedom might look like. This is indeed an odd omission if Marx is assumed (as he usually is) to be operating with a dialectical conception of freedom. For it is after all a familiar criticism of Idealism, indeed one made by Marx himself, that it deploys an abstract conception of the self or subject. Thus our ordinary notion of a person is pared down by Kant into that of bare non-physical self-consciousness (the 'experience-in-general' of the *First Critique*), and Hegel's notion of *Geist* is similarly detached from any essential individual physical subject. From the Idealists' point of view this was, of course, by no means a philosophically gratuitous move. The rationale lay in the fact that they were convinced that a dialectical relation between self and world, a relation able to accommodate and express freedom in an appropriately strong non-contingent sense, was possible only between the self abstractly conceived and the world. The problem facing Marx is focused in the first thesis on Feuerbach where it is proposed that the 'abstractness' of Idealism needs to be modified by the 'sensuousness' (i.e. the empirical physicality) of materialism in such a way that the passivity associated with the latter may be rectified by the Idealist notion of the active self—precisely the combination of empirical concreteness and free activity rejected as being *a priori* impossible by the Idealists themselves.

To understand the dimensions of the philosophical challenge facing Marx we need perhaps to linger a moment over some of the details of the Idealist conception of the self. One important source is to be found in Kant's rejection of Descartes' view of man as essentially a spiritual substance. Kant rejects it largely on the grounds that it is a metaphysical postulate quite incapable of furnishing empirical criteria for self-identity. In Kant's opinion the crucial feature of self-identity is the sense of being an enduring subject to which the succession of experiences is ascribed as 'mine', and he holds that this sense of continuity is explicable in one way only—it must arise out of the characteristic activity of the self. Since the self as consciousness is necessarily subject (that which experiences) and is never object (that which is experienced) it cannot be part of the experienced world. So far he agrees with Descartes. But the self is none the less constitutively related to the world in that its existence is explicable only by reference to its activity in creating an objective world of experience which furnishes the conditions of its own enduring identity as a self. This activity takes the form, of course, of interpreting experience under the *a priori* forms of space and time and of imposing categories of the Understanding upon that experience.[6] As the self can never fall under the cate-

---

[6] The best treatment of the philosophical issues concerning individuation raised by Kant's approach is to be found in P. F. Strawson's *The Bounds of Sense* (London: Methuen, 1966). The key idea here is that the notion of an enduring self is logically parasitic upon a prior recognition of an independently existing world furnishing physical object reference points which can be encountered and re-encountered in the course of a 'subjective experiential route through an objective world' (125). Kant psychologizes as the 'activity' of the transcendental ego in 'imposing' categories upon experience what Strawson more austerely regards as logical conditions for the intelligibility of the idea of the self.

gories of empirical experience precisely because it is 'abstract', i.e. non-physical, it cannot fall under the category of causality. Hence it may in this respect be said to be 'freely creative'. So, according to Kant's account of the conditions for the possibility of free self-creative activity, the freedom of the self is inextricably bound up with its abstractness. Moreover, the conditions grounding the freedom of Kantian abstract self-consciousness also entail its universality. For not only is the self transcendentally elevated beyond the category of causality, it is projected beyond all empirical determinants of experience, including the categories of substance and quantity, i.e. the categories of empirical individuation and identification. The upshot is that though the Kantian self is an enduring self, it does not endure as *a* self or as *several* selves. Instead, the self (or, more accurately, just 'self') is best understood as an enduring process or activity rather than as any one thing or number of things to which individuating concepts can apply.[7] In this sense, then, the self is both abstract and universal, and its freedom is conditional upon both. This is, of course, an extremely rarefied, not to say mysterious, idea of the self—it is abstract (non-physical consciousness) and it is universal (neither one self nor many). Even in the *First Critique* Kant seems unwilling to digest all the implications, employing personal pronouns ('I', 'my', 'mine', etc.) apparently quite literally to denote what is strictly speaking abstract unindividuated self-consciousness. In his ethical writings what might be construed as an oversight in his epistemology becomes a necessity, as it is clearly senseless to talk about moral responsibility, which in his view presupposes freedom (i.e. determination by the transcendental self rather than by heteronomous causes), unless the subject who freely acts is identifiable as this individual rather than that. It has even been suggested (by R. C. Solomon[8]) that Hegel's conception of the philosophical subject as *Geist* is best understood as a response to precisely these Kantian difficulties over individuation. *Geist*, Solomon argues, is transcendental ego, the literally general or universal consciousness, what it ought to have been for Kant had he been consistent. With Marx in mind we might put it slightly differently: Hegel recognized that a relation of dialectical self-identity between subject and object (and hence the prospects for dialectical freedom) demands the unequivocal rejection of the idea of the self as an empirically individuated person. The price extracted by dialectical freedom is a revolution in our conception of what it is that can be free in

---

[7] Some of the problems involved in introducing individuating terms into the notion of 'experience-in-general' are discussed by Strawson in *The Bounds of Sense*, 162, 170, and at greater length in my 'Concepts of the Sceptic: Transcendental Arguments and Other Minds', *Philosophy* **49** (1974), 149–168.

[8] 'Hegel's Concept of "*Geist*"' in A. MacIntyre (ed.), *Hegel* (New York: Anchor Books, 1972), 125–150.

this sense. Hence Hegel's systematic anti-individualism—freedom must be predicated in the first instance of *Geist* and only derivatively and in a highly qualified manner of actual empirical individuals. When placed in this context the tendency to assume that all Marx needs to do is to extract the notion of self-creative activity from Idealism and attach it to the idea of the physical individual characteristic of materialism to solve the problem of *praxis* must strike one as being philosophically naive. Without some attempt at an explanation of how the combination is conceivable Marx (and Marxists) stand open to the charge of repeating Kant's original error and of failing to comprehend Hegel's reasons for universalizing the self. And, whatever form that account might take, it cannot avoid bearing implications for a Marxian position on the question of individual freedom.

III

Before going on to consider whether it is possible to fabricate an acceptable conception of the individual person from the materials Marx apparently has available we need to clear some preliminary ground; in particular the peculiarly limited scope of the dialectic in question must be noted. Kant and Hegel purport to offer a general solution to a general question—they attempt to show how the self may be said to be free in a law-governed world. Indeed, even the positivist version of freedom introduced by Mill operates at the same level of philosophical generality. Marx is far less ambitious. Except from a brief period when writing his doctoral thesis on the ancient Atomists he never indicates much interest in this general problem. Even the account of proletarian freedom (sense (i)) revolves in a narrower orbit than Mill's, for unlike Mill who addresses the question both of the social and physical determination of man, Marx is concerned only to show how (some) men can be free in respect of the social determination of human nature. And whereas the essence of Idealism is that freedom is possible because self and world arise as conditions of and along with each other in a process of creative self-activity, Marx, however much he believed that men change the face of the physical world, never thought that they actually created it. Consequently the kind of dialectical self-identity taken by the Idealists to hold generally can, given Marx's commitment to a materialist view of physical reality, hold only between men and society. The condition which furnishes the stronger, non-positivistic, conception of freedom holds only within the human sphere: a dialectic exists because societies are human creations, the product of human labour and, conversely, human beings are created (or, at least, what is distinctively human about them is created) by society. So, Marx lowers his sights and confines himself to the question of human social freedom, the kind of dialectical self-identity of subject and object characteristic of the metaphysics of Idealism being reproduced on the social plane between men who, in creating their social world, express who and what they are, the society they create reflecting back upon them as the objective medium through which they express themselves rather than as an external obstacle to their creative activity.

Our first (and indeed our most important) question must be: does the dialectic hold between individual persons and society, or between men collectively and society? By no means can it be the former: the notion that the constituents of society are individuals atomistically detached from their social context implies a contractual conception of society quite foreign to Marx's thinking. On the other hand, if freedom is predicated simply or unequivocally of men collectively the individual is submerged and lost in the universal in precisely the way to which Marx objects in the Idealists. The dilemma arises, however, only when we assume that the individual must either be detached from society or be submerged by it. In an interesting but annoyingly brief aside in the *Grundrisse* Marx appears to suggest that these alternatives misrepresent the truth: 'Society', Marx says, 'does not consist of individuals, but expresses the sum of interrelations, the relations within which these individuals stand'.[9] Perhaps one can make what one wants of this, but it does seem to suggest a line between the horns of the dilemma—the way out is to reconceptualize the individual to capture both sides. As we have seen, Kant develops his notion of the freely creative self by abstracting 'self-consciousness' from our 'ordinary' or 'common-sense' conception of an individual person, but the above quotation might be taken to suggest that this is a philosophical starting-point bound by the narrow and erroneous assumptions of what Marx elsewhere calls 'civil society'. For the *apparently* concrete entity from which Kant starts (the physical individual) is in fact itself an abstraction—an abstraction from the real, i.e. social, individual. Society consists exclusively neither of individuals nor of social relationships, but rather of individuals in social relationships. The empirical individual, identified and distinguished from others primarily by reference to the physical characteristics of his body, is a being already abstracted from the nexus of his social relationships, and hence from the conditions constituting him as a human individual. The so-called 'common-sense' conception of the individual person, the notion from which Kant begins his transcendental argument for freedom, and which terminates in

[9] *Grundrisse* (Harmondsworth: Penguin, 1973), 265. It is worth noting the difference between this and the position expressed in the sixth thesis on Feuerbach where the 'single individual' seems to be reduced to the 'ensemble of social relations'. ('Seems to be' because it is the 'human essence' that is directly assimilated to the latter and it is unclear whether Marx thinks that the 'single individual' has an essence or not.)

Hegel in the characteristically universal subject of Idealism, is itself merely an abstraction from the logically and ontologically more basic idea of a *physical* individual constitutively engaged in *social* relationships.

It is beyond the scope of this paper to pursue the ramifications of this approach, the most that can be done is to indicate the general line of the possible Marxian solution to the problem of individual freedom in communism[10] and to note the major (and perhaps crippling) difficulty facing it. The individual is, as we have seen, to be conceived of as a *locus* of a set of intersecting social relationships—he occupies a determinate position in a network of social relationships which constitute him on the one side and society on the other. From this perspective he is, in a sense, a universal—a function of social relations displaying the kind of dialectical self-identity typical of the Idealist conception of freedom. This mutual interpenetration of individual and society furnishes the ontological premise upon which may be based characteristically Marxian ethical and political views about men's *Gemeinwesen* nature. On the other hand, the individual is prevented from being logically assimilated without trace into the universal because his identity as a social individual is ultimately grounded in the spatio-temporal physicality of his body. *Qua* physical individual his identity cannot be reduced without remainder to any set of social relations; *qua* social individual the reduction cannot be made in the opposite direction either. We seem here to have at least the beginnings of an account of how dialectical freedom might be predicable of the individual person. A paradox immediately arises, however, in that it is far from clear how it can be applied within communist society, as Marx describes it.

A key difference between class societies and communism is that whereas in the former social relations are, so to speak, chosen for the individual by the contingencies of the social and economic system, in the latter he chooses his own. In class societies 'social relationships take on an independent existence . . . the individual's position in life and his personal development are assigned to him by his class and he becomes subsumed under it'.[11] In communism, however, social relations cease to be coercive and the individual participates in the community as an individual rather than as an involuntary member of a class.[12] For liberal contractarians holding the 'common-sense' view of personal individuality the idea that the individaul may be left free to choose his own relationships is logically unproblematical —the physical individual adopts and discards social persona as he wishes,

---

[10] A more developed account along these lines would parallel, at a more abstract level, the kind of interpretation of the 'dialectic of labour' so brilliantly presented by G. A. Cohen. See 'Marx's Dialectic of Labour', *Philosophy and Public Affairs* **3** (1974), 236–261.

[11] *German Ideology*, 83 and 82.

[12] Ibid., 82–86.

and there can be no problem in class societies from the Marxian point of view as social relations are given rather than chosen anyway. But once the thesis as to the largely social nature of personal identity is annexed to the idea that involuntary social relations are abolished in communism, the possibility of accounting for the enduring individual seems to evaporate much in the way that it does with the Idealists. In communism social relations presumably must persist, for if they vanished the social individual, who owes his identity at least in part to those social relations, would disappear with them. The effect would be the kind of 'abstraction' of the individual Marx deplores in Kant and Hegel.[13] If social relations remain in communism and the exercise of true freedom and individuality consists basically in choosing those relationships then we have to make some sense of the idea of an individual who creates his own identity by acts of social choice. Yet once again the individual seems necessarily to disappear, for how can he intelligibly be said to endure through a series of changing relationships which constitute him as an individual person? One might be tempted at this point to emphasize the contribution made by the enduring physical body to personal identity. Instead of figuring as a logically residual element, as simply a kind of reminder that we are dealing with a materialist rather than an Idealist, the physical body might be called upon to carry a heavier (perhaps the main) philosophical burden of identification. But this is scarcely an attractive option, if only because it smacks of a return to Kantian bourgeois individualism, reducing the prospects for dialectical freedom for individuals so characterized to the kind involving precisely the abstraction from the physical body to self-consciousness of which Marx so strongly disapproves. The drift of the Marxian position seems inevitably to be towards attenuating, perhaps even fragmenting, the individual self of 'common-sense'.

Of the two claims, central to historical materialism, that Marx makes about freedom—that the revolutionary proletariat is in an important sense more free than its class opponents, and that communists are freer than either—only the first has been found to be logically coherent. As to the second claim, both critics and defenders of Marxism remain largely oblivious to the difficulty and intractability of the issues involved. The point may be put by way of a standard liberal objection. Liberals often accuse Marx of suppressing the individual in the name of communal solidarity, and they typically see this suppression as taking the form of forcibly subordinating the individual to the general will. Those Marxists who do not profess to disdain individual liberty usually reply by maintaining

---

[13] Marx faces, at the metaphysical level, difficulties similar to the sociological problems Cohen identifies in his ambition to transcend both the 'submergence' and the 'detachment' of the individual in 'community' whereby he is to step out of inhibiting social roles without stepping out of society.

that, on the contrary, individual liberty is fully and completely realized only in communism. Both parties in fact badly under-rate the conceptual revolution implied for our inherited ways of looking at ourselves and others in Marx's metaphysics of freedom. To claim that the individual is neither suppressed nor liberated in communism because he cannot conceivably exist there in the first place is perhaps excessive, but the exaggeration might at least serve to raise a question rarely asked with seriousness, namely: In what way is the 'new man' of communism recognizable as a man?

University of Lancaster

Althusser: How to be a Marxist in Philosophy

TIMOTHY O'HAGAN

Two Definitions of Philosophy

Althusser called a recent essay: 'Is it simple to be a Marxist in philosophy?' My title, intentionally provocative, echoes that question. Following Althusser, I shall answer it in the negative and, in so doing, shall raise a series of further questions concerning the nature of and connections between politics, science and philosophy. My lecture will keep turning on these three points, just as Althusser's own work has turned on them, ever since his first book, a monograph on Montesquieu, up to his most recent critical interventions on the role and organization of the French Communist Party in the 1970s. In an interview given in 1968, characteristically entitled 'Philosophy as a revolutionary weapon', Althusser linked the three points in an autobiographical comment:

> In 1948, when I was thirty, I became a teacher of philosophy and joined the French Communist Party. Philosophy was an interest; I was trying to make it my profession. Politics was a passion; I was trying to become a communist militant.
>
> My interest in philosophy was aroused by materialism and its critical function: for *scientific* knowledge, against all the mystifications of *ideological* 'knowledge' (LP 15).[1]

[1] Works of Althusser referred to in the text, with abbreviations: Louis Althusser, *For Marx*, trans. Ben Brewster (London: New Left Books, 1977) (trans. originally published by Allen Lane, 1969) (Fr. *Pour Marx*, Paris: Maspéro, 1965) (FM). Louis Althusser, Etienne Balibar, *Reading 'Capital'*, trans. Ben Brewster (London: NLB, 1968) (first Fr. edn Paris: Maspéro, 1965) (RC). Louis Althusser, *Lenin and Philosophy and Other Essays*, trans. Ben Brewster (London: NLB, 1971) (LP) (containing the 'Interview' with Macciocchi, 1968). Louis Althusser, *Essays in Self-Criticism*, trans. Grahame Lock (London: NLB, 1976) (ESC) (translations of *Réponse à John Lewis* (Paris: Maspéro, 1973) (RJL), *Eléments d'Autocritique* (Paris: Hachette, 1974), 'Est-il simple d'être marxiste en philosophie?' *La Pensée*, 1975 (IISTBAMIP). Louis Althusser, *Philosophie et Philosophie Spontanée des Savants* (1967) (Paris: Maspéro, 1974) ('Cours de Philosophie pour Scientifiques') (PPSS). Louis Althusser, *Politics and History*, trans. Ben Brewster (London: NLB, 1972) (*Montesquieu: Politique et Histoire*, Paris: PUF, 1959) (PH).

Later in the interview, his questioner condensed this central problem of Althusser's work like this: 'You have said two apparently contradictory or different things: (1) philosophy is basically political; (2) philosophy is linked to the sciences. How do you conceive this double relationship?' (LP 21). In what follows I shall try to formulate an answer to that question.

There is a continuity in Althusser's project since the 60s: that of combining philosophical commitment to the sciences with political commitment to the working class movement. Yet within that continued project we have to set the profound break in his orientation, both philosophical and political, dating from 1967. From that date on, he has attempted to distance himself from what he was to call his 'theoreticist deviation', propounded and practised in *For Marx* and *Reading 'Capital'*. He has highlighted the break in a series of aphoristic formulations and in one full-length book, the *Elements of Self-Criticism* (1974). But few of those texts make clear just what was philosophically wrong with the 'Old Definition' of philosophy as the 'theory of theoretical practice' or precisely what errors in that definition are corrected in the 'New Definition' of philosophy, now conceived as 'political intervention in the field of theory'. Althusser has, in fact, explored the complexity of the 'New Definition' in only one text, the 'Philosophy Course for Scientists',[2] delivered in 1967, but not published until 1974 and still not translated into English: I shall make considerable use of that text in the pages that follow.

In *For Marx* and *Reading 'Capital'* Althusser was attempting to pose and solve a revolutionary philosophical problem with relatively antiquated philosophical moves.[3] That problem had two components: (a) how to combine a realist thesis of the priority of the material world to knowledge of it with a recognition that scientific breakthroughs inaugurate radical discontinuities of conceptualization, which repeatedly put that realism in question; (b) how to establish an absolute difference between 'the real object' and 'the object of knowledge' and to combine that thesis with a non-normative account of the 'mechanism of knowledge production'. In this latter attempt, Althusser aimed to dismantle a model of philosophi-

---

[2] Full title: *Philosophy and the Spontaneous Philosophy of Scientists*. This gap in the corpus of Althusser translations means that the full novelty, subtlety and fragility of the new position has not been widely appreciated. In his most recent philosophical text ('Is it Simple to be a Marxist in Philosophy?', 1975), Althusser has made one further important shift in his position on the relation of 'command' between philosophy and science. In what follows I expound both the 'New Definition' of 1967 and the 'Command Problem' of 1975 suggesting some of the implications of the new positions but leaving many questions open.

[3] The original version of this paper contained an account of those moves and expounded in more detail the emergence of the 'New Definition' in response to defects in the 'Old'. I hope to publish that section, which had to be excluded from the present text for reasons of space, elsewhere.

cal practice, deeply entrenched since Descartes, according to which philosophy (particularly epistemology) stands in judgment on the sciences, establishing 'criteria' of validity external to them, to which their practices must measure up. In his opposition to this traditional self-image of philosophy, Althusser found uncomfortable historical allies, notably Spinoza, Nietzsche and (barely acknowledged) Heidegger.[4]

But the philosophical programme of *For Marx* and *Reading 'Capital'* ended in a series of *impasses*, ontological, epistemological and metaphilosophical. The theses that the material world has priority to knowledge of it and that science can establish a correspondence between concepts and their objects, allowing knowledge of that world, were left suspended in a philosophical vacuum, to be filled either by dogmatic reassertion of the theses or by resort to traditional and unsatisfactory forms of argumentation. The void was caused because Althusser wanted to reject the normative search for 'guarantees' of knowledge, but could not yet show how philosophy could characterize its own practice.

We can pause at this moment to note that those difficulties were not a peculiarity of Althusser's programme, but were encountered by a number of philosophers, Marxist and non-Marxist, in both English and French language traditions. These philosophers, particularly in the philosophy of science, were to establish a new trend towards realism, which attained some dominance in the 70s, following the same requirement as Althusser, that we respect the integrity and validity of scientific practice, starting from the existence of that practice as a premise. Two variants of this realism have emerged in the English language literature: *transcendentalism* and *continuism*. *Transcendentalists* demand that we must 'reason from the effect, science, to the conditions of its possibility'. They argue that those conditions are (1) that there exists 'a world of enduring and transfactually active mechanisms', independent of, and prior to, our knowledge of them and (2) that the knowledge yielded by science is indeed knowledge of (1): it is not simply efficient, elegant, economical ordering of experience.[5] The problem with transcendental arguments like this, whatever their degree of sophistication, is that they cannot fail to be circular, what

[4] Cf. the following characteristic question from *Being and Time*: '... what higher court is to decide whether and in what sense there is to be any problem of knowledge other than that of the phenomenon of knowing as such and the kind of being which belongs to the knower?' (Heidegger, *Being and Time*, trans. J. Macquarrie and E. Robinson (Oxford: Blackwell, 1962), 88).

[5] Roy Bhaskar, *A Realist Theory of Science* (Leeds: Leeds Books, 1975), 208. André Glucksmann, one of Althusser's earliest critics, argued that Althusser's early epistemology presupposed a tacit transcendental argument with respect to correspondence ('The Althusserian Theatre' in *New Left Review* No. 72 (1972), 73–74).

Althusser calls 'no more than the *fait accompli* of mirror recognition' (RC 56), since, given the form of the argument, the transcendentalist's premise ('Science exists') already contains the realist component (i.e. 'Science exists and it provides objective knowledge of an objective world'), which makes the 'derivation' of the realist conclusion trivial. If, on the other hand, it does not contain the realist component, then the derivation is invalid.[6]

More in keeping with Althusser's position in *Reading 'Capital'* is some variant of *continuism*, which makes materialist philosophy simply continuous with the sciences. The advantage of continuism, of turning philosophy into a 'summing-up of the most general results'[7] of the sciences, is that it appears to be a direct way of avoiding the idealist subversion of scientific practice, for it can no longer stand outside the sciences and impugn their credentials by reference to external normative criteria.

However, continuism has major shortcomings when it attempts to capture the reality of philosophical practice. In particular, it does not come to terms with the Kantian challenge to explain why in philosophy we make, strictly speaking, no progress and 'constantly move round the same spot, without gaining a single step' (*Prolegomena*, 256). It does not account for the *ever recurring* necessity for philosophical interventions. If we agree with Althusser that the foundation of a new science is an irreversible event (ESC 151), then, if philosophy were continuous with science, we should expect that those philosophical categories which emerge directly from the new scientific concepts would have the same irreversible quality as their scientific counterparts.

Yet the reality of the history of science and philosophy points in the opposite direction. In physics in particular, each new breakthrough has delimited certain *new* frontiers of knowledge, yet at the same time has precipitated a *recurrence* of old debates about the reality of the external world and the objectivity of our knowledge of it.

Furthermore, if, in the words of one outstanding continuist, materialism shares a 'unity of approach or outlook' with the sciences, so that 'to look at the world materialistically is to look at it as a scientist', since materialism alone genuinely 'expresses the spirit of science',[8] why should it be that scientists themselves so constantly resort to idealist philosophical positions and should need philosophers (non-scientists) to help them recognize the

---

[6] I have taken this conclusive argument from D. H. Ruben, *Marxism and Materialism* (Hassocks: Harvester Press, 1977), 101–102.

[7] K. Marx and F. Engels, *German Ideology* in K. Marx and F. Engels, *Collected Works*, 5 (London: Lawrence & Wishart, 1976), 37. Interpretation of this somewhat ambiguous passage plays an important part in Ruben's attribution of continuism to Marx.

[8] D. H. Ruben, op. cit., 108, 191.

'appropriateness' of materialist philosophy to their scientific practice?

It is in attempting to reach answers to these questions that Althusser moves to the more explicit and more radical formulations of the 'New Definition'.

The 'New Definition of Philosophy': Politics in the Field of Theory

Althusser's 'New Definition' has three levels, which are logically separable, so that philosophical and political critics may want to accept one or other of them, while rejecting the rest. Although here, for reasons of space, I must concentrate on the distinction between the levels, I must emphasize that it is not just their joint assertion, but precisely their combination, that makes Althusser's position novel and explosive.

The three levels are the following:

(1) The logical status of philosophical propositions.
(2) The connection between philosophy and the sciences.
(3) The connection between philosophy and the political class struggle.

Level 1. The Logical Status of Philosophical Propositions

Let us allow Althusser to introduce his 'New Definition' in his own words, from the opening pages of the 'Course for Scientists.'

> In this course we shall begin by pronouncing a certain number of didactic and dogmatic propositions . . . These propositions are *dogmatic*: this adjective is linked to the very nature of philosophy. I define as *dogmatic* any proposition which has the form of a *Thesis*. I add: 'Philosophical propositions are Theses'. Therefore they are dogmatic propositions.

> That proposition is itself a philosophical Thesis.

> Thus

> *Thesis 1*. Philosophical propositions are Theses (PPSS 13).

What is meant by 'dogmatic'? In Spinozan style, Althusser supplies an *explicatio* to the *definitio* by first marking off philosophical from scientific propositions:

> . . . philosophical propositions can be said to be dogmatic in the *negative* sense that they cannot be demonstrated in the *strictly* scientific sense. (In the sense in which we talk of demonstration in mathematics or logic) or proved in the *strictly* scientific sense (in the sense in which we talk of proof in the experimental sciences).

From this explanation, Althusser proceeds to Thesis 2:

> Philosophical Theses, not being able to the object of scientific demonstration or proofs, cannot be said to be 'true' (demonstrated or proved, as in mathematics or physics). They can only be said to be 'correct' ('*justes*').

> *Thesis 2.* Every philosophical Thesis is said to be correct or incorrect (ibid., 14).

He then explains the term 'correct':

> What can 'correct' mean?

> To give a first idea, let's say that the attribute 'true' implies primarily a relation to theory; the attribute 'correct' primarily a relation to practice (cf. a correct decision, a correct war, a correct line) (ibid., 14).

I have presented Theses 1 and 2 and some of Althusser's comments on them quite fully since they are found only in the 'Course for Scientists' and are not reproduced in such explicit form elsewhere. Yet without them, the 'New Definition' is of little philosophical interest. Let us begin by examining these theses. Thesis 1 is expanded into the statement that philosophical theses are not demonstrable or provable. Thesis 2 states that philosophical theses are correct or incorrect rather than true or false. These theses can be connected only by making a radical *identification* between lack of demonstrability and lack of truth value. Such an identification is initially puzzling, since there seem to be many *particular* propositions which have a truth value, even though that truth value cannot be demonstrated in any scientific fashion. For instance, the proposition 'This piece of paper is white' is true, but its truth is hardly demonstrable.[9]

To solve the puzzle, we have to move to one of the central insights of Althusser's 'New Definition' and understand Thesis 1 and Thesis 2 as two specifications of a more primitive 'Thesis 0':

> Philosophical propositions, though grammatically indicative, are disguised injunctions.

This seems to me to be the best way of understanding Althusser's particular

---

[9] Intuitionist mathematics does explicitly identify truth-value with demonstrability (or, perhaps more accurately, replaces the conception of truth by one of demonstrability): see W. and M. Kneale, *Development of Logic* (Oxford, Clarendon Press, 1962), 680. But Althusser does not seem to have any mathematical model in mind here.

conceptions of philosophy as a struggle[10] and philosophy as a game.[11] Philosophical propositions are *both* unprovable *and* lacking in truth value in so far as they are (a) *particular*, having a function and meaning only in relation to the political and scientific conjuncture in which they are made and (b) *practical*, enjoining us to adopt conceptualizations, analogies, models and, in particular, lines of distinction and demarcation, which foster or hinder the emergence and development of particular phases of scientific knowledge, but do not themselves constitute such knowledge.

The properties of the objects of the sciences are, on Althusser's realist and rationalist view of the sciences, demonstrable or experimentally provable, whereas those of philosophy are not. Indeed, in the strong sense, '*philosophy, strictly speaking, has no object* in the sense that a science has an object . . . ' (ibid.).

Yet, though it does not have its own object, philosophy has its own functions and its own field of intervention. Althusser lists the *functions* of philosophy under the headings of division (Plato) or demarcation (Lenin), i.e. making the critical distinctions that mark the history of philosophy: ideal/phenomenal, necessary/contingent, analytic/synthetic, materialist/idealist . . . Forms of demarcation include classification, separation of ideas from one another, forging ideas 'suitable to allow us to perceive these separations and the necessity of making them', ideas which make distinctions 'manifest or visible' (PPSS 15).[12] He sees philosophy's *field of intervention* as follows:

> Philosophy intervenes in a certain reality: 'Theory' . . . in the indistinct reality constituted by the sciences, theoretical ideologies and philosophy itself . . . The result of the philosophical intervenion . . . is to trace, within this indistinct reality, a demarcation line which, in each case, separates the scientific from the ideological . . . Philosophy acts by modifying words and their organization . . . this change of words allows something *new* in reality to appear, to be seen, where previously it was hidden and covered (PPSS 62–63).

[10] 'Philosophy represents the class struggle in theory. That is why philosophy is struggle . . . and basically a *political* struggle: a class struggle . . . The philosophical struggle is a sector of the class struggle between world-views . . .' (Interview. Q.5 LP 21).

[11] 'The forms and arguments of the fight may vary, but if the whole history of philosophy is merely the history of these forms, they only have to be reduced to the immediate tendencies that they represent for the transformation of these forms to become a kind of *game for nothing*' (LP 56).

[12] In linguistic terminology, as Tony Trew suggests, philosophical theses are irreducibly 'deictic' or 'indexical', the objects *to which* they point, *of which* they are the index, being already elaborated in scientific and political practice.

But is this conception of philosophy not immediately self-defeating? For, if theses are propositions that are neither true nor false and if proposition p: 'Philosophical propositions are theses' is itself a thesis, then p is neither true nor false, therefore it does not merit rational consideration. Althusser admits that there is a circle here, but claims that it is not the vicious one implied in the objection. In order to understand the nature of philosophy, he says, it is necessary to go outside of philosophy, into the sciences, in particular into historical materialism, which gives a theoretical explanation of the role and history of philosophy. But any process of going outside philosophy towards an objective knowledge of philosophy represents at the same time a position in philosophy, a position which is materialist, in so far as it asserts and endorses the possibility of a particular kind of objective knowledge and which is thus a thesis in and on philosophy. It is impossible to reach a definition or a knowledge of philosophy which can *radically* escape philosophy in the realm of a so-called 'science of philosophy' (PPSS 56). I have already suggested that we should regard the first two theses as injunctions to regard philosophy as interventionist and injunctional or as the rational application of injunctions. If that view is correct, then it is perfectly rational to adopt a set of injunctions (the philosophical theses of Louis Althusser) which illuminate and assert the objectivity of a particular form of scientific practice (historical materialism); this scientific practice can in turn both give us knowledge of the objective role and functioning of traditional philosophy and can found the self-consciously interventionist practice of contemporary materialist philosophy.

At Level 1, then, Althusser stresses that philosophical interventions are particular, inconclusive, recurring, polemical, modelled on struggle and eristic, yet at the same time supported by 'rational justifications of a particular distinct type' (PPSS 15). I detect some ambivalence in Althusser's view of the degree and nature of rationality in philosophical interventions. At some points, when addressing the philosophical establishment, '*pour épater la bourgeoisie*', he seems to advocate the irrationalist programme of 'philosophizing with a hammer':

> If science unites, and if it unites without dividing, philosophy divides and it can only unite by dividing ... there is no such thing as philosophical communication, no such thing as philosophical discussion ...
> (LP 31–32).

But his actual philosophical practice belies this extreme position, operating according to quite conventional logical and semantic rules which allow for 'communications' and 'discussion', even if that does not lead to demonstrable conclusions. Philosophical reasoning, on this model, has much in common with legal reasoning. Legal practice can be seen as arising from, and constantly re-forming, systems that are rational but inconclusive. Its rationality is always relative to other demands which are irreducibly particular and contingent. Its content is always given by social, political, economic practices: practices which are other than its own and within which it has the function of intervening, demarcating, drawing lines.[13]

Level 2. The Connection Between Philosophy and the Sciences

Althusser moves from Level 1 to Level 2 via three theses from Lenin:

(i) Philosophy is not a science.
 Philosophy is distinct from the sciences.
 Philosophical categories are distinct from scientific concepts (LP 50).
(ii) If philosophy is distinct from the sciences, there is a privileged link between philosophy and the sciences. This link is represented by the materialist thesis of objectivity (LP 53).
(iii) The history of philosophy is the history of an age-old struggle between two tendencies: idealism and materialism (LP 55).

The close link between the discovery of 'scientific continents' and the emergence of philosophical positions has been a constant theme of Althusser's work since the beginning:[14]

Marx founded a new science: the science of history. Let me use an image. The sciences we are familiar with have been installed in a number of great 'continents'. Before Marx, two such continents had been opened up to scientific knowledge: the continent of Mathematics and the continent of Physics. The first by the Greeks (Thales), the second by Galileo. Marx opened up a third continent to scientific knowledge: the continent of History.
 The opening up of this new continent has induced a revolution in philosophy. That is a law: philosophy is always linked to the sciences.
 Philosophy was born (with Plato) at the opening up of the continent of Mathematics. It was transformed (with Descartes) by the opening up of the continent of Physics. Today it is being revolutionized by the opening up of the continent of History by Marx. This revolution is called dialectical materialism (Interview Q.4 LP 18–19).

---

[13] It is interesting that, when Althusser discusses the epistemologists' search for absolute 'guarantees' of knowledge, he criticizes it for following an erroneous juridical model, that of the search for natural laws, for a set of absolute norms which can ultimately validate a legal system. At the same time, his own new, interventionist model of philosophical practice has much in common with the view of legal practice and reasoning put forward by some contemporary legal theorists, notably by Neil MacCormick, *Legal Reasoning and Legal Theory* (Oxford: Clarendon Press, 1978), Ch. 10.
[14] See e.g. the Foreword to *Montesquieu: Politics and History*, PH, 13–15.

Timothy O'Hagan

Philosophy, on this view, always comes on the scene *post festum, after* the emergence of a science. Althusser sums up its function in two theses:

> A major function of philosophy is to trace a demarcation line between the ideological component of ideologies on the one hand and the scientific component of the sciences on the other.

> All the demarcation lines traced by philosophy are reducible to modalities of a fundamental line: between the scientific and the ideological (PPSS 26, 50).

But what kind of demarcation lines are available to Althusser's interventionist, non-normative philosophy? Evidently nothing so abstract or 'external' as Popperian falsifiability or empiricist verification criteria will be acceptable. In fact, Althusser has always claimed in Spinozan style, that scientifically founded propositions are *index sui*, in need of no external 'justification'. Philosophy characteristically intervenes at points of so-called 'crisis' in a science, when there is

> a contradiction between the new problem and the existing theoretical materials. When the whole theoretical edifice is shaken (PPSS 67–68).

Althusser alludes to the 'crises' of irrational numbers in Greek mathematics, of modern physics at the end of the nineteenth century and of modern mathematics and logic at the time of Cantor and Zermelo and he instances various reactions which scientists may have to these 'crises'. These include the reaction of *capitulation*, when the scientists 'go outside' science altogether and consider it from some extra-scientific moralistic standpoint, abandoning their belief in *both* the validity of scientific knowledge *and* (in the case of physics) the existence of matter independent of the knowing subject. They also include the more sophisticated reaction of an *immanent move to idealism*, the criticism of science from within science by scientists who erect their own philosophy of science against the 'old', 'outmoded' philosophy of science, labelled 'dogmatic', 'mechanist', 'naive', 'materialist', etc. But these moves too always take place within a strong philosophical tradition, whether empiricist, Kantian or some other variant of idealism (PPSS 74). The materialist philosophical intervention, then, does not produce the distinction between science and ideology, since that distinction is already present, once there is scientific practice, but in establishing and applying the philosophical, categorial distinction between *the* scient*ific* and *the* ideolog*ical* in a particular area, it allows us to *see* where the distinction lies, by distinguishing the materialist from the idealist components within a particular discourse.

Althusser's radical separation between philosophical and scientific questions is designed to prevent the traditional exploitation of scientific problems to produce idealist, anti-scientific positions:

> Philosophical questions are not scientific problems. Philosophy does not infringe on the domain of the sciences (PPSS 50).

Yet does not the conception of philosophical *correctness* (*justesse*) embody all the normative content of the old conception of philosophical truth under a new name? Althusser argues that philosophical interventions have a 'relative autonomy', so that, though philosophy has no right to intervene in the *content* of scientific research, yet it does have the right to assess the limits of scientific discourse in particular conjunctures. Thus in his polemic with the eminent biologist Monod, Althusser attempts to isolate the materialist content of his scientific work from the idealist applications of it, made by popularizers of science, including Monod himself, and, in particular, to mark off wholly mythical models (e.g. the noosphere) erected on the basis of the science. Althusser claims that philosophy does have the right to intervene on such questions, and on a number of other 'new philosophical questions', e.g.:

> what is the application of one science to another, how is one science constituted by some other? . . . (PPSS 50).

But these examples suggest that Althusser may still have trouble in making his strong distinction between the illicit intervention of philosophy into the *content* of scientific work and its justified intervention on the *frontiers* and *boundary lines* that divide science from non-science. By virtue of his general position on philosophical method, he can hardly lay down an abstract, *a priori* criterion for deciding where this distinction must be made. But in so far as his fragmentary list of legitimate philosophical questions includes such apparently intra-scientific questions as 'the application of one science to another', I am not confident that Althusser has a sufficiently elaborate philosophical armoury to prevent his own interventions from becoming as metaphysically authoritarian as those of traditional philosophy.

The 'new ordering' or 'command' problem

We have recorded the major break in Althusser's position dating from 1967 and formulated in his 'New Definition' of philosophy. But that 'New Definition' contained important elements of continuity with the previous position, in particular the view that

> Transformations of philosophy are always rebounds from great scientific discoveries. Hence in essentials, they arise after the event. That is why philosophy has lagged behind science in Marxist theory (Interview Q.4 LP 19).

253

Indeed, in his lecture on *Lenin and Philosophy* (1968), Althusser reinforces this view, with a reiterated claim that there is necessary time-lag (*retard*) between the emergence of a science and the emergence of a philosophy, even though there may be a degree of reciprocal aid from the side of philosophy once the scientific breakthrough is underway:

> ... the work of philosophical gestation is closely linked with the work of scientific gestation, each being at work in the other (LP 45).

We are reminded here of Marx's obstetric image, in which society can 'shorten and lessen the birth pains' but not radically alter the 'natural phases of its evolution'.[15] The parallel between Marx's and Althusser's metaphors is suggestive. In Marx's notoriously fatalistic formulation, the overall trend of economic development of a society, including contradiction and collapse, are beyond the power of political intervention, though its form and timing can be so affected. Althusser's formulation suggests a similarly autonomous, reified progress of scientific research and discovery, and a similarly subordinate role for philosophical intervention.

Althusser's next metaphor suggests that there may sometimes be a more active role for philosophy:

> But it is also true that in certain cases (to be precise, Plato, Descartes) what is called philosophy also serves as a theoretical laboratory in which the new categories required by the concepts of the new science are brought into focus (*mises au point*) (ibid.).

But even on this account, philosophy arrives strictly *post festum*. In fact, the whole distinction between philosophy, on the one hand, and ideological world-views on the other, depends on the assumption that philosophy handles (exploits[16] or defends) scientific concepts, on the basis of which it constitutes philosophical categories. Hence a central thesis of the *Course for Scientists* states that

> (Th. 24): The relation of philosophy to the sciences constitutes the *specific* determination of philosophy ... Apart from its relation to the sciences, philosophy would not exist ... (PPSS 65, 66).

It comes as a complete surprise, therefore, to read in the *Reply to John Lewis* (ESC 68–69 Fr. 56) that

> Marx's philosophical revolution governed (*a commandé*) Marx's 'episte-

---

15 K. Marx, *Capital*, I (London: Lawrence & Wishart, 1970), 9–10.
16 In the pejorative sense in which a ruling class exploits a subordinate class, not in the neutral sense in which producers exploit a raw material like a coal mine.

mological break': it was one of the conditions of the possibility of the break.[17]

Althusser then refers to his previous position, that philosophy always appears *post festum* and agrees that it can be argued for. But,

from another point of view, which is important here, one has to say the opposite, and argue that in the history of Marx's thought, the philosophical revolution necessarily governed the scientific discovery and gave the latter its form; the form of a *revolutionary science* ... In the case of Marx, both the philosophical revolution and the epistemological break take place 'at the same time'. But it is the philosophical revolution that 'governs' the scientific 'break'.

But furthermore, according to Althusser, Marx's philosophical evolution is not independent of his political evolution. Althusser traces a three-stage political evolution in Marx's career between 1841 and 1845 (radical bourgeois liberalism/petty bourgeois communism/proletarian communism), 'governing' a three-stage philosophical evolution (subjective neo-Hegelianism/theoretical humanism/materialist revolutionary philosophy). This in turn ultimately 'governed' his scientific discovery.

It is not too difficult to 'locate' Althusser's *new ordering* of the couple, scientific break/philosophical revolution. It is associated with his increasing emphasis on the class struggle as the key to understanding both historical development and present political practice.

But what of the particular problem that concerns us? How does Althusser's new emphasis affect the general relationship between philosophy, the sciences and politics? If philosophy is to be understood as a kind of intervention, which has, strictly speaking, no object and does not yield knowledge, how can it 'govern' (*'commander'*) the emergence of scientific concepts? It should be noted that Althusser is careful to restrict the 'New Ordering' to a single philosophy/science couple, the couple formed by Marx's philosophy and Marx's discovery of historical materialism. He does not suggest that the 'New Ordering' is applicable in other cases. If that is correct, then it must be because historical materialism is in some important respect different from the other sciences. To understand that difference we shall now turn to the third and final level of the 'New Definition' which relates politics to philosophy.

Before that transition to Level 3 is made, it should be re-emphasized that, for Althusser, the link between the sciences and materialist philo-

---

[17] I have retranslated these passages. The English translation renders *A a commandé B* first as *A preceded B* and later as *B was based on A*. Both versions are misleading.

sophy is a fragile, conjunctural one. There is no strictly logical relation between the two: materialism is not a 'science of sciences' from which the particular sciences could be derived, nor does it provide formulae which can be 'applied' in them (ESC 58). Thus the efficacy of materialist interventions is assessed *ex post facto*, by reference to the particular historical occasions when such interventions 'opened the way to further scientific progress'. During the Enlightenment, says Althusser, 'the philosophers' materialism undeniably served the scientific progress of the time . . . against the religious impostures . . . which were currently dominant . . . The scientists' alliance with materialism served the sciences' (PPSS 109). But, as Althusser goes on to show, that particular alliance was fragile and short-lived, as the particular materialist positions of the *philosophes* were rapidly incorporated by the dominant idealism. In each case, the credentials of an alliance between a given philosophical position and a given scientific movement can only be established historically, conjuncturally.

Level 3. The Connection Between Philosophy and the Political Class Struggle

We come finally to the most controversial level of Althusser's position, the thesis that 'Philosophy is politics in the field of theory' (LP 68), which is expanded into the double thesis that

> Th. 20: philosophy represents politics in the field of theory . . . and vice versa philosophy represents scientificity in politics, with the classes engaged in the class struggle (ibid., 65).

The bald slogan 'philosophy is politics' is misleading unless the specificity of 'in the field of theory' is immediately understood. For Althusser, the 'field of theory' is divided into different levels, so that in one and the same field ideas at one level can conflict with, correspond with or be 'represented by' ideas at another level:

> The class positions in confrontation in the class struggle are 'represented' in the domain of practical ideologies (religious, ethical, legal, political, aesthetic ideologies) by world views of antagonistic tendencies: in the last instance idealist (bourgeois) and materialist (proletarian) . . .
>
> World outlooks are represented in the domain of theory (science + the 'theoretical' ideologies which surround science and scientists) by philosophy. Philosophy represents the class struggle in theory. That is why philosophy is a struggle . . . and basically a political struggle: a class struggle. (Interview Q.5 LP 21).

It is in the light of distinctions like these that Althusser begins to give an answer to the question why scientists resort to idealist philosophy and why they should need non-scientists (materialist philosophers) to counter that idealism, a question which seemed to be particularly embarrassing for continuity theorists. In the course of his answer, Althusser envisages a particular scientist as the point of intersection of a number of different theoretical strands: (1) a scientific practice as such, (2) a 'spontaneous philosophy', arising in the course of (1) and determining his perception and presentation of (1), but with its content co-determined by (3) elements of philosophy proper, which in turn are 'organically linked' to (4) a world-view, a more or less immediate ideological grasping of the world and the individual's place in it. Within (2), Althusser identifies contradictory elements, materialist and idealist: *the relative weight of these elements is determined by the whole range of extra-scientific factors reflected through levels (3) and (4)* and, in turn, reflects the scientist's own rating of the objectivity of his object, his knowledge and his methods (PPSS 100–101). These external factors, predominantly political–ideological rather than scientific, can none the less constitute (or be destructive of) the productive forces of scientific knowledge.

At issue in philosophical struggle is ultimately 'the ideological hegemony of the ruling class, whether it is to be organized, strengthened and defended, or fought against' (IISTBAMIP=ESC 167). But the terminology of representation and hegemony only sharpens the central problem: just why should there be any link between Level 2, the thesis that philosophy is necessarily connected with the sciences, whose autonomy and objectivity are defended by materialist philosophy, and Level 3, the thesis that the struggle between philosophical tendencies is connected with the political struggle for ideological hegemony between proletariat and bourgeoisie? In the reply just quoted, Althusser links the two levels via the intermediary of world-views and a casual use of brackets: '*world-views* of antagonistic tendencies: in the last instance, idealist (bourgeois) and materialist (proletarian)'. For Althusser and for many Marxists, the answer is perhaps so obvious that it hardly needs stating. Indeed, Althusser provides it almost as an aside later in the interview, when he says:

> Philosophy represents the people's class struggle in theory. In return it helps the people to distinguish in theory and in all ideas (political, ethical, aesthetic, etc.) between true ideas and false ideas. In principle, true ideas always serve the people; false ideas always serve the enemies of the people (Interview Q.7 LP 24).

Now we have already followed Althusser through the complexities of Level 1 and seen that he rejects any Enlightenment identification of materialist philosophy with truth and idealist philosophy with falsehood and the correlative view of convergence between political progress and materialism as two facets of 'the truth'. But if Althusser does not envisage a *convergence* between political and scientific progress, he does look for a constantly renewed *alliance*, whose credentials cannot be demonstrated *a priori*.

Given its particular interventionist function, *between* the sciences and the class struggle, there could well be sceptical objections from either side of the proposed alliance. From the side of the sciences, it could be objected that on Althusser's own view,

> . . . if philosophy . . . is subject to certain values which rest on practical ideologies, . . . then in the name of what philosophy can we (materialists) denounce the exploitation of the sciences by ideology? Does it so happen that the philosophy which we profess is freed from . . . this dependence on practical ideologies and is consequently preserved *a priori*, from the risk of exploiting the sciences, as other philosophies do? (PPSS 95).

Althusser answers this objection by acknowledging that materialism, as much as any other philosophical position, embodies a normative attitude with respect to the sciences; but in the case of materialism alone that attitude is a positive defence of the sciences against exploitation.[18] Moreover dialectical materialism can be 'relied on' here in virtue of its privileged link with historical materialism, which alone yields

> knowledge of practical ideologies, a knowledge which finally allows philosophy to control and criticize its organic link with practical ideology, and so to rectify its effects in accordance with a 'correct' line (PPSS 97).

Dialectical materialism is also linked, according to Althusser, to 'the political positions of the working class'. But now the sceptic from the political side might object that we have still not been given an explanation of that link. Just in what sense is it true to say that 'In principle, true ideas always serve the people; false ideas always serve the enemies of the people'? This thesis is plausible only if presented in a carefully nuanced fashion, as the thesis that in class-dominated societies *particular* scientific breakthroughs make *particular* threats to the monopoly of ruling ideas by the ruling class at *particular* historical moments.

Left at such a level of abstraction, Althusser's definition of philosophy is very 'exposed'. Each of its three levels still stands more or less alone, unintegrated with the next. The levels can still be relatively easily detached, causing the collapse of the definition as a whole. But in order to make the definition more concrete and so integrate the levels, we should have to develop its 'social-theoretic content'[19] in two directions.

(1) A *general* explanation of the role of science and ideology within the general theory of historical materialism.

18 See note 16.
19 This formulation and most of what follows are due to Tony Trew.

(2) A *particular* explanation of the role of philosophical interventions relative to politics and the sciences.

(1) *General Explanation*

Here we must develop Marx's insights into the contrast between the scientific and the ideological: scientific practice as the active elaboration of adequate concepts, revealing the underlying structures of the material world, an autonomous process, with standards of adequacy laid down from within the discipline; ideological practice as, the passive reflection of commonsense dogma, seeking to 'accommodate science to a viewpoint which is not derived from science itself . . . but from outside, from alien, external interests'.[20] We must go on to demonstrate the link between ideology and the class struggle, by showing that a ruling class necessarily relies on mystificatory ideological cognitive forms, in particular those which eternalize and universalize transitory and particular social relations. We must then theorize the recurring challenge of particular scientific discoveries to those universalizing world views and the recurring re-integration of those discoveries into the dominant ideologies of the ruling classes.

(2) *Particular Explanation*

Here we must show how philosophy is a struggle, in the sense that it is the practice of establishing or resisting the hegemony of a (class) world view over a scientific practice: a struggle which is a necessary consequence of scientific breakthroughs within class formations. In detailed philosophical work, we must illuminate the form in which each philosophical intervention is irreducibly particular, conjuncturally determined by the intersection of scientific production and class struggle.

Within the confines of the present paper, there is no space for this neces-sary concrete elaboration. Since so much traditional Marxist thinking has tended to collapse distinct levels, e.g. philosophical practice into either scientific or political or ideological practice, my first task throughout has been the analytical one of making precise lines of demarcation between levels, since only when that is done can their mode of interaction be properly understood. But I am only too painfully aware of the distance existing between the present abstract, analytical presentation and a fully integrated theory.

Given the correctness of that general account, according to which, in particular conjunctures, idealism both obstructs scientific practice by

[20] K. Marx, *Theories of Surplus Value*, Part II (London: Lawrence & Wishart, 1969), 119.

capitalizing on scientific 'crises' and serves to refine and reinforce the ideological mystification of the exploited classes, then both 'sides' (the sciences on the one hand and the movement of the revolutionary working class on the other) have good reasons to seal the 'alliance'. But it must be re-emphasized that an alliance is not a fusion, that Althusser is neither identifying philosophical with political interventions nor collapsing either of those interventions into scientific practice itself. Nor is he claiming that any particular philosophical intervention will embody 'pure' materialism or 'pure' idealism:

> . . . even if only because every philosophy must, in order to take up its own theoretical class positions, surround those of its principal adversary. But one must learn to recognize the dominant tendency which results from its contradictions, and masks them (ESC 61).

Althusser's view (unlike that of some more 'scientistic' Marxists) is quite consistent with the fact that on many fronts in the struggle against imperialism the people's interests can be represented and furthered in religious ideological forms and that the forces of repression are quite capable of adopting not only the jargon but also the concrete applications of scientific practice. What is at issue, always, is the struggle for certain ideas which, at the particular moment, provide the key to the successful struggle for liberation.

Now that we have reached this third level of Althusser's 'New Definition', we can re-pose the problem of the 'New Ordering' of the philosophy/science couple. Althusser's general schema, before the 'New Ordering', gave a plausible account of a number of great scientific breakthroughs, in particular of Galilean mechanics, which was followed by a politico-ideological ferment, which in turn was followed by a strictly philosophical struggle: on the one side, Cartesian dualism, the philosophical defence of the theology of the immortal soul endowed with free will; on the other side, the remorseless mechanistic monism of Hobbes.[21] A similar story can be told of other great scientific breakthroughs in history: an attempted *recuperation* by idealism of ground it has *lost* in the emergence of the new science, an attempt to block the insights made available in the breakthrough, by resorting to new forms of mystification. If Althusser is right that, in general, the great philosophical battles are fought out in the aftermath of scientific breakthroughs, but that that order is reversed in the case of the emergence of historical materialism, how can we explain this

[21] See Quentin Skinner, 'The Context of Hobbes' Theory of Political Obligation' in M. Cranston and R. S. Peters (eds), *Hobbes and Rousseau: A Collection of Critical Essays* (Garden City, New York: Anchor Books, 1972), and T. Spragens, *The Politics of Motion: the World of Thomas Hobbes* (London: Croom Helm, 1973).

reversal? The answer must lie in the peculiar character of historical materialism, 'the form of a revolutionary science' (ESC 69). As Althusser says, echoing Hobbes, 'Geometry unites men, social science divides them' (RC 185). In the case of Galilean mechanics just noted, the ideological and then philosophical battle came *post festum* (though not long *post festum*, as Galileo knew to his cost), as religious ideology intervened to establish the limits of applicability of the scientific discoveries and even their epistemological and ontological status[22] and philosophy then struggled over the categories to be formed in reaction to them: monism/dualism; mechanical determinist causation/freewill, etc. It was at this level, at one remove from the scientific discoveries themselves, that we can locate the battle for these ideas which would provide the instruments of class rule or class liberation. In the case of historical materialism, in contrast, the historically determined forms of class exploitation constitute the very subject matter of the science. There is thus not the same time-lag between the formation of the scientific concept and the application of that concept to provide insight into the class struggle, since historical materialism itself conceptualizes and so provides knowledge of the modalities of class exploitation and class struggle.

In *Reading 'Capital'* Althusser discussed (RC 21) Marx's comments on the problems involved in formulating the concept of sale of labour-power to represent the central transaction of the capitalist mode of production. That required a change of perspective impossible for political economy 'so long as it sticks in its bourgeois skin' (*Cap.* I, 542). The obstacle was the fact that the new concept *directly* brought to light the relation of *exploitation* underlying the transaction, and so the mode of production as a whole, and so permitted the working class a theoretical insight into the mechanism whereby it produces surplus value for the benefit of the capitalist class.

While these considerations point clearly to the specificity of historical materialism as a scientific discipline, they do not in themselves explain or justify Althusser's 'New Ordering' of the philosophy/science couple in the case of historical materialism. The analysis certainly shows that a struggle at the politico-ideological level of world views may have to be settled before a radically new concept can be accepted into the scientific corpus. But it does not show how that struggle can be strictly philosophical, unless Althusser's fundamental view of philosophy is substantially transformed.

The correct suggestion of the 'New Ordering' is that philosophy may have a much more dynamic, interactive role to play *vis-à-vis* the sciences: the rough formulation of a scientific concept can be illuminated and de-

---

[22] Notorious here is Osiander's re-writing of Copernicus' discoveries as 'hypotheses'. For the text of his 'Preface' see A. Koestler, *The Sleepwalkers* (Harmondsworth: Penguin, 1968), 573.

fended against ideological infanticide by the elaboration of a philosophical category, which in turn can open the way to further scientific developments.[23]

This rather vague conception of 'interaction', suggested by the 'New Ordering' brings me to a final question concerning Level 3 of the 'New Definition'. In connecting philosophical interventions so closely with the class struggle, Althusser gives an account of the recurring, non-progressive nature of philosophy:

> In the history of philosophy, as in very long periods of the class struggle, one cannot really talk about a point of no return. So I shall use the term: philosophical 'revolution' ... This expression is more correct: for, to evoke once again the experiences and terms of the class struggle, we all know that a revolution is always open to attacks, to retreats and reverses, and even to the risk of counter-revolution.
>
> Nothing in philosophy is *radically* new, for the old theses, taken up again in new form, survive and return in a new philosophy. Nor is anything ever settled definitively: there is always the struggle of antagonistic tendencies, there are always 'comebacks' and the oldest philosophies are always ready to mount an offensive disguised in modern—even in the most revolutionary—trappings (RJL = ESC 72 Fr. 61).

Does this mean that in the limiting case of communism, when class exploitation is liquidated, there will be no more philosophy, since there will be no more reason or opportunity for exploiting the results of the sciences? The problem of envisaging the 'withering away of philosophy' mirrors that of envisaging the 'withering away of the state'. Althusser marks off philosophy from the juridico-political superstructure in several ways: it is not a superstructural level, but a form of activity (Level 1) and, in virtue of its privileged link with the sciences, it is not a mere ideological 'form of social consciousness' (Level 2). Yet, like the superstructures, it is closely tied to the class struggle at Level 3.

A rather uninteresting answer might be that philosophy would retain certain 'innocent' residual functions, of classification, clarification, popularization, etc., parallel to the 'innocent' 'administration of things' inherited by communism after the supersession of the class struggle.

A more serious answer would be that neither political nor ideological tendencies are ever definitively overcome; that in so far as communism embodies the highest level of development of the material productive forces, a 'return' to class exploitation is always inscribed as a possibility within it; that similarly, in so far as advanced science embodies the highest

[23] This line of thought is developed by Pierre Raymond, philosophically perhaps the most original of those inspired by Althusser's 'New Definition' in his book *Le Passage au Matérialisme* (Paris: Maspéro, 1973).

level of development of the theoretical productive forces, so there too a 'return' to idealist positions is always possible. To establish such a link between the disappearance of the class struggle and the disappearance of philosophy, we must of course first make good the 'social-theoretic content'[24] of the theses propounded abstractly in the present paper. On that basis, our view of the possibility of the 'supersession' of philosophy and of its 'return' would follow not just tautologically from certain arbitrary definitions, but from a total theoretical account of the connection between, on the one hand, mystification as a necessary component of ideological hegemony in the class struggle and, on the other hand, philosophy as an interventionist practice which allows the sciences to play a particular conjunctural role relative to ideological hegemony.

Does Althusser's 'New Definition' provide an adequate way out of the *impasses* of his 'Old Definition'? Clearly not, by any traditional standards of philosophical adequacy. But that is hardly surprising, since the 'New Definition' precisely rejects those traditional standards. The form of 'solution' offered by the 'New Definition' is this: once we start on the path of an entirely general search for 'guarantees' of either the ontological or the epistemological status of the material world and the practice of the sciences in yielding knowledge of it, we necessarily end up with idealism. The practice of materialist philosophy is twofold. *First*, it wages polemical attacks on the idealist opposition, at the level both of immanent critique (unmasking contradictions, etc.) and of locating idealist philosophical positions in the context of the practical ideologies from which they are derived and which they in turn sustain. *Second*, if the truth of scientific practice is *index sui*, in need of no external guarantee, yet vulnerable to exploitation and subversion at moments of internal 'crisis', then the positive role of materialist philosophy is to 'clear the way' for the sciences, to make scientific truths 'visible', 'recognizable', etc. Althusser maintains that any materialist philosophical intervention must draw a line which is precise relative to the particular scientific development, but must also attain a 'minimum of generality', so as to establish 'the thesis of the primacy of the real object over the object of knowledge' (an ontological thesis, which must have primacy over the epistemological thesis which establishes the distinction between the two at the level of knowledge) (IISTBAMIP=ESC 193).

Althusser's aim is to steer his 'Definition' between the Scylla of normatively judging the sciences and the Charybdis of passively relaying the scientists' own image of their own practice. How does Althusser steer his course? His own philosophical practice bears out his aphorism that 'in philosophy you can think only through metaphors' (ESC 140). His practice takes the form of a continuing struggle to destroy misleading metaphors

---

[24] As envisaged programmatically on p. 259 above.

and replace them by fruitful ones. To understand the process of knowledge, he inveighs against metaphors inspired by legal ideology and strives for a metaphor drawn from material production. To understand philosophical practice as a whole, he elaborates and acts upon a model of guerrilla warfare: he constantly refuses pitched battles against entrenched philosophical positions, but fights 'on the run', making a light defence of an exposed position, then rapidly dismantling it, before moving on to another. The result of the manoeuvre in each case is to wear down the enemy by exposing his weaknesses and forcing him into defensive positions not of his choosing, which turn out to be contradictory. The commentator has to follow these moves over a specific piece of philosophical 'terrain', before standing back to take stock of the overall campaign. Like all philosophical moves, this assessment of mine is necessarily provisional, itself an intervention, which may perhaps for a moment alter the balance of forces in the continuing struggle.[25]

University of East Anglia

[25] Interventions by G. A. Cohen and D. H. Ruben after the presentation of this lecture allowed me to correct some obvious errors. Many of the remaining correct formulations are due directly to my friend and colleague Tony Trew. The text was completed while the author was Fellow to the Alexander von Humboldt-Stiftung in the Federal Republic of Germany.

Index

Index

Index

self, identity of, 236–237
Singer, P., 88
Skillen, A., 31n.
Skinner, Q., 260n.
Smith, G. W., 17–18
socialism, ethical, 3, 16, 24, 30–31, 178, 187
society, civil, 130, 133, 135, 141, 198
Solomon, R. C., 237
Solzhenitsyn, A., 194, 204
Sombart, W., 190
Sorel, G., 7, 72–73, 90–94
speech situation, ideal, 16, 175–176, 214–216, 224
Spinoza, B. de, 11–12, 17–19, 245, 252
Spragens, T., 260n.
Stalin, J. V., 2, 80
Stammler, R., 189
state, nature of, 10–11, 129–143
Staudinger, F., 186
Steiner, G., 174n., 175n.
Stephenson, M. A., 77n.
Strawson, P. F., 236n., 237n.
structure, 5, 151–152
superstructure, *see* basis and super-structure
Sweezy, P., 50

Taylor, C., 1, 196n., 201n.
teleology, 13–15, 72–73, 90, 168–171, 174

tendencies, 4–5, 49–54
theory, 160–161, 163
theory and practice, unity of, 4, 13, 33–38, 95, 157, 163
Thompson, E. P., 9, 192–194
Tillich, P., 162
toleration, 32
Toulmin, S., 211n.
Trew, A., 249n., 258n.
Trotsky, L., 191–192, 201, 204
truth, 15–16, 210–219, 222
Tucker, R., 142n.

Urry, J., 44n.
utilitarianism, 223–224, 226

Valéry, P., 107
value, fact and, 3–4, 14–15, 171, 186
value, labour theory of, 87
Verne, J., 150
Vorländer, K., 187

Warnock, Mary, 8–9
Weber, M., 36, 44, 82, 161
Weinstein, D. and M. A., 175n.
Wetter, G. A., 157n., 159n.
Wiggins, D., 210
Williams, R., 172n.
Wood, A. W., 196n., 197n.

268